"Scholars and policy analysts have spent the last 20 years or so focused on institutions that create transnationalism and cross-cultural integration. They have overlooked the most obvious institution—marriage. Juan Díez Medrano's important new book explores how transnational marriage creates dynamic cosmopolitan social forms. This meticulously researched book is a landmark study that scholars of nationalism and cross culturalism will cite for years to come."

— *Mabel Berezin, Department of Sociology, Cornell University*

"With the political project of building Europe failing, we may need to look to everyday life to see if EU integration is having any irreversible sociological consequences. The obvious place to look is international marriage and family life, as a core building block of the cross-border kinship networks that might sustain a more cosmopolitan future. In this, the very first systematic study of intra-EU love across borders, Díez Medrano again pioneers a new kind of transnational sociology. Notably he challenges easy assumptions that successful cosmopolitanism is the exclusive preserve of upper and middle classes. This quite literally sexy study deserves wide attention for the virtuoso methodology and analysis on display throughout."

— *Adrian Favell, Chair in Sociology and Social Theory, University of Leeds*

"This very important book explores a crucial but under-researched dimension of the Europeanisation of everyday life; the author unearths some often surprising and counter-intuitive results. Social scientists concerned with the further development of a European society will want to read this study, and it should inspire much further work."

— *William Outhwaite, Emeritus Professor of Sociology, Newcastle University, UK*

"Juan Díez Medrano continues to dig deeper into the social and cultural underpinnings of European integration by focusing on binational couples – a strategic minority in the redefinition of nation-based habitus, lifestyles and identifications. *Europe in Love* is another must read for anybody interested in the future of Europe beyond the controversies and vagaries of EU politics."

— *Ettore Recchi, Professor of Sociology, Sciences Po Paris*

EUROPE IN LOVE

Inter-marriage both reflects and brings social change. This book draws on a unique survey of randomly selected samples of national and European binational couples to demonstrate that the latter are core cells of a future European society.

Unrestricted freedom of movement has enabled a rise in the number of lower-class and middle-class binational couples among Europeans. Euro-couples fully integrate in their host cities but secure less support in solving everyday problems than do national ones, partly because of a relatively small network of relatives living close-by. Embeddedness in a dense international network and a cosmopolitan outlook also distinguish them from national couples. The book challenges the view of cosmopolitanism as exclusively middle-class and high-lights contrasts between lower-class and middle-class binational couples. Furthermore, it shows that social cosmopolitanism among binational couples is not matched by a commensurate weaker national identification that would enhance support to a more federal Europe.

This book is primarily addressed to the general public interested in contemporary European society and to academics interested in inter-marriage. Since the chapters are quasi stand-alone pieces devoted to specific topics, it provides suitable reading material for social stratification, social networks, civil society, popular culture, and European integration undergraduate and graduate courses.

Juan Díez Medrano is Professor of Sociology at the Universidad Carlos III de Madrid (Spain). The focus of his research is the study of nationalism and European integration. His publications include *Divided Nations* (1995) and *Framing Europe* (2003).

Routledge Advances in Sociology

277 On the Genealogy of Critique
Or How We Have Become Decadently Indignant
Diana Stypinska

278 Nostalgia Now
Cross-Disciplinary Perspectives on the Past in the Present
Edited by Michael Hviid Jacobsen

279 Magical Realist Sociologies of Belonging and Becoming
The Explorer
Rodanthi Tzanelli

280 Queer Campus Climate
An Ethnographic Fantasia
Benjamin Arnberg

281 Children in Social Movements
Rethinking Agency, Mobilization and Rights
Diane M. Rodgers

282 The Global Citizenship Nexus
Critical Studies
Edited by Debra D. Chapman, Tania Ruiz-Chapman and Peter Eglin

283 People, Care and Work in the Home
Edited by Mohamed Gamal Abdelmonem and Antonio Argandona

284 Europe In Love
Binational Couples and Cosmopolitan Society
Juan Díez Medrano

For more information about this series, please visit: www.routledge.com/ Routledge-Advances-in-Sociology/book-series/SE0511

EUROPE IN LOVE

Binational Couples and
Cosmopolitan Society

Juan Díez Medrano

LONDON AND NEW YORK

First published 2020
by Routledge
2 Park Square, Milton Park, Abingdon, Oxon OX14 4RN

and by Routledge
52 Vanderbilt Avenue, New York, NY 10017

Routledge is an imprint of the Taylor & Francis Group, an informa business

© 2020 Juan Díez Medrano

The right of Juan Díez Medrano to be identified as author of this work
has been asserted by him in accordance with sections 77 and 78 of the
Copyright, Designs and Patents Act 1988.

All rights reserved. No part of this book may be reprinted or reproduced
or utilised in any form or by any electronic, mechanical, or other
means, now known or hereafter invented, including photocopying and
recording, or in any information storage or retrieval system, without
permission in writing from the publishers.

Trademark notice: Product or corporate names may be trademarks
or registered trademarks, and are used only for identification and
explanation without intent to infringe.

British Library Cataloguing-in-Publication Data
A catalogue record for this book is available from the British Library

Library of Congress Cataloging-in-Publication Data
Names: Díez Medrano, Juan, author.
Title: Europe in love: binational couples and cosmopolitan society /
Juan Díez Medrano.
Description: Abingdon, Oxon; New York, NY: Routledge, 2020. |
Series: Routledge advances in sociology | Includes bibliographical
references and index.
Identifiers: LCCN 2020001671 (print) | LCCN 2020001672 (ebook) |
ISBN 9780367478568 (hardback) | ISBN 9780367478575 (paperback) |
ISBN 9781003036951 (ebook)
Subjects: LCSH: Nationalism—European Union countries. |
Dual nationality—European Union countries. | Married people—
European Union countries. | Cosmopolitanism—European Union
countries. | Transnationalism.
Classification: LCC JC311 .D5175 2020 (print) | LCC JC311 (ebook) |
DDC 306.84/5094—dc23
LC record available at https://lccn.loc.gov/2020001671
LC ebook record available at https://lccn.loc.gov/2020001672

ISBN: 978-0-367-47856-8 (hbk)
ISBN: 978-0-367-47857-5 (pbk)
ISBN: 978-1-003-03695-1 (ebk)

Typeset in Bembo
by codeMantra

For Selene

CONTENTS

List of tables	*x*
Acknowledgments	*xvii*

1	Introduction	1
2	When Willem met Laura: who enters national and binational couples?	26
3	Sociability	47
4	Making a living	79
5	Civil and political engagement	105
6	Taste and cultural practices	126
7	Identities	151
	Conclusion	192

Appendix 1: survey methodology	*201*
Appendix 2: in-depth Interviews	*209*
Appendix 3: variables Used in the Statistical Analysis	*211*
Index	*219*

TABLES

2.1	Distribution of Respondents by Type of Couple, Education, and Country of Residence (%)	33
2.2	Distribution of Foreign Individuals (Respondents or Partners) in Binational Couples, by Nationality (N)	34
2.3	Average Age When Partners Started Life Together, by Type of Couple, Education, and Country	35
2.4	Average Number of Children with Current Partner, by Type of Couple, Education, and Country	35
2.5	Mean Age Gap between Partners, by Type of Couple, Education, and Country	36
2.6	Place of First Meeting for Individuals in Binational Couples, by Education, and Country (%)	36
2.7	Average Number of Years Foreign Partner Spent in Country of Residence before Meeting Partner, by Education and Country (Information Provided by Foreign Partners to Binational Couples)	37
2.8	Average Number of Years Foreign Partner Spent in Country of Residence before Meeting Partner, by Education and Country (Foreign Partners Who Met in Country of Residence only; Information Provided by Foreign Respondent)	37
2.9	Reasons for Coming to Country, by Nationality of Reporting Respondent, Place Where Partners Met, and Education (Partners in Binational Couples Only) (%)	38
2.10	Gender Distribution, by Type of Couple, and Education (% Women)	40
2.11	Parents Born in Different Countries, by Type of Couple, Education, and Country (%)	42

Tables **xi**

2.12 Average Number of Countries Visited Before Turning 17, by Type of Couple, Education, and Country 42

2.13 Average Number of Countries Visited Between the Age of 17 and the Age When Met Partner, by Type of Couple, Education, and Country 43

2.14 Average Number of Languages Known before Meeting Partner, by Type of Couple, Education, and Country 43

3.1 Relatives, In-Laws, and Friends *in Country of Residence*, by Type of Couple and Education (Unweighted Average % across the Four Countries) 49

3.2 Origin of Respondent's Friends in *Country of Residence*, by Type of Couple and Education (Unweighted Average % across the Four Countries) 50

3.3 A Close Friend among the Respondent's Five Closest Ones in the Country of Residence Has a Different Nationality from the Country of Residence's, by Type of Couple, Education, and Country (%) 52

3.4 Average Frequency of Contact with Relatives and In-Laws who live *in Country of Residence*, by Type of Couple and Education (Average of the Country Means) 53

3.5 Average Frequency of Contact with Friends who live *in Country of Residence*, by Type of Couple and Education (Average of the Country Means) 53

3.6 Mean Perceived Degree of Help (1–7) Received by Respondents When Conducting Specific Tasks, by Type of Couple and Education (Average of the Country Means) 54

3.7 Association between Having Family and Friends in Country of Residence and Meeting Frequency with Family and Friends, and Amount of Help received, Controlling for City of Residence and Education (National Couples Only) (OLS) 55

3.8 Relatives, In-Laws, and Friends *in the European Union*, by Type of Couple and Education (Unweighted Average % across the Four Countries) 55

3.9 Average Frequency of Contact with Friends who live *in the European Union*, by Type of Couple, Education, and Country 56

3.10 Association between Being in a Binational Couple and Having Relatives, In-Laws, and Friends *in Country of Residence, EU, and outside the EU*, Controlling for City of Residence and for Country of Nationality, Socio-Demographic and Transnational Experience and Skills Variables (OLS) 58

3.11 Association between Socio-Demographic Variables and Availability of Family in Country of Residence and How Many Native Close Friends Foreign Partners in Binational Couples have (OLS) 61

xii Tables

3.12 Association between Being in a Binational Couple and the Frequency of Contact *with Relatives/In-Laws,* Controlling for City of Residence, for Socio-Demographic Variables, and for the Presence of Relatives and In-Laws in CoR (OLS)　64

3.13 Association between Being in a Binational Couple and the Amount of Help Received When Solving Problems or Conducting Specific Tasks, Controlling for City of Residence, Socio-Demographic Variables, and Social Networks in the Country of Residence (OLS)　66

3.14 Association between Being a *Foreign Partner* in a Binational Couple and the Frequency of Contact *with Relatives/In-Laws* and Friends *in other EU States*, Controlling for City of Residence and for Socio-Demographic, and Transnational Experience and Skills Variables (OLS)　70

3.15 Association between Being in a Binational Couple and the Number of States Visited Since with Partner, the Number of Trips to Border Countries, and the Number of Trips to other European Union Countries in the 12 months before the Interview, Controlling for City of Residence and for Socio-Demographic Variables and Transnational Experience and Skills Variables (OLS)　71

4.1 Employment Status, by Type of Couple and Education (Employed–Unweighted Average % across the Four Countries)　83

4.2 Employment Status, by Type of Couple and Education (Employed–Unweighted Average % across the Four Countries) (Women)　84

4.3 Employment Status, by Type of Couple and Education (Employed–Unweighted Average % across the Four Countries) (Men)　84

4.4 Employed in Managerial, Professional, or Technical Occupations (Unweighted Average % across the Four Countries) (Currently Employed)　84

4.5 Employed in Managerial, Professional, or Technical Occupations (Unweighted Average % across the Four Countries) (Currently Employed-Women)　84

4.6 Employed in Managerial, Professional, or Technical Occupations (Unweighted Average % across the Four Countries) (Currently Employed Men)　85

4.7 Works for a Multinational, by Type of Couple and Education (Currently Employed)　86

4.8 Association between Being in a Binational Couple and Work for a Multinational, Controlling for City of Residence, Gender, Education, and Specific Nationality (OLS) (Employed respondents only)　87

Tables **xiii**

4.9 Association between Being in a Binational Couple and Personal Income, Controlling for City of Residence, Gender, Education, Nationality, Work for a Multinational, and English Knowledge (OLS) — 89

4.10 Association between Being in a Binational Couple and Personal Income, Controlling for City of Residence, Gender, Education, Specific Nationality, Work for a Multinational, and English Knowledge (OLS) — 90

4.11 Association between Being in a Binational Couple and Personal Income, Controlling for Years of Residence, City of Residence, Gender, Education, Specific Nationality, Work for a Multinational, and English Knowledge (OLS) (Subsample of Male Respondents with known years of residence in Country of Residence) — 92

4.12 Mean Level in Society, by Type of Couple and Education (Unweighted Average of Country Means) — 95

4.13 Association between Being in a Binational Couple and Perceived Social Position, Controlling for City of Residence, Gender, Education, Specific Nationality, Work for a Multinational, and English Knowledge (OLS) — 96

5.1 Participation in Civil Activities and Associations, by Type of Couple and Education (Unweighted Average of Country %) — 111

5.2 Association between Being in a Binational Couple and Participation in Civil Activities and Associations, Controlling for City of Residence, and for Socio-Demographic Variables, Transnational Skills and Experience, Social Support Network Embeddedness, Identification, and Socio-Psychological Variables (OLS) — 112

5.3 Interest in City, Country of Residence, European, World Politics, and Country of Nationality, by Type of Couple, Education, and Country (% Very and Extremely Interested) — 115

5.4 Association between Being in a Binational Couple and Interest in Politics on Different Scales, Controlling for City of Residence and for Socio-Demographic, Social Support, Network Embeddedness, and Psychological Variables (OLS) — 117

5.5 Association between Years of Residence and Interest in Politics in the Country of Nationality relative to Interest in Politics in the Country of Residence, Controlling for City of Residence and for Socio-Demographic, Social Support, Network Embeddedness, and Psychological Variables (OLS) (Foreign Partners Only) — 118

5.6 Political Participation, by Type of Couple and Education (Unweighted Average of Country %) — 120

xiv Tables

5.7 Association between Being in a Binational Couple and Political Participation, Controlling for City of Residence, Socio-Demographic Variables, Transnational Skills and Experience, Social Support Network Embeddedness, Identification, and Psychological Variables (OLS) — 121

6.1 Musical Taste, by Type of Couple and Education (Unweighted Average of Country %) — 129

6.2 Association between Being in a Binational Couple and Taste for Different Music Genres, Controlling for City of Residence, Socio-Economic Variables, and the Number of Spoken Languages (OLS) — 131

6.3 Film Taste, by City of Residence, Type of Couple, and Education (%) — 133

6.4 Association between Being in a Binational Couple and Taste for Films from Different World Regions, Controlling for City of Residence and for Socio-Demographic Variables and the Number of Spoken Languages (OLS) — 135

6.5 Preference for Films in Original Version, by City of Residence, Type of Couple, and Education (%) — 136

6.6 Association between Being in a Binational Couple and Taste for Films in Original Version, Controlling for City of Residence and for Socio-Demographic Variables and the Number of Spoken Languages (OLS) — 137

6.7 Read a Book in a Foreign Language the Previous Year, by City of Residence, Type of Couple and Education (%) — 139

6.8 Association between Being in a Binational Couple and Reading Books in Foreign Languages, Controlling for City of Residence and for Socio-Demographic Variables, and the Number of Spoken Languages (OLS) — 139

6.9 Number of National Cuisines Liked and Taste for Asian Food, by Type of Couple and Education (Unweighted Average of Country Means) — 141

6.10 Association between Being in a Binational Couple and both the Number of National Cuisines Liked and Taste for Asian Food, Controlling for City of Residence and for Socio-Demographic and Transnational Experience and Skills Variables (OLS) — 141

6.11 Taste for Host Country's Cuisine, by Type of Couple, Education, and Country (%) — 143

6.12 Association between Being in a Binational Couple and Liking Different Cuisines, Controlling for Socio-Demographic Variables, and for Having a Partner of a Particular Nationality or from a particular European Region (Respondents who have the Country of Nationality Only) (OLS) — 143

Tables **xv**

6.13	Association between Taste in Music, Taste in Film, Reading Habits, and Taste for Cuisine and Being in a Binational Couple instead of a National Couple (Multinomial Logit Model—Logit Coefficients).	146
6.14	Associations between Years of Residence and Duration of Relationship on Taste for Music, Film, and Cuisine among Foreign Partners in Binational Couples, Controlling for City of Residence, Gender, Age, Education, Parents' Education, and the Number of Spoken Languages (OLS Regression Coefficients)	147
7.1	Average European Identification, by Type of Couple, Education, and Country	155
7.2	Association between being in a Binational Couple and European Identification, Controlling for City of Residence and for Socio-demographic and Transnational Background and Experience Variables (OLS)	157
7.3	Choice of European over Other Identifications, by Type of Couple, Education, and Country (%)	161
7.4	Association between being in a Binational Couple and Choice of European Identification, Controlling for City of Residence and for Socio-demographic and Transnational Background and Experience Variables (OLS)	162
7.5	Average Levels of Solidarity with Country of Residence Region by Type of Couple, Education, and Country	165
7.6	Average Levels of Solidarity with European Region, by Type of Couple, Education, and Country	166
7.7	Association between being in a Binational Couple and Regional and European Solidarity, Controlling for City of Residence, and for Socio-demographic and Transnational Background and Experience Variables (OLS)	167
7.8	Respondents Who "Would be Very Sorry" if the European Union were to Dissolve, by Type of Couple, Education, and Country (%)	170
7.9	Association between being in a Binational Couple and Anticipation of Regret if the European Union were Dissolved, Controlling for City of Residence and for Socio-demographic and Transnational Background and Experience Variables (OLS)	171
7.10	Average Identification with Country of Nationality, by Type of Couple, Education, and Country	175
7.11	Association between being in a Binational Couple and Identification with Country of Nationality, Controlling for City of Residence and for Socio-demographic and Transnational Background and Experience Variables (OLS)	176

xvi Tables

7.12 Average Levels of Identification with Country of Residence, by
Type of Couple, Education, and Country   178

7.13 Association between Socio-demographic, Temporal,
Network, Well-Being, and Cultural Assimilation Variables
and Identification with the Country of Residence (Foreign
Partners) (OLS)   181

7.14 Average Levels of Identification with City of Residence,
by Type of Couple, Education, and Country   184

7.15 Association between being in a Binational Couple and
Identification with City of Residence, controlling for
Socio-demographic and Transnational Background and
Experience Variables (OLS)   186

ACKNOWLEDGMENTS

In 2003, as I was finishing a book on the role of frames in the explanation of attitudes toward European integration, I became uncomfortable with the idea of approaching European integration as just a political process in need of explanation. Frequent travelling across Europe while writing *Framing Europe*, my personal life, and my professional experience in different countries had convinced me that the European Union bears the potential for a dramatic transformation of Europe's social structure and culture that will, in the long run, result in the emergence of a European society. It became clear to me that these changes could mean to Europe what the development of internal markets and the growth of states in the nineteenth and early twentieth centuries meant for national societies. Yet the great majority of my colleagues in sociology, married as they still largely are to methodological nationalism, had shown no interest whatsoever in these changes. There was thus a big intellectual gap to fill and a great opportunity for me to assert my professional identity as a sociologist. It turned out that I was not alone in thinking that major social transformations were taking place in Europe, which sociologists were best suited to study. Around that time, Adrian Favell, Neil Fligstein, Ettore Recchi, and Steffen Mau embarked on similar projects and, by 2011, Adrian Favell and Virginie Guiraudon had edited a book that outlined a sociological agenda for the study of both European integration and the social transformation of Europe.

Europe in Love resulted from this interest of mine in the emergence of a European society. I chose to focus on binational couples among Europeans because of the rise in the prevalence of these couples in countries like Spain, which have experienced a large influx of immigrants from other European countries, and because exogamy is the foundation of society. I was fortunate to come into contact with a group of prominent scholars in Spain and other European countries willing to embark on a collaborative research project: Teresa Castro,

xviii Acknowledgments

Helga de Valk, Jörg Rössel, and Leo van Wissen. *Europe in Love* would not have been written without their enthusiastic participation in the implementation of public opinion surveys in seven European cities in Belgium, the Netherlands, Spain, and Switzerland, which provided systematic information regarding the social lives of *Euro-couples*. Therefore, my deepest gratitude goes to them and to their research teams as well as to my closest collaborators, Clara Cortina, Ana Safranoff, Roque Álvarez, and Irina Ciornei. My appreciation for making the public opinion surveys possible also extends to the *European Science Foundation*, which evaluated the research proposal and recommended it for funding by the national research foundations of the four countries in the project (EUI2010-04221) and to the national research foundations themselves (Flanders' Fund for Scientific Research or FWO, the Netherlands Organization for Scientific Research or NWO, Spain's former Ministry of Science and Innovation, and the Swiss National Science Foundation or FNS-SNF), which provided the funds.

Many other institutions and people have made this book possible. The IBEI (Institut Barcelona d' Estudis Internacionals) provided valuable administrative assistance during the execution phase of the public opinion survey and space for regular meetings between the research team's members. Meanwhile, the Kolleg-Forschergruppe "The Transformative Power of Europe" at the Freie Universität Berlin, the Alexander von Humboldt Foundation, and the Institut für Soziologie at the Freie Universität Berlin provided me with funding, research resources, and a great intellectual environment while I wrote some of the chapters in *Europe in Love*. I am particularly thankful to Tanja Börzel, Thomas Risse, and Jürgen Gerhards for making this possible. I also owe a great debt to my colleagues at the Department of Social Sciences of the Universidad Carlos III de Madrid. This department was created while I was writing this book, and what a fantastic creation! I never imagined that I would have the privilege to work in an inter-disciplinary department with so much talent and scholarly ambition. The tremendous productivity and intellectual rigor of my colleagues have been a constant source of ideas and motivation over these years. Finally, in the last stages of this project, I benefitted from useful feedback provided by Mabel Berezin, the external reviewers, and Routledge's editorial team. I thank all of them for making this a better book.

My biggest source of strength and joy has been my family and my friends. Writing a book is like running a marathon. One needs discipline, resilience, dedicated coaching, and good nourishment. I somehow acquired the first two at some point in my early twenties. As for the coaching and the nourishment, I have obtained them from good books, intellectual conversation, fun, and affection. My parents and siblings, as well as my friends, Akos, John, and many more (including my virtual friends on FB!), have provided them in regular and adequate amounts. It is unfortunate that my good friend and journalist José Manuel Costa, with whom I had so many exchanges over musical taste in the context of Europeanization, is no longer with us. The real booster to my performance, however, have been my son Pascal and my wife Selene. Their love for me and my love for them have made the task of writing this book a most enjoyable experience.

1

INTRODUCTION

> I also want to say this… if Anne's prediction comes true, if one day a stronger feeling grows between you and Muriel and you both deign to recognize it, I'll not be against it, personally…though I have my doubts about international marriages.
>
> (Ms. Brown to Claude, *Les Deux anglaises et le continent;* Truffaut, 1971)

Although events in Truffaut's film, based on the novelist Henri-Pierre Roché's wonderful period drama set early in the 20th century, will in the end confirm Ms. Brown's misgivings, contemporary British parents would have probably been more optimistic about the future of Muriel and Claude's relationship. Binational relationships between Europeans are nowadays much more prevalent than in the past and last almost as much (or as little) as those between co-nationals. Like the French director's film, *Europe in Love* deals with binational marriage. Its focus, however, is not on the stability of binational marriage, a well-researched topic anyway, but on the lives of partners in binational couples. Longstanding interest in the process and historical significance of European integration as well as in its social foundations led me to a topic about which there is no systematic research.[1] Binational married and cohabiting couples formed by Europeans are core cells of a future European society. Partners in these couples not only self-select for open-mindedness and cosmopolitan lifestyles, taste, and identification, but also become more cosmopolitan the longer they stay together. At the same time, they lead distinct lives and face unique everyday problems. This distinctiveness contributes to the on-going gradual division of national middle and lower classes into local and cosmopolitan social segments, already noted in the political sociology literature.[2] One of the book's major contributions to this literature is, indeed, to demonstrate that this emerging social and political

2 Introduction

cleavage does not reflect a market-related distinction between *winners* and *losers* of globalization only, as leading scholars have emphasized (e.g. Fligstein, 2008; Kriesi et al., 2004), but also broader social changes, such as the greater prevalence of binational couples. The book also challenges the assumption in much of the literature that cosmopolitanism is only a middle-class phenomenon. A segmentation between nationals and cosmopolitans is also taking place among the lower classes and binational marriage and cohabitation is one of the vehicles for this social transformation.

There are many definitions of the terms "cosmopolitan" and "cosmopolitanism" in the literature.[3] Although analytically useful, many among them, however, deviate from Durkheim's precept that the definition of a sociological concept must be "sufficiently kin to" and not break with "common usage" (Durkheim, 1952 [1905], p. 42). In order to differentiate the concept "cosmopolitan" from related ones such as cultural openness and curiosity, cultural relativism, or ethnic or racial tolerance, I define it narrowly by building on the distinction between that which is national (i.e. from the state) and that which is foreign, as the stem "poli" from "polis" (city-state; group of citizens) implies. Cosmopolitanism is, first of all, a competence that results from having visited many foreign places and interacted and established bonds with many foreign nationals. It manifests itself in comfort, in ease while going around when abroad and while interacting with foreign nationals. It can also be understood as an identification, that is, as the feeling of belonging to actual or projected communities that stand above the dominant—in our world, national—political community. As Gerhards notes, the referent political community, or "social field," which serves as the benchmark to describe an identification as "cosmopolitan"—the local, the national, and so on—varies historically (Gerhards, 2012). The two elements in the definition of "cosmopolitanism" above are precise and correspond to common usage. Individuals can be cosmopolitan in terms of competence but non-cosmopolitan on the basis of identification, and *vice-versa*.[4]

The European Union is an ideal setting for the unfolding of cosmopolitanism and for the study of the role that binational couples play in the process. The absence of barriers to the mobility of citizens of the European Union means that the motivations that enter into the formation of *Euro-couples* follow a similar logic to that which enters into the formation of national ones. It also means that the structure and character of the partners' national and transnational social networks is most unhindered by bureaucratic, political, and economic barriers. At the same time, the significant scope and depth of European integration means that the European Union comes closest to the idea of a cosmopolitan polity and that Europe has become a meaningful object of identification. Finally, the freedom of movement for European Union nationals and the salience of European Union political institutions reduce pressure on foreign partners to assimilate to the country of residence's culture and identity.

Euro-couples embody "cosmopolitanism" in practice and become more cosmopolitan as a consequence of being together. I pay particular attention to the social segmentation potential of cosmopolitanism as competence and identification.

Especially since the publication of Kriesi et al.'s seminal book *West European Politics in the Age of Globalization* (Kriesi et al., 2004), scholars have emphasized the politicization of cosmopolitanism, the emergence of a new political cleavage opposing nationals and cosmopolitans. This emphasis on the political dimension of cosmopolitanism, however, obscures the new political cleavage's social foundations, the fact that it is not just a reflection of conflict between winners and losers of globalization but, also, the expression of a deep social transformation to which binational couples are contributing.

We gain historical perspective on the emergence of this new cleavage between nationals and cosmopolitans, if we look back at the formation of nation-states in the 19th and 20th centuries. The crystallization of nations and nation-states was more than just a shift in political loyalty from the local or regional group to a more broadly conceived nation; it also meant the emergence of a national layer in the social structure which superseded the local, as evidenced by Kocka's work on the German bourgeoisie (Kocka, 1999; see also Kaelble, 2004). Some of the most relevant social and political conflicts in the 19th century pitted in fact local and national fractions of the same social class (e.g. the Spanish Carlist wars in the Basque Country) (Díez Medrano, 1995). Political conflicts crystallize and become enduring cleavages to the extent that they rest not only on differences regarding policies or ideological programs but also on social distinctiveness. By social distinctiveness, I mean a distinct socio-economic status as well as distinct social networks, lifestyles, and world outlook. The literature on nationalism, for instance, has emphasized that ethnic and national differences become politically salient when they coincide with class and Mann's work highlights the special significance for the formation of nations and nation-states of coinciding ideological, economic, military, and political networks as opposed to cross-cutting ones (Hechter, 1975; Mann, 1992). Inspired by this insight, I approach the study of *Euro-couples* with an eye to the extent to which they constitute a basic social unit in an emergent segmentation process toward the formation of cosmopolitan and national social groups.

I move beyond the current literature on transnationalism, not only by examining how partners in binational couples differ from partners in national couples on various dimensions of cosmopolitanism, but also by examining how they differ on various other social dimensions, like socio-economic status, social networks, the capacity to deal with everyday problems, seasonal or yearly routines, civil engagement, and consumer taste and practices. Recchi approaches the study of mobile Europeans in the same spirit, comparing their social mobility and civil and political engagement to those of non-mobile Europeans (Recchi, 2015). My study of binational couples differs from Recchi's in that I focus on binational couples instead of mobile Europeans, I examine a broader range of sociological dimensions, and, above all, I interpret the findings from the perspective of social segmentation between nationals and cosmopolitans.

Europe in Love relies on data provided by random online surveys conducted in seven European cities in 2012. I coordinated the project and then Teresa Castro and I executed it in Spain while Helga de Valk, Jörg Rössel, Leo van Wissen

4 Introduction

executed it in Belgium, Switzerland, and the Netherlands, respectively.[5] *Europe in Love* shows that, just like the mobile Europeans that Favell, Recchi, and their co-contributors have studied in recent years, partners in Euro-couples are pioneers in the road toward a cosmopolitan world. They stand-out for their thick transnational social networks and for their international taste, world outlook, and emotional attachment to the European Union. Their lives, especially those of foreign partners in these couples, are also more complicated, partly because their families and friends are more scattered than those of partners in national couples and partly because of the logistic complications that arise from this scatter of relatives and friends.

The book also reveals significant contrasts between foreign partners in binational couples, based on education and geographic origin. Less educated foreign partners benefit from more emotional support and help in addressing the ordinary problems of daily life than do more educated ones. Also, whereas less educated foreign partners, especially if from poorer European countries, are likely to experience their move to a new country as upward social mobility, more educated ones often experience the move as downward social mobility. Having or not having blood relatives in the country of residence and comparisons with relative opportunities and collective well-being in the country of origin explain these contrasts.

Social segmentation between locals and cosmopolitans along class lines is thus taking place. We are still, however, in the early stages of a long process. This explains that, contrasts notwithstanding, binational and national couples still resemble each other: their socio-economic position is determined by cultural and other forms of capital to about the same extent and they are strongly attached to their country of nationality.

Nationals into cosmopolitans—year one

The study of inter-group marriage in contemporary sociology is inextricably linked to that of assimilation or integration of foreign partners to the host state's national culture. This focus on assimilation and integration is justified as an answer to pressing political problems and demands in the countries that concentrate most of research on the topics of migration and inter-group marriage. *Europe in Love* invites the reader to approach European integration and inter-group marriage from a different angle, to integrate the book's findings into a *longue durée* narrative about how societies have been transforming in the past one thousand years.

Nations

At the end of the Middle Ages, human groups around the world began an uninterrupted expansion beyond family and village. This tectonic process, major, slow, and of varying speed eventually produced a world of nations and national states in the 20th century and has continued and accelerated since then, roughly pre-figuring what a cosmopolitan society may look like in a distant future. In this narrative, nations and national states are neither the beginning nor the end of history—and it is easy to forget that they are no more than 150 years old! Once we relativize nations and national states in this way, once we turn our focus to the continuous expansion of social networks across the earth and start asking questions about the logic that drives this process and the social mechanisms that channel or obstruct expansion, the study of inter-group marriage, just like that of geographic mobility with which it is bound, acquires new meaning. It becomes relevant to the description and explanation of the process of expansion, an entry point to the study of cosmopolitanism in all its forms, of how people come to develop an interest in and appreciate otherness, of how they decide to cross group boundaries, and of how they come to develop group transcending and more encompassing identifications. Inter-group couples formed across the ages, linking families, villages, regions, and states, have been the specific micro-nodes, ephemeral and not necessarily recreated by these inter-group couples' offspring, which have propelled the slowly moving centrifugal process toward the formation of nations and cosmopolitan society forward.

Past research provides us already with a good understanding of the historical process through which entire populations transcended their village identifications and came to see themselves as members of national imagined communities. This transition is brilliantly captured in Eugen Weber's book title *Peasants into Frenchmen*.[6] The resumption of trade in the 12th century, followed by print capitalism in the 15th and 16th centuries, created extensive and expansive exchange and communication networks that gradually drew the contours of *imagined communities* roughly bounded by state borders. After the 17th century, the state played an increasing role in propitiating the development of these imagined communities and their coincidence with states: the centralization of power, language and legal homogenization policy, national conscription, and the creation of internal markets through the elimination of internal borders and the unification of weights and measures paved the way. Simultaneously, in extra-European colonies and at the fringes of some older states like Spain or Britain, the combination of print capitalism (e.g. local newspapers) and state centralization efforts propitiated the emergence of dissident and politically contentious imagined communities. Then, in the 19th and early 20th centuries, dramatic social and political change contributed to a new transformation, that of state-bounded imagined communities into nations.

The industrial revolution uprooted thousands of peasants from the countryside into cities, where they met, befriended, and married people from everywhere in the states where they lived, just as they developed a working class consciousness; meanwhile successful local capitalists conquered national markets, associated with capitalists from other regions, moved their residence to large urban centers, and intermarried with members of the ruling political class and the old landowning aristocracy, thus transforming into a national capitalist class.

6 Introduction

Meanwhile, the state experienced a dramatic increase in size, scope, and depth, becoming a major presence in people's lives and minds, a central source of material and physical security. Social upheaval leading to the transition from Absolutism to Constitutionalism transferred sovereignty to what was called the nation, initially largely conceived as the state's inhabitants, but by the end of the 19th century metamorphosed into a culturally distinct group of people in or across state boundaries. National sovereignty meant that state and nation became inextricably united in discourse, if not in the minds of those on whose names political elites or contenders spoke. Furthermore, Napoleon's military prowess persuaded ruling and aspiring state elites all over Europe of the formidable power of mobilizing and speaking in the name of the nation. When in power, they mobilized political discourse, symbols, commemoration, official rituals, universal education, universal conscription, and welfare policies to culminate the centuries' old process that had transformed local peasants into members of amorphous, shifting, and nameless imagined communities, by making them see themselves now as members of fully fledged and eternal nations.

In the synthesis above, which borrows from the most relevant texts published in the past 50 years, I have taken the liberty of adding the sentence segment "where they met, befriended, and married people from everywhere in the states where they lived, just as they developed a working-class consciousness." I draw from Deutsch's application of communication theory to account for how rural–urban migration during industrialization contributed to the emergence of national communities (Deutsch, 1953). Deutsch emphasizes the role of migration in promoting a break with local culture and of inter-group marriage in promoting the gradual emergence of common understandings, a common world outlook, and common values. The cumulation of these micro-processes eventually led to the emergence of new identifications. Deutsch did not test his theory empirically and, to my knowledge, no study has empirically analyzed intermarriage between people coming from different geographical locations in industrializing countries, and how these propitiated and sedimented national identifications. The most important book connecting demography to national development, Cotts-Watkins's *From Provinces into Nations: Demographic Behavior in Western Europe, 1870–1960* just focuses on demographic convergence (Cotts-Watkins, 1991).[7] More recently, Botev's study of intermarriage in Yugoslavia in the decades before the outbreak of the civil war in 1990 has not been replicated in other countries and extended to earlier times (Botev, 1994).

Globalization

The world did not stop when nations and nation states came to cover the entire surface of the earth, with the exception of the Antarctic region. While nation-states make the emergence of supranational polities more difficult, while they hinder the emergence and diffusion of cosmopolitan identifications, the same, or similar, centrifugal social processes that contributed to the emergence of national states and nations have remained at work in the 20th and 21st centuries. And these forces have seen mobility and inter-marriage play similar roles as in the past.

What some people refer to as the second globalization wave has significantly uncoupled economic, political, ideological, and military networks. All of them now transcend the boundaries of national states to some extent. From a socio-logical perspective, this second globalization wave has dramatically intensified the flow of goods, services, capital, and people across countries and around the globe, just as the 19th and 20th centuries witnessed these flows' dramatic inten-sification within states. In addition to this, new types of economic organization (i.e. the transnational corporation) and new forms and kinds of cross-national mobility have emerged or at least changed from trivial to mass phenomena (among the forms, circular, and commuting mobility; among the kinds, tour-ism, student mobility, the mobility of retirees). This expansion of world markets and cross-national flows has coincided with a proliferation of international or supranational civil associations and, if not with the emergence of a common language, at least with the emergence of English as the international language of communication.[8] Meanwhile, surpassing the power of print capitalism since the 16th century, new technologies of communication have paved the way for the development of imagined communities that extend well beyond the nation and national states. From a political perspective, efforts to introduce order in and control regional and world markets have facilitated exponential growth in the number of international governmental and non-governmental organizations and of international regulatory agencies. Just as the state played a major role in the emergence of nations, international and supranational governance institutions promote standardized scripts around the world that reduce institutional and cul-tural heterogeneity (Krüchen and Drori, 2009).

In Europe, the transformations described above have been more dramatic and deeper: instead of free trade areas, a fully fledged internal market; instead of multiple currencies, one currency; instead of a liberalization of immigration policy, Schengen, a free space for the movement of European citizens; instead of multilateral governance institutions, supranational ones requiring a pooling of sovereignty (Fligstein and Mérand, 2002). And, on top of this, an affluent, well-educated, and polyglot population by world standards, a population more familiar with cultural diversity and with the history and geography of different parts of the world and better prepared to communicate across borders.

The second wave of globalization and its political-institutional correlates have started to transform nationals into cosmopolitans. This is mainly because of ex-ponential growth in the concentration of people in large urban centers and in cross-national mobility, and because of the telecommunications revolution. A formidable increase in the prevalence of binational acquaintances and friendships and in the number of binational marriages and cohabiting relationships illus-trates this change. Also, from what we know from quantitative and qualitative empirical research, a significant proportion of the population has developed a

8 Introduction

genuine cosmopolitan outlook. The fact that it is still small, however, justifies the assertion that the world is only at a very early stage (Year 1) in the transition from national to cosmopolitan society. In order to describe the character of this transition and to explain trends and variation across places and individuals, social scientists have focused mainly on geographic mobility, both as an expression of cosmopolitanism and as an independent variable for the explanation of cosmopolitan identification. Inter-group marriage as cosmopolitanism-in-practice or as independent variable features in most studies but, until very recently, on a very secondary plane, as I show below.

Mobility, binational couples, and cosmopolitan society

Mobility

Cross-border mobility in all its forms, from permanent international migration to shopping trips, is the behavioral dimension of globalization that has concentrated most of the social scientists' attention in recent decades.[9] Since the 1990s, scholars have focused on the ties between migrants and the countries and locations that structure their biography, on how they contribute to transforming these countries and locations, and on their contribution to forging enduring transnational connections. This literature has paid particular attention to identity, which, when the focus is outside Europe, tends to express itself as hybrid, hyphenated, bi-national, sometimes even as pan-ethnic (e.g. Asian or Latino in the USA).[10]

Although research has concentrated on migrants from the less developed countries, it has also begun to examine the mobility experiences of citizens of wealthy industrialized states, with emphasis on the highly skilled, highly educated segment (Smith and Favell, 2006). Human geographers, urban sociologists, and social anthropologists have asked about the meaning of increasing mobility for people's relationship to the various places in which they live and for the role of place in people's sense of belonging. Savage has proposed that people's attachments in today's hypermobile world depend less on being born and raised in a particular place than on the role that different places play in one's biography. Andreotti, Le Galès, and Moreno, on the other hand, emphasize that highly educated, highly skilled professionals can lead fairly transnational lives and yet be strongly rooted in their places of origin (Andreotti et al., 2015; Savage et al., 2009).

At a more empirical level, sociologists have started to pay attention to different forms of cross-border mobility. Some have explored intra-organizational and other forms of cross-border mobility by scientists and highly skilled professionals (Saxenian, 2007). They are mainly interested in the economic returns to studying abroad, knowing foreign languages, and knowing people in other countries, and in the strategies and logistics involved.

In Europe, sociologists have focused on the different forms of trans-European mobility of individuals whose exclusive motivation for moving is not necessarily or primarily economic. Favell calls them "free-movers" or *Eurostars*. The main question that drives this research is the extent to which cross-border mobility contributes to weaken national attachments and replace them with cosmopolitan ones (i.e. European) (Favell, 2008; Gerhards et al., 2017; Roudometof, 2005). Some authors broaden it to examine the effect of other variables, such as transnational background, transnational skills, or being in a binational couple on people's identifications. Others broaden the question even more to examine the effect of cross-border mobility on solidarity with, trust in, and affinity to citizens from other countries. The work of Favell, Recchi, Kuhn, and Fligstein takes these questions as its starting point and then moves on to address larger sociological or political questions.[11] Favell, for instance, asks whether international mobility in the borderless space of the European Union allows highly educated individuals to pursue a de-nationalized life project. Fligstein and Kuhn ask why only a small and stable segment of the population identifies as European. Both borrow from Kriesi et al.'s distinction between winners and losers of globalization to conclude that the winners of Europeanization, highly skilled, highly educated, multilingual, Europeans are still a very small group. Kuhn and, also, Norris and Inglehart, respectively, add to this that the more a country is inserted in the global economy, society, and polity, and the more prevalent cosmopolitanism and self-expression values become, the more the losers of globalization tend to resist it (Kriesi et al., 2004; Kuhn, 2015; Norris and Inglehart, 2019).

Intermarriage

The literature on inter-group marriage has paid little attention to the implications that the increase in the prevalence of intermarriage has for the transition to a cosmopolitan society.[12] Meanwhile, scholars who study new forms of mobility among the highly educated and highly skilled, and their link to cosmopolitanism, have only occasionally referred to the role of intermarriage. Recchi, Favell, and Santacreu, among others, highlight that romance often underlies the mobility of highly educated, highly skilled Europeans (Favell and Recchi, 2009; Santacreu et al., 2009). Kuhn and Delhey et al. use composite indices of cosmopolitanism that include having or having had a foreign partner as one of the indicators (Delhey et al., 2015; Kuhn, 2015). Fligstein conceives of binational marriage as a vehicle to a sense of Europeanness (Fligstein, 2008).

Scholars find themselves at odds about the role that binational couples play in the transition to a cosmopolitan society: Mau predicts that "binational couples and the children of foreign parents are predestined to become the core cells of a transnational movement" (translated from Mau, 2007, p. 118). Favell's appraisal of binational couples is just the opposite of Mau's: For him, intermarriage is a vehicle that helps *Eurostars* overcome the informal barriers they encounter as they strive for the good life in a foreign European city, but at the price of sacrificing their initial de-nationalized project (Favell, 2008, p. 164). Mau's and Favell's contradictory statements, just as empirical examinations of the impact of transnationalism on cosmopolitan identification, have inspired, orient, and set

10 Introduction

the agenda for this book. For although there is great awareness that binational couples must enter the picture in analysis of the social, cultural, and political transformations brought by globalization, no worldwide or regional study has measured trends and contrasts in their prevalence, and none has situated them at the center of the analysis of how globalization contributes, and under what conditions, to the transition to a cosmopolitan society.

Inter-group marriage transforms the partners' world outlook and practices as they become familiar and adapt to the other's cultures. Under some circumstances inter-group marriage can also transform the partners' group identification. Like other transformations in the partners' world outlook and practices, this is partly because of the high emotional intensity of the marriage bond. Love can motivate the partners to find a shared collective identification or can increase the salience of some category of identification that they shared but that they did not pay much attention to. Inter-group marriage also bears the potential for intensified contact with members of the other partner's group and with the other partner's culture, which, if realized, can have a transformative effect on one's sense of group membership. If we follow social psychological research, this is first, because regular voluntary contact improves communication, which in turn leads to a reduction in perceived cultural distance and, second, because perceptions of similarity are the foundation of identification (Benet-Martínez and Haritatos, 2005; Gordon, 1964; Taft, 1957; Turner, 1987).

The analytical framework above does not say anything about what new collective identifications and identities will emerge and whether inter-group marriage will transform the identifications and identity of the two partners' or of just one of them. Bi-cultural, hybrid, hyphenated, pan-ethnic, and supranational are some of the forms that the new identifications have taken in the past. Also, in situations where only the identification and identity of one of the partners changes, one alternative scenario is that he or she drop his or her former group identification and identity and take on the partner's.

This book verses on a particular type of inter-group marriage, marriage between nationals from different countries. Binational couples are a major contributing force to the transition to a cosmopolitan society. Frequent and intense contact between the partners and family and friends living in other countries, makes it likely that partners in binational couples are quite competent, cosmopolitan, in navigating different places and cultures. The same applies to the binational couples' offspring, who, because of knowing several languages, because of their familiarity with different countries and people, may also eventually marry or cohabit with a foreign national, and thus propel the process forward. In addition to this, the emotional intensity of marriage, combined with cosmopolitan competence and a reduced perception of cultural distance between national groups, may also propitiate the transformation of people's identification into a cosmopolitan one.

In *Europe in Love*, I focus on binational couples between European citizens. Europe provides the most conducive context for the simultaneous diffusion of cosmopolitan competence and identification. This is because of the unique visibility and power of European political institutions compared with other instances of international governance. This visibility and power provide citizens with a focal point that they can use to make sense and give a name to cosmopolitan feelings. The European Union itself has actively promoted this identification through its symbols, statements, and policies.[13]

Two other factors make Europe, and especially the Schengen space of passport free movement, a most favorable environment for the development of a cosmopolitan identification.[14] One is the concept of European citizenship, which formally makes all its members equal in status, rights, and obligations. One-way acculturation processes, as well alternative types of cosmopolitan identifications, hyphenated, bi-cultural, hybrid, or pan-ethnic are thus less attractive or needed. In particular, there is no great pressure on foreign European citizens to assimilate to the host country's culture. The second factor, I would argue, is the relatively similarity of Europe's cultures relative to non-European ones. Surveys like the World Values Study demonstrate this with respect to values, with Europe concentrated in the Rational-Secular Authority region of Inglehart's Traditional Authority versus Rational-Secular Authority values axis (Inglehart, 1997).[15] One can argue that hyphenated identifications express some unique or unbreachable difference between two cultures, which requires to preserve them in name. Because of this, the greater two groups' cultural proximity, the easier it is for individuals to discard hyphenated identifications in favor of all-encompassing, umbrella, synthetic ones to symbolize a common identification. In a nutshell, the European Union and the Schengen space are an ideal setting for the development of a cosmopolitan identification (i.e. European) instead of hyphenated ones among partners in binational couples.

Europe in Love examines the extent to which the lives, taste, and identification of partners in binational couples are indeed more cosmopolitan than those of partners in national couples. I push the comparison into analyzing the extent to which binational couples distinguish themselves from national ones in other important social aspects, aspects that are relevant to ordinary citizens' lives, such as work, income, social networks, the capacity to solve everyday problems, civil and political engagement, and leisure, and the extent to which part of this distinctiveness can be traced to the binational nature of the couple. Drawing on a long sociological tradition that emphasizes the role of coinciding social and cultural cleavages in promoting group cohesion, one can anticipate that the more distinct the binational couple's lives are, the more this distinctiveness owes to the structural nature and demands of the binational bond, the more self-conscious and cohesive binational couples will be as a group, and the more their cosmopolitan disposition and identification can be mobilized for political purposes to spread cosmopolitan identification to other groups and to sustain a cosmopolitan political project. In other words, Mau's vision above is all the more conceivable if binational couples are socially segmented on relevant dimensions from other segments of the population.

12 Introduction

The context: binational couples in the European Union

The prevalence of binational couples largely depends on cross-national mobility in all its forms. This is the reason why the European Union, by granting freedom of movement to citizens and removing obstacles to mobility between member states, should be at the forefront of the transformation toward a cosmopolitan society. Since WWII, intra-European migration has been mainly driven by traditional push–pull economic and work-related factors, flowing from relatively poor countries to relatively rich ones and more intense in periods when there were labor shortages in the latter. One can thus distinguish two periods of intense migration: the period from the late 1950s to the mid-1960s, when fast economic growth in North-Western Europe attracted immigrants from Southern Europe, and the first decade of the new millennium, when labor-intensive sectors of the economy in some wealthier European countries attracted a large flow of immigrants from poorer Central and European countries (Castro-Martín and Cortina, 2015; Recchi, 2015). In this new wave, Poland and Romania have been the main sending countries, whereas the United Kingdom, Spain, Italy, and Germany have been the main destinations. For all its significance, however, intra-European migration in the last two decades has been outpaced by migration from non-European Union states in Africa, Latin America, and Asia. In this sense, in the last three decades, many European Union member states have not only become more European but, especially, more global. Germany stands out in this respect, given the massive influx of refugees from the Middle East in this country.

In addition to a new intra-European migration wave, recent decades have witnessed a dramatic increase in other forms of intra-European mobility, like tourism, retiree migration, and student mobility. This greater mobility has exponentially multiplied opportunities for contact, friendships, and love relationships between Europeans, and indirectly contributed to another kind of migration, less intense, less driven by economic motivations and more by a desire for adventure or in order to live with one's partner.

Although the overwhelming majority of weddings or consensual unions in a given year still involve two co-nationals, although Euro-couples represent no more than a tiny one-digit percentage of the total number of married and cohabiting couples in a given country, steady intra-European migration and stepped-up mobility have propitiated a trickle of binational marriages between Europeans year after year. The *Eumarr* project, on which this book draws its empirical information, was in fact the first systematic effort to examine trends in Euro-marriages since the creation of the European single market. In a special issue of the journal *Population, Space, and Place*, we focused on the Netherlands, Sweden, Belgium, Switzerland, and Spain (de Valk and Díez Medrano, 2014). We demonstrated that in countries like Spain, where the number of European foreign residents has increased dramatically, the yearly number of binational Euro-marriages has also increased over time. The same probably applies to other high immigration countries like the United Kingdom, Italy, and Germany.

Both Euro-marriages and international binational marriages contribute to a transnational expansion of the Europeans' social networks, which increases their familiarity with other countries and peoples. One intriguing question is whether, in addition to this, Euro-marriages and international binational marriages contribute to the same extent to cosmopolitan identifications becoming more prevalent. In an effort to optimize the use of resources devoted to conducting the survey on which this book rests, the team of researchers that designed the *Eumarr* project chose to focus only on Euro-couples.[16] *Europe in Love* compares Euro-couples to national couples. It is particularly interested in the contrast between Euro-couples formed by less educated individuals and those formed by more educated ones and in the contrast between Euro-couples formed with foreign nationals from poorer European Union countries and those formed with foreign nationals from richer European Union countries. With rare exceptions, the literature has assumed that cosmopolitanism is only a middle-class phenomenon. *Europe in Love* demonstrates that this assumption is wrong. First, because the less educated and citizens from poorer European Union countries have benefitted from the liberalization of the transportation and telecommunications sector and thus, when in binational couples, also travel to foreign places and communicate frequently with people abroad; second, because the European Union is salient enough in political, symbolic, and cultural, terms as to instill a cosmopolitan identification in partners in binational couples, regardless of education or country of origin. In the book's last chapter, I argue that this focal point is easily activated by the act of marrying or cohabiting with a foreign European national.

Pioneers in the study of pioneers

Scholarly work on mobile Europeans is scarce, and work on binational couples formed by European nationals is even scarcer. The *Eumarr* project has started to fill this last gap, by analyzing trends in the incidence of Euro-marriages in a selected number of countries and through surveys of randomly selected 30- to 46-year-olds, married or in a consensual union, in Brussels, Antwerp, Amsterdam, the Hague, Barcelona, Madrid, and Zurich. Whereas Belgium, the Netherlands, and Spain are part of both the European Union and Schengen, Switzerland has only signed to the Schengen Treaty. Chapter 2 below provides details on the surveys and on the analytical strategy that I follow in the book. Since the finalization of the data collection process in 2012, participants in the project and other researchers have published articles whose content prefaces some of the topics addressed in the book. This published work is largely oriented to examining traditional sociological or psycho-sociological themes in order to explore whether the attitudes, behavior, and psychological condition of binational couples formed by Europeans conform to theoretical expectations; also, to analyze how the distinction between partners in binational couples formed by Europeans and partners in other types of couples, national or international, throws new light on traditional research topics. Because much of the literature has focused on

14 Introduction

migrants, some of these contributions solely target the foreign partner in binational couples. A socio-psychological perspective characterizes Van Mol's and de Valk's and Koelet's and de Valk's work on satisfaction in the relationship and on subjective perceptions of social loneliness, respectively (Koelet and de Valk, 2016; Van Mol and de Valk, 2016). Van Mol and de Valk use the Dutch city surveys to show that foreign European partners in binational couples are generally happier in their relationship than Dutch partners in Dutch-Dutch and Dutch-Other European couples. Meanwhile, Koelet and de Valk use the Belgian city surveys to show that first generation European migrants married or cohabiting with the Belgian partner are more likely to feel socially lonely than are Belgian-born married or cohabiting individuals.

Other publications by participants in the *Eumarr* project more squarely focus on sociological themes that bear on this book. Schroedter, de Winter, and Koelet, for instance, use the Belgian, Swiss, and Dutch city surveys to examine the role of transnational experience in the likelihood that individuals will enter or not a binational relationship between Europeans (Schroedter et al., 2015). One does not expect this effect to be big, among other things because the percentage of individuals with significant transnational experience is small and because when one lives in a large European city one does not need to be mobile in order to meet other Europeans. Nonetheless, the authors find a small but statistically significant relationship between frequent stays abroad in early adulthood and the probability of being in a binational couple. Contrary to theoretical expectations, however, early socialization transnational experience has no impact on the probability of being in a binational couple.

Transnational social networks contribute to and are an expression of familiarity with foreign places and people, a major dimension of cosmopolitanism. Koelet, de Valk, and Van Mol, however, are not as interested in this question as in the question of how migrants gradually integrate in local family and friendship networks and distance themselves from those in their home country (Koelet et al., 2017). In order to examine this question, they use the Dutch and Belgian city surveys to focus on first generation European migrants in binational couples and analyze their local and transnational networks compared with those of married or cohabiting natives. They find that time indeed plays a role in the relative significance of local and transnational networks. As time goes by, some of these migrants' relatives also move to the Netherlands or Belgium and migrants make friends with locals, especially when they have children, so that local networks become more important in relative terms. In another, quite original, piece, Van Mol and de Valk focus on the Dutch data to examine language use between partners in binational couples and with their children (Van Mol and de Valk, 2018). Their statistical analysis shows that partners generally use the Dutch language when communicating between them and with their children and that they do so more often, the longer they have been together. In addition, they demonstrate that foreign partners, especially women, transmit their native language to their children.

Of all the themes associated with cosmopolitanism, European identification is the one that has received most attention in the literature. Schroedter, Rössel, and Datler with the Zurich survey and then Van Mol, van Wissen, and de Valk, with the Dutch and Belgian cities surveys, have broken new ground by analyzing the impact of being in a binational couple on European identification (Schroedter et al., 2015; Van Mol et al., 2015). Schroedter, Rössel, and Datler bank on their comparatively rich Swiss dataset, which includes couples formed by Swiss partners and non-Europeans and binational couples between non-Swiss nationals. Of interest to this study is that they demonstrate that partners in Swiss-EU couples tend to express a slightly higher level of identification as Europeans than do individuals in other couples. Clearly, it makes a difference for cosmopolitan identification who marries who, and in what political context. The salience of Europe as a category of identification clearly explains Schroedter's and Rössel's findings.

The argument

Europe in Love examines the extent to which the lives, taste, and identification of partners in binational couples are indeed more cosmopolitan than those of partners in national couples. I push the comparison into analyzing the extent to which binational couples distinguish themselves from national ones in other important social aspects, aspects that are relevant to ordinary citizens' lives, such as work, income, social networks, the capacity to solve everyday problems, civil and political engagement, and leisure, and the extent to which part of this distinctiveness can be traced to the binational nature of the couple.

The book demonstrates that "middle class" and "lower class" binational couples are cosmopolitan social groups in the making. Compared with national couples, they are more cosmopolitan in their lifestyles and in their identifications. That is, they are integrated in more international social networks and they feel more at ease when traveling to other countries and meeting people from other countries. They are also more likely to identify as European. This greater "cosmopolitanism" coincides with other contrasts, both social and cultural. Binational couples are less likely to have children and less likely to have relatives from both partners. This is consequential for their social life. Their social networks in the place of residence are more work related, less anchored in the family, in the neighborhood, and in different stages of their personal biography than those of partners in national couples. They also participate somewhat less in local civil and political life. On the other hand, partners in binational couples express more interest in European and world politics, as well as in foreign cultural consumption, whether film, literature, or food.

Binational couples are divided along "class lines," however, with education, mode of family formation, and distinct moral economies playing an important structuring role. "Lower class" binational couples generally involve traditional migrants who have spent a good number of years in the country of residence before meeting their national partner and who sometimes have relatives and friends from

16 Introduction

their country of origin. The lives of these couples tend to be centered in the private sphere of friends and family and contacts abroad are more likely to be with relatives than with friends. The frequent availability of friends and relatives, and immersion in a moral economy where mutual assistance replaces what money cannot buy, means that these binational couples get as much support as they need with their everyday problems. A life centered in the give-and-take of mutual assistance with friends and relatives, a life immersed in the private sphere, expresses itself in more limited interest in politics and in civil and political engagement than one finds among "middle class" binational couples and among national "lower class" couples and in a greater level of identification with city and country of residence than one finds among "middle class" binational couples. Also, "lower class" binational couples identify slightly less as Europeans, are less interested in the consumption of foreign culture, and appreciate local culture (e.g. national film) more than do "middle class" ones. In socio-economic terms binational couples do as well as national ones, except when the foreign male partner originates in the new European Union member states. Nevertheless, foreign partners in these couples generally express a strong sense of social achievement, probably because they compare their current life with memories from or projections about life in their country of origin.

Compared with lower class migration and intermarriage between members of this class, the increase in "middle class" international mobility and a greater prevalence of "middle class" binational couples are recent phenomena, propitiated by technological and institutional changes like the telecommunications and transportation revolutions and the creation of the Schengen space for the freedom of movement. Compared with "lower class" binational couples, the partners in these couples often met abroad, as students or during short professional stays. They are more likely to be "free movers," people who, if and when they move to another country, do so for exclusively individual reasons. Because of this, the foreign partners in "middle class" binational couples rarely have blood relatives in their new country of residence and have to build their local friendship network from scratch. Initially at least, they depend a lot on the national partner's circle of friends and relatives. They are also more likely to be on their own when dealing with everyday problems than are "lower class" binational couples. Perhaps to compensate for a shallower family life, "middle class" binational couples are comparatively more interested in politics and more engaged in civil and political activities than are partners in "lower class" binational couples. They also identify more as Europeans and identify less with the city and the country of residence. Finally, partners in these couples do as well as nationals in socio-economic terms, but this does not translate into commensurate self-perceptions of social achievement among the foreign partners in these couples. They often perceive their social position as lower than that of locals with similar jobs and incomes.

Europe in Love not only demonstrates that Euro-couples are "core cells" of the transition to a cosmopolitan society, as Mau predicts, it also speaks to discussion and debate on the impact of globalization on identification and engagement with the local, with the place where one lives. First of all, it shows that cosmopolitan lives are indeed associated with the development of cosmopolitan identifications, as countless authors have predicted for the European case (i.e. Andreotti et al., 2015; Fligstein, 2008; Kuhn, 2015; Mau, 2007; Recchi, 2015). Most of the work so far has concentrated on the impact of mobility. While this book testifies to the power of mobility, for foreign partners in binational couples actually tend to be those who are more likely to identify as Europeans, it also shows that marrying or cohabiting with a foreign national impacts on the national partners to these couples, who tend to identify more as Europeans than do national partners in national couples.

The book speaks to the winners–losers argument that articulates both Fligstein's and Kuhn's explanatory narrative. Fligstein and Kuhn emphasize that the Europeans are mainly the highly educated, highly skilled, those who allegedly "benefit" more from the economic conditions created by globalization and from greater opportunities to move abroad. *Europe in Love* qualifies this argument, by showing that the Europeans also comprise a large group of less-educated, less-skilled individuals who, in Fligstein's and Kuhn's account, would fall under the category of "losers." Greater opportunities to migrate across the European Union has brought segments of the European "lower class" in contact with other migrant Europeans and made possible the formation of binational couples, which have then expanded their national partners' life and identity horizons, beyond their country of residence and nationality.

Scholars have debated the question of whether globalization and the associated greater mobility promotes a cosmopolitan outlook or simply triggers processes of de-nationalization. *Europe in Love* definitely sides with those who, like Fligstein or Andreotti et al., emphasize the former. The analysis below demonstrates that partners in binational couples, while more European, do not identify less with their country of nationality than do partners in national couples. Actually, the analysis reveals that foreign partners in binational couples identify more with their country of nationality as time passes and that this does not come at the price of a decline in European identification. Cosmopolitan identifications are thus compatible with national ones, as previous work has shown.

In *Eurostars and Eurocities*, Favell outlines a slightly different de-nationalization argument. He claims that *Eurostars* are bearers of a de-nationalized life project, a strong desire to emancipate from one's material and emotional dependence on the state. As stated above, he also claims that by marrying or cohabiting with a national, *Eurostars* surrender their de-nationalized project in exchange for the comfort of integrating in local society. This book calls for calibrating Favell's assessment. It shows that those *Eurostars* who marry or cohabit with a national partner still face great obstacles when dealing with everyday problems like finding childcare for their children. At the same time, it also shows that *Eurostars* do not necessarily compromise their de-nationalized project when marrying or cohabiting with a local: they retain strong ties to friends abroad, they are not absorbed by the partner's circle of relatives, they do not assimilate to local culture and they do not identify with the country of residence. Meanwhile, their consumer and political interests lie beyond the country of residence and encompass the world

18 Introduction

at large. They may not lead a life project that is as de-nationalized as that of their single co-nationals, but they are far from assimilating to the national lifestyle, outlook, and identifications.

Finally, the book speaks to debate on the impact that transnational mobility and practices have on people's attachment to place, as studied by authors like Savage and Andreotti, Le Galès, and Moreno, among others. *Europe in Love* confirms most of Andreotti et al.'s findings in their qualitative study of highly educated executives in Paris, Lyon, Milan, and Madrid. Highly educated nationals in national couples in the *Eumarr* samples often lead transnational lives but are still deeply rooted in local urban life and national culture. This is not the case among those who marry or cohabit with a foreign European, but Andreotti et al.'s object of inquiry was the most prevalent segment among the highly educated, that is, people who live in their place of birth but still take advantage of the opportunities offered by global society. Hardly any of the respondents in their study was married to a foreign national.

Europe in Love contradicts some of Savage's findings, while providing some confirmation of others. Savage's main argument, based on ethnographic work in four suburbs around Manchester, is that in today's mobile world people's attachment to place is connected to the extent to which they can meaningfully link the place where they live to their biography. This is the sense he attaches to the concept "elective belonging." Very often, he shows, it is not those who were born and grew up in a particular place who identify most with it but, instead, those who can connect a place, or how they imagine this place, to a life project, a particular outlook, or a set of values. *Europe in Love* is not an ethnography, nor did it collect information on people's attachment to their neighborhood. The unit of observation in the book is the city. Viewed from this angle, the study shows that identification with the city is lower than other identifications but remains high, as Savage et al. and Andreotti et al. have observed. At the same time, the analysis of the survey data reveals that nationals, and more specifically, nationals in national couples, identify more with the city than do partners in binational couples, whether national or foreign.

In sum, *Europe in Love* is a significant contribution to contemporary intellectual debate surrounding the impact of globalization. While it addresses this debate, however, its aim and contribution are to situate it in a larger historical-sociological discussion, one that takes us beyond the study of globalization and focuses instead on the gradual emergence of ever larger and more territorially inclusive social groups. Establishing whether the process is inevitable or not and studying the factors that propel it forward, slow it down, or even reverse, is the research program to which this book contributes.

Book structure

The book comprises six main substantive chapters. The introduction, Chapter 1, outlines the problem, situates it in contemporary scholarly debates, synthesizes the argument, and provides an outline of the book's contents. It works as an extended synopsis of this book's contents. Chapters 2–5 cover structural aspects of people's lives whereas Chapters 6 and 7 cover more cultural ones. Chapter 2 outlines the research design for the seven surveys and provides descriptive background and socio-demographic information about the participants in the survey as well as information on when, how, and under what circumstances they met their partners. The chapter shows that most of the partners in binational couples met in the country where they now reside. This is especially the case, however, for binational couples whose partners are less educated in relative terms, which speaks to a running theme throughout the book: although binational couples share many things in common, the binational couple's social position and the foreign partners' country of origin impacts on how binational couples integrate in the country of residence, both socially and culturally. The chapter also reveals that heterosexual binational couples tend to settle in the male's country of nationality. Finally, another significant finding is that binational couples tend to have fewer children on average than do national ones. This, as shown in Chapter 3, impacts on the couples' social life.

Chapter 3 examines the local and transnational social networks of partners in national and binational couples as well as how they structure their lives and the support that they provide. The chapter reveals that partners in binational couples benefit from dense local and transnational networks. The latter clearly distinguish them from national couples. At the same time, it shows that transnational friendship and family networks restrict the freedom that binational couples have to organize their free time. The chapter engages with Favell's highly influential book *Eurostars and Eurocities*. It confirms his insights about the less than satisfying lives of highly educated movers in European cosmopolitan cities and expands on his contribution by revealing that less educated movers adjust somewhat better to life abroad, partly because they are more likely to benefit from the presence of blood relatives.

Chapter 4 analyzes contrasts in the employment and income opportunities of partners in national and binational couples, as well as in people's perceptions of their social position. In particular, it explores the roles of language skills and discrimination in channeling natives and foreigners to particular jobs and in explaining contrasts in the returns to educational cultural capital to foreign partners in binational couples. The chapter also provides indirect information as to the very important role that economic opportunities in the country of origin play in structuring the foreign partners' perception of their social-economic position in the country where they now reside.

Chapter 5 evaluates the de-nationalization thesis, that is the assertion that migration and frequent transnational mobility come at the price of engagement and identification with the local, by comparing the extent of civil and political participation by partners in national and binational couples. This analysis shows that partners in binational couples are indeed less engaged in local civil and political life than are partners in national ones. This does not mean, however, that they are a de-politicized group. In fact, they display more interest in European and world politics than do partners in national couples.

20 Introduction

Chapter 6 focuses on consumer taste and practices, a sociological subfield that still wrestles with Bourdieu's legacy (Bourdieu, 1984). It explores a wide range of forms of consumption: music, film, taste in food, and reading habits and show that partners in binational couples have a more developed taste for that which is foreign. This mainly reflects that partners in binational couples are self-selected for openness. Chapter 6 is most relevant, however, for providing evidence as to the transforming potential of being part of a binational couple. Just as individuals in binational couples tend to learn their partner's language, just as they socialize their offspring to be fluent in more than one language, they also develop an appreciation for their partners' national cuisine. Micro-changes like these illuminate how binational couples can exogenously contribute to the long-term transition to a cosmopolitan society.

Finally, Chapter 7 examines identification from different angles: from the angle of the development of cosmopolitan identifications, but also from the angle of city and national identifications, the adoption of the host country's identification on the part of foreign partners in binational couples, attachment to the European Union, and transnational solidarity. It thus speaks as much as to the Europeanization as to the de-nationalization theses. Joint analysis of the data for *Eumarr*'s seven cities shows that partners in binational couples identify more as Europeans and are more emotionally attached to the European Union than are partners in national couples, but that they do not express greater willingness to help other Europeans. The chapter illustrates again the transformative power of being in a binational couple by demonstrating that average European identification among national partners in binational couples is higher the longer the couples have been together.

Although partners in binational couples have a more developed sense of being European, Chapter 7 also demonstrates that cosmopolitan lives and identification are not bought at the price of a reduced level of national identification. In fact, foreign partners in binational couples identify more with their country of nationality the longer they have lived abroad. Also, the chapter's statistical analysis shows that although being in a binational couple instead of in a national couple is associated to less identification with the city of residence, both among the national and foreign partners in these couples, it remains quite strong.

The book ends with a concluding chapter, which summarizes the findings, reflects on their generalizability to the world at large, integrates them in the recent literature on European transnational mobility, and reflects on the relationship between social and political cosmopolitanism.

Notes

1 I first approached this topic in two previous publications (Díez Medrano, 2010, 2011). See also William Outhwaite's and Hartmut Kaelble's pioneering studies on the topic of European society (Kaelble, 2004, 2011; Outhwaite, 2008).
2 For political analyses of this emerging cleavage (see Fligstein, 2008; Kriesi et al., 2004).

    I define cosmopolitanism narrowly by building on the distinction between that which is national (i.e. from the state) and that which is foreign, as the stem "poli" from "polis" (city-state; group of citizens) implies. Cosmopolitanism is, first of all, a habitus that results from having visited many foreign places and interacted and established bonds with many foreign nationals. It manifests itself in comfort, in ease while going around when abroad and while interacting with foreign nationals. It can also be understood as an identification, that is, as the feeling of belonging to actual or projected communities that stand above the dominant--in our world, national--political community.

3 Unfortunately, the range of definitions is too broad to be covered here in detail. Useful, but not all-encompassing lists and typologies are provided in Vertovec and Cohen (2002), Delanty (2012), Szerszynski and Urry (2002). See also Beck (2006), Beck and Grande (2004), Calhoun (2002), Held (1995) and Rumford (2014).

4 From a technical, statistical view, the two variables that contribute to the definition of the term cosmopolitan are better conceived as *cause indicators* than as *effect ones*: Cause indicators do not need to be correlated. They separately contribute to determine the value of a latent variable of interest (in this case, "cosmopolitanism"). Effect indicators, on the other hand, depend on the latent variable (which they measure with error) and must be correlated, the stronger, the better (see Bollen, 1989, p. 222).

5 The remaining team members were Suzana Koelet, Clara Cortina, Julia Schroedter, and Liesbeth Herring.

6 The synthesis that follows draws from a long list of books on the topic, of which I would highlight the following: Deutsch (1953), Weber (1976), Poggi (1978), Gellner (1983), Anderson (1983), Hobsbawm (1990), Mann (1992), Wimmer (2018).

7 For a historical overview of inter-marriage, through case studies (see Dumanescu et al., 2014).

8 For a short sample of books dealing with these subjects (see Castells, 1996; DiMaggio, 2003; Lechner and Boli, 2015; Katzenstein. 2005; Robertson, 2003; Sheler and Urry, 2003; Urry, 2007).

9 Selected examples of this huge literature are: Massey et al. (1998), Portes et al. (2009), van Tubergen et al. (2004), García Polavieja et al. (2018), Brown (2006), Hainmueller and Hiscox (2007), Guiraudon and Lahav (2007), Koopmans et al. (2015).

10 See Waters (1990), Espiritu (1992), Mora (2014), Bélanger and Verkuyten (2010).

11 Examples of this work are: Favell and Recchi (2009), Favell (2008), Fligstein (2008), Kuhn (2015), Roose (2010). The basic research program that guides this bibliography was articulated in Favell and Guiraudon (2011).

12 I here list some examples: Kalmijn (1998), Beck-Gernsheim (2007), Hu (2016), Balistreri et al. (2017), Choi and Tienda (2017), Dribe and Lundh (2008), Yodanis et al. (2012). There is also a vast literature on Jewish-Gentile intermarriage, scientific and popular, which focuses on the normative barriers that stand between them and the effects of challenging these norms.

13 See Calligaro (2013), MacNamara (2015), Risse (2010), Checkel and Katzenstein (2010).

14 Schengen overlaps but does not coincide with the European Union. It was created in 1985 and currently comprises 26 countries. Switzerland, for instance, does not belong to the European Union but is part of the Schengen area. The United Kingdom, on the other hand, never signed to Schengen.

15 Perceived differences are certainly more important and I do not know of data that would provide a world picture of perceptions of cultural distance between countries. Nonetheless, my previous research shows that the British population has a more developed sense of cultural distinctiveness relative to the rest of Europe than do Germans or Spaniards (Díez Medrano, 2003) One would thus expect that when in binational couples they are less prone in relative terms to develop a European identification (although a European identification may select Britons for marriage or cohabitation with another European citizen).

16 The Zurich survey is the exception, for it also includes binational Swiss—Non-European couples.

References

Anderson, Benedict. 1983. *Imagined Communities*. London, UK: Verso.

Andreotti, Alberta, Patrick Le Galès, and Francisco Javier Moreno-Fuentes. 2015. *Globalized Minds, Roots in the City*. Oxford, UK: Wiley Blackwell.

Balistreri, Kelly, Kara Joyner, and Grace Kao. 2017. "Trading Youth for Citizenship? The Spousal Age Gap in Cross-Border Marriages: The Spousal Age Gap in Cross-Border Marriages." *Population and Development Review* 43(3): 443–466.

Beck, Ulrich. 2006. *Cosmopolitan Vision*. Cambridge, UK: Polity Press.

Beck, Ulrich and Edgar Grande. 2004. *Cosmopolitan Europe*. Cambridge, UK: Polity Press.

Beck-Gernsheim, Elizabeth. 2007. "Transnational Lives, Transnational Marriages: A Review of the Evidence from Migrant Communities in Europe." *Global Networks* 7(3): 271–288.

Bélanger, Emmanuelle and Maykel Verkuyten. 2010. "Hyphenated Identities and Acculturation: Second-Generation Chinese of Canada and The Netherlands." *Identity* 10(3): 141–163.

Benet-Martínez, Verónica and Jana Haritatos. 2005. "Bicultural Identity Integration (BII): Components and Psychosocial Antecedents." *Journal of Personality* 73: 1015–1050.

Bollen, Kenneth. 1989. *Structural Equations with Latent Variables*. New York: Wiley.

Botev, Nikolai. 1994. "Where East Meets West: Ethnic Intermarriage in the Former Yugoslavia, 1962 to 1989." *American Sociological Review* 59(3): 461–480.

Bourdieu, Pierre. 1984. *Distinction: A Social Critique of the Judgement of Taste*. Cambridge, MA: Harvard University Press.

Brown, Stuart. 2006. "Can Remittances Spur Development? A Critical Survey." *International Studies Review* 8(1): 55–75.

Calhoun, Craig. 2002. "The Class Consciousness of Frequent Travelers: Toward a Critique of Actually Existing Cosmopolitanism." In Steven Vertovec and Robin Cohen (eds.), *Conceiving Cosmopolitanism: Theory, Context and Practice*. Oxford, UK: Oxford University Press, pp. 86–109.

Calligaro, Oriane. 2013. *Negotiating Europe: EU Promotion of Europeanness since the 1950s*. New York: Palgrave MacMillan.

Castells, Manuel. 1996. *The Rise of the Network Society*. Oxford, UK: Blackwell.

Castro-Martín, Teresa and Clara Cortina. 2015. "Demographic Issues of Intra-European Migration: Destinations, Family and Settlement." *European Journal of Population* 31(2): 109–125.

Checkel, Jeffrey and Peter Katzenstein (eds.). *European Identity*. Cambridge, UK: Cambridge University Press.

Choi, Kate and Marta Tienda. 2017. "Marriage-Market Constraints and Mate-Selection Behavior: Racial, Ethnic, and Gender Differences in Intermarriage: Marriage Market and Intermarriage." *Journal of Marriage and Family* 79(2): 301–317.

Cotts-Watkins, Susan. 1991. *From Provinces into Nations: Demographic Behavior in Western Europe, 1870–1960*. Princeton, NJ: Princeton University Press.

Delanty, Gerard. 2012. "A Cosmopolitan Approach to the Explanation of Social Change: Social Mechanisms, Processes, Modernity." *The Sociological Review* 60(2): 333–354.

Delhey, Jan, Emanuel Deutschmann, and Katharina Cirlanaru. 2015. "Between 'Class Project' and Individualization: The Stratification of Europeans' Transnational Activities." *International Sociology* 30(3): 269–293.

Deutsch, Karl. 1953. *Nationalism and Social Communication*. Cambridge, MA: MIT Press.

Díez Medrano, Juan. 1995. *Divided Nations: Class, Politics, and Nationalism in the Basque Country and Catalonia*. Ithaca, NY: Cornell University Press.

Díez Medrano, Juan. 2003. *Framing Europe*. Princeton, NJ: Princeton University Press.

Díez Medrano, Juan. 2010. "A New Society in the Making." *Working Paper* 12. KfG The Transformative Power of Europe. Berlin, Germany: Free University.

Díez Medrano, Juan. 2011. "The Present and Future of Social Classes." In Adrian Favell and Virginie Guiraudon (eds.), *Sociology of the European Union*. New York: Palgrave MacMillan, pp. 25–50.

DiMaggio, Paul (ed.). 2003. *The Twentieth-Century Firm*. Princeton, NJ: Princeton University Press.

Dribe, Martin and Christer Lundh. 2008 "Intermarriage and Immigrant Integration in Sweden." *Acta Sociologica* 51(4): 329–354.

Dumanescu, Luminia, Daniela Marza, and Marus Eppel (eds.). 2014. *Intermarriage throughout History*. Newcastle, UK: Cambridge Scholars Publishing.

Durkheim, Emile. 1952 [1905]. *Suicide*. Glencoe, IL: The Free Press.

Espiritu, Yen. 1992. *Asian American Panethnicity: Bridging Institutions and Identities*. Philadelphia, PA: Temple University Press.

Favell, Adrian. 2008. *Eurostars and Eurocities*. Oxford, UK: Blackwell.

Favell, Adrian and Ettore Recchi (eds.). 2009. *Pioneers of European Integration*. Northampton, UK: Edward Elgar.

Favell, Adrian and Virginie Guiraudon (eds.). 2011. *Sociology of the European Union*. New York: Palgrave MacMillan.

Fligstein, Neil. 2008. *Euro-clash*. Oxford, UK: Oxford University Press.

Fligstein, Neil and Frédéric Mérand. 2002. "Globalization or Europeanization? Evidence on the European Economy since 1980. *Acta Sociologica* 45: 7–22.

García Polavieja, Javier, Mariña Fernández-Reino, and María Ramos. 2018. "Are Migrants Selected on Motivational Orientations? Selectivity Patterns amongst International Migrants in Europe." *European Sociological Review* 34(5): 570–588.

Gellner, Ernest. 1983. *Nations and Nationalism*. Ithaca, NY: Cornell University Press.

Gerhards, Jürgen. 2012. *From Babel to Brussels: European Integration and the Importance of Transnational Linguistic Capital*. Berlin Studies on the Sociology of Europe (BSSE) 28. Freie Universität Berlin.

Gordon, Milton. 1964. *Assimilation in American Life. The Role of Race, Religion and National Origins*. New York: Oxford University Press.

Guiraudon, Virginie and Gallya Lahav (eds.). (2007). *Immigration Policy in Europe: The Politics of Control*. New York: Routledge.

Hainmueller, Jens and Michael Hiscox. 2007. "Educated Preferences: Explaining Attitudes toward Immigration in Europe." *International Organization* 61(2): 399–442.

Hechter, Michael. 1975. *Internal Colonialism: The Celtic Fringe in British National Development*. Berkeley: University of California Press.

Held, David. 1995. *Democracy and the Global Order*. Cambridge, UK: Polity Press.

Hobsbawm, Eric. 1990. *Nations and Nationalism since 1780*. Cambridge, MA: Harvard University Press.

Hu, Yang. 2016. *Chinese-British Intermarriage: Disentangling Gender and Ethnicity*. London, UK: Palgrave-MacMillan.

Inglehart, Ronald. 1997. *Modernization and Post-Modernization*. Princeton, NJ: Princeton University Press.

Kaelble, Hartmut. 2011. *The Social History of Europe, 1945–2000: Recovery and Transformation after Two World Wars*. New York: Berghahn.

Kaelble, Hartmut (ed.). 2004. *The European Way: European Societies during the Nineteenth and Twentieth Centuries*. New York: Berghahn.

Kalmijn, Matthijs. 1998. "Intermarriage and Homogamy: Causes, Patterns, Trends." *Annual Review of Sociology* 24: 395–421.

24 Introduction

Katzenstein, Peter. 2005. *A World of Regions.* Ithaca, NY: Cornell University Press.

Kocka, Jürgen. 1999. *Industrial Society and Bourgeois Culture in Modern Germany.* New York: Berghahn.

Koelet, Suzana and Helga AG de Valk. 2016. "Social Networks and Feelings of Social Loneliness after Migration: The Case of European Migrants with a Native Partner in Belgium." *Ethnicities* 16(4): 610–630.

Koelet, Suzana, Christof Van Mol, and Helga A. G. De Valk. 2017. "Social Embeddedness in a Harmonized Europe: The Social Networks of European Migrants with a Native Partner in Belgium and the Netherlands." *Global Networks* 17(3): 441–459.

Koopmans, Ruud, Bram Lancee, and Merlin Schaeffer (eds.). 2015. *Social Cohesion and Immigration in Europe and North America. Mechanisms, Conditions, and Causality.* New York: Routledge.

Kriesi, Hans-Peter, Edgard Grande, Romain Lachat, Martin Dolezal, Simon Bornschier, and Frey, Timotheos. 2004. *West European Politics in the Age of Globalization.* Cambridge, UK: Cambridge University Press.

Krücken, Georg and Gili Drori (eds.). 2009. *World Society: The Writings of John W. Meyer.* Oxford, UK: Oxford University Press.

Kuhn, Theresa. 2015. *Experiencing European Integration.* Oxford, UK: Oxford University Press.

Lechner Frank and John Boli. 2015. *The Globalization Reader.* Oxford, UK: John Wiley and Sons.

MacNamara, Kathleen. 2015. *The Politics of Everyday Europe.* Oxford, UK: Oxford University Press.

Mann, Michael. 1992. *The Sources of Social Power,* Vol. 2. Cambridge, UK: Cambridge University Press.

Massey, Doug, Joaquín Arango, Graeme Hugo, Ali Kouaouci, and Adela Pellegrino. 1998. *Worlds in Motion: Understanding Migration at the End of the Millennium.* Oxford, UK: Oxford University Press.

Mau, Steffen. 2007. *Transnationale Vergesellschaftung.* Frankfurt am Main: Campus.

Mora, Cristina. 2014. *Making Hispanics.* Chicago, IL: University of Chicago Press.

Norris, Pippa and Ronald Inglehart. 2019. *Cultural Backlash: Trump, Brexit, and Authoritarian Populism.* New York: Cambridge University Press.

Outhwaite, William. 2008. *European Society.* Cambridge, UK: Polity Press.

Poggi, Gianfranco. 1978. *The Development of the Modern State: A Sociological Introduction.* Palo Alto, CA: Stanford University Press.

Portes, Alejandro, Cristina Escobar, and Renelinda Arana. 2009. "Divided or Convergent Loyalties?: The Political Incorporation Process of Latin American Immigrants in the United States." *International Journal of Comparative Sociology* 50(2): 103–136.

Recchi, Ettore. 2015. *Mobile Europe: The Theory and Practice of Mobility in the EU.* Basingstoke, UK: Palgrave MacMillan.

Risse, Thomas. 2010. *A Community of Europeans?* Ithaca, NY: Cornell University Press.

Robertson, Robbie. 2003. *The Three Waves of Globalization: A History of a Developing Social Consciousness.* London, UK: Zed Books.

Roose, Jochen. 2010. *Vergesellschaftung an Europas Binnengrenzen.* Wiesbaden: VS Verlag.

Roudometof, Victor. 2005 "Transnationalism, Cosmopolitanism and Globalization." *Current Sociology* 53: 113–135.

Rumford, Chris. 2014. *Cosmopolitan Borders.* London, UK: Palgrave.

Santacreu, Oscar, Emiliana Baldoni, and Maria Carmen Albert 2009. "Deciding To Move: Migration Projects in an Integrating Europe." In Adrian Favell and Ettore Recchi (eds.), *Pioneers of European Integration.* Northampton, UK: Edward Elgar, pp. 52–71.

Savage, Mike, Gaynor Bagnall, and Brian Longurst. *Globalization and Belonging*. London, UK: Sage.

Saxenian, AnnaLee. 2007. *The New Argonauts*. Cambridge, MA: Harvard University Press.

Schroedter, Julia, Jörg Rössel, and Georg Datler. 2015. "European Identity in Switzerland: The Role of Intermarriage, and Transnational Social Relations and Experiences" edited by Dan Rodríguez-García. *The ANNALS of the American Academy of Political and Social Science* 662(1): 148–168.

Schroedter, Julia, Tom De Winter, and Suzana Koelet. 2015. "Beyond l'Auberge Espagnole: The Effect of Individual Mobility on the Formation of Intra-European Couples." *European Journal of Population* 31(2): 181–206.

Sheler, Mimi and John Urry. 2003. *Tourism Mobilities*. New York: Routledge.

Smith Michael Peter and Adrian Favell (eds.). 2006. *The Human Face of Global Mobility: International High Skill Migrants in Europe, North America and the Asia Pacific*. New Brusnswick, NJ: Transaction Press.

Szerszynski, Bronislaw and John Urry. 2002. "Cultures of Cosmopolitanism." *The Sociological Review* 50(4): 461–481.

Taft, Ronald. 1957. "A Psychological Model for the Study of Social Assimilation." *Human Relations* 10: 141–156.

Tubergen, Frank van, Ineke Maas, and Henk Flap. 2004. "The Economic Incorporation of Immigrants in 18 Western Societies: Origin, Destination, and Community Effects." *American Sociological Review* 69(5): 704–727.

Turner, John. 1987. *Rediscovering the Social Group: Self-Categorization Theory*. New York: Blackwell.

Urry, John. 2007. *Mobilities*. Cambridge, UK: Polity Press.

Valk, Helga de and Juan Díez Medrano (eds.). 2014. "Meeting and Mating Across Borders: in the European Union: Union Formation in the European Union Single Market." Special Issue of *Population, Space, and Place* 20(2): i–ii, 103–199.

Van Mol, Christof and Helga A. G. de Valk. 2016. "Relationship Satisfaction of European Binational Couples in the Netherlands." *International Journal of Intercultural Relations* 50: 50–59.

Van Mol, Christof and Helga A. G. de Valk. 2018. "European Movers' Language Use Patterns at Home: A Case-Study of European Bi-National Families in the Netherlands." *European Societies* 20(4): 665–689.

Van Mol, Christof, Helga A. G. de Valk, and Leo van Wissen. 2015. "Falling in Love with(in) Europe: European Bi-National Love Relationships, European Identification and Transnational Solidarity." *European Union Politics* 16(4): 469–489.

Vertovec, Steven and Robin Cohen (eds.). 2002. *Conceiving Cosmopolitanism: Theory, Context and Practice*. Oxford, UK: Oxford University Press.

Waters, Mary. 1990. *Ethnic Options*. Berkeley: University of California Press.

Weber, Eugen. 1976. *Peasants into Frenchman*. Palo Alto, CA: Stanford University Press.

Wimmer, Andreas. 2018. *Nation Building: Why Some Countries Come Together While Others Fall Apart*. Princeton, NJ: Princeton University Press.

Yodanis, Carrie, Sean Lauer, and Risako Ota. 2012. "Interethnic Romantic Relationships: Enacting Affiliative Ethnic Identities." *Journal of Marriage and Family* 74(5):1021–1037.

2

WHEN WILLEM MET LAURA

Who enters national and binational couples?

Romanian woman, mid-thirties; formerly married to Romanian man with whom she has a young daughter; moved to Spain in the early 2000s; cohabits with a Spaniard since last year, early thirties. He was raised partly in Spain, partly in South America (Interview # 3).

"I have lived in Spain for exactly eight years. Before, I was married to another person. Last year, we formalized the divorce, the division of property. Everything was settled in Romania. The court case and everything else was settled there. Because we had three houses there, an issue that has no value to me anymore. It means nothing to me. I only care for my daughter. She is five years old; well, she is soon turning six…

…I did not move here in search of adventure, I moved here to rejoin my spouse. To see what is there to see in Spain, what Spain is. And I was fascinated, I like it, and I think of this as my home.

…I finished high school in Romania and then I started to study Management, for two years. I don't know what was wrong with me, however, but I dropped out. And I am sorry that I stopped, because I realize now, in Spain; well, in Spain I have also enrolled in workshops—nurse assistant, marketing, management through goals--but it is just workshops, not a proper degree…

…When I came [to Spain] I did not know anybody. I had some acquaintances, people who hosted me at the beginning, who offered me a bed, but after a while I decided that I wanted to be independent, not to be a burden to anybody, and searched for work. And two weeks later, I had a job.

…This was 2004. He [former husband] was here. But, of course, he and I were estranged from one another from the beginning. We lasted many years, but… He moved to Spain in 2003. When I came here, we did not meet for about the first ten days. He is like this, he did not seem to care that we had not seen each other for half a year. I don't know where he was; he is cold, just like this, he has a very cold personality. I don't know whether it is like this with the majority of Romanian men. I told myself: "If I am starting my life again, it will not be with a Romanian."

...[current partner] and I still need to get to know each other better, learn how to communicate with one another. Because my first marriage lasted seventeen years, but we communicated poorly. We were different. [Partner] and I are lucky, we even share the same zodiac sign! I am somewhat older than he is."

Romanian woman, early forties, married to a Spaniard her age, born and raised in Spain. Two young children; met at the turn of the millennium in a Western European country and married just a few years later; in Spain since 2004 (Interview # 8).

...We both work at the university...We have two young children, the youngest has just started pre-school and the girl is in first grade. ...I got my undergraduate degree in Romania. Then, I wrote my PhD dissertation in [Western European country]. My husband was already there, on a post-doc fellowship. This is how we first met. And then, after that, we were only able to find work together in [Northern European country]. We each received a post-doc. I stayed two and a half years and he stayed one and half years. Then, he came back to Spain and I started my struggle to get a Spanish post-doc to be able to join him...It was easier for him. He was already affiliated to Spain's [research/academic institution] by the time we first met. ...When he went back to Spain, he did so with a fellowship targeted to returning scientists. ...This funding lasted two years and then he won a Senior Research fellowship. I entered the Spanish system with a Spanish post-doc fellowship. ...I was affiliated at the [Name of a research institution in the hard sciences] from 200X to 200X and, just one year before my post-doc expired, I was also awarded a Senior Researcher fellowship by the Spanish government. With it, I was able to secure a job in the same department where my husband was already employed...Everything turned out for the best. We were very lucky that the University [Name omitted] was investing in attracting young talent ...My husband is actually from this city...His parents also live here. One of his brothers lived here too but he recently moved to [Another Spanish region].

Notwithstanding predictions to the contrary, the "family," broadly conceived as the relatively permanent emotional bonds and cohabiting arrangements between two persons, remains a core social institution, whose changes reverberate across society. One recent change, which one can relate to globalization, has been the increase in the incidence of intermarriage. In this book, I examine the lives of partners in binational couples formed by Europeans. I depart from the literature on inter-, cross-border-, bi-ethnic binational, transnational marriage and cohabitation, which has tended to focus on couples formed by Western and non-Western individuals. This focus is justified: the removal of barriers to the flows of goods, capital, services, and people has been faster and more sweeping in Europe than anywhere else in the world (Fligstein and Mérand, 2002). The European Union has passed laws, created institutions, and sponsored policies that have greatly facilitated mobility between its member states. Signatories of the Schengen Treaty have eliminated passport controls between their countries. More than one million university students have spent at least a semester in another member state through the ERASMUS program. De-regulation of air transport and in tele-communications has lowered the costs of traveling and spending holidays throughout Europe. The liberalization of capital flows, combined with the freedom of movement, has made it possible for thousands of European retirees to spend part of the year or live permanently in another country. Millions of Europeans from Central and Eastern Europe, and from Southern Europe, have moved for relatively long periods or permanently to other European Union member states in search of better economic opportunities.

Meeting people from other European countries is easier than ever, and this should have consequences for the development and increase in friendship and love relationships. We know next to nothing, however, about changes in the incidence of binational marriages or cohabitation arrangements between Europeans. A rare exception is the *Population, Space, and Place* special issue that Helga de Valk and I co-edited, with contributions by all of the *Eumarr* project's team members (de Valk and Díez Medrano, 2014). The special issue revealed that thousands of Europeans intermarry every year. In European Union states like Spain, which since the early 2000s have become host to large numbers of migrants from Central and Eastern European countries, the incidence of binational marriages between Europeans has actually increased dramatically. Neither the in-flow of migrants from these countries nor the increase in the incidence of Euro-marriages would have reached the same levels had these Central and Eastern European countries remained outside the European Union (Díez Medrano et al., 2014). It is obvious that the European Union's institutional, legal, and policy context is conducive to an increase in the prevalence of binational couples formed by Europeans.

I also depart from the literature in thematic focus. Whereas the literature on migration and inter-marriage in mainly interested in the assimilation of immigrants to the host society, in marriage dissolution rates, and in the complex legal disputes surrounding divorce or child custody in couples formed by nationals from different countries, I concentrate on the Euro-couples' ordinary lives. Sociology has always paid particular attention to conflict. There is also a political and policy bent to much sociological research. The obsession with immigrant assimilation and cultural conflict of much contemporary sociology risks becoming tedious and self-limiting. Society is much more than that. It also encompasses the mundane, the ordinary, areas of life to which historians since Braudel or Duby and sociologists since Simmel and the early 20th century Chicago school (Wirth, Park, White, Burgess) have devoted some of their most memorable pages.

One running theme in this book is the need to differentiate between Euro-couples formed by less educated partners and Euro-couples formed by more educated ones. Indeed, as the quotes that open the chapter already hint at, binational couples are not a homogeneous social category. Both education and country of origin distinguish the experiences and lifestyles of partners in binational couples. Binational couples formed by individuals with less education generally involve traditional migrants whereas those formed by individuals with more education tend to involve what Favell describes as "free movers." Although Favell does not systematically elaborate on the analytical distinction between traditional migrants and free-movers (Favell, 2008), I would argue that what distinguishes the two the most is that the former's moves are part of family- or community-based strategies, while the latter mainly reflect individual choice and strategizing. So, for instance, whereas the first respondent above moved in Spain to join her Romanian husband who had migrated a year before her and already knew some people, the second respondent moved to Spain because her husband was Spaniard and had settled back in Spain after a short period abroad. She had no Romanian relatives or acquaintances in Spain. She actually had never visited the country before. The book's narrative will thus alternate comparisons between national and binational couples and comparisons between binational couples involving less educated partners and binational couples involving more educated ones.

Europe in Love analyzes information collected through a survey conducted in seven European cities (Antwerp, Brussels, Barcelona, Madrid, Amsterdam, The Hague, and Zurich), and in-depth interviews conducted in Spain with some of the sample's respondents. The choice of four different countries aimed at capturing some of the socio-economic and cultural diversity of the European countries where binational couples are most prevalent in order to then focus on what is common across national settings. Because of this analytic choice, the samples in each country are relatively small and comparisons across cities and countries only play a secondary role in the book's narrative. I have only mentioned contrasts across cities or countries when these are significant and theoretically justifiable. Three criteria guided the city selection: a relatively high prevalence of Euro-couples in the chosen cities, diversity in the composition of the European population of the different cities, so that the nationality combinations in the overall sample of binational couples would be as diverse as possible, and the availability and quality of population registers to randomly select individuals in national and binational couples. The population register in each country indeed provided the sampling frame that the national teams used to select respondents. The book draws inductively from the data collected for this survey and is written in the logic of discovery. When contrasts emerge, I have pushed the analysis in an explanatory direction, but only so far as the nature of the research design allows. In general, I have kept the statistical analysis as simple as possible, and relied mainly on bivariate percentage tables, in order to maximize readability and a clear visualization of the order of magnitude of differences across groups. I always complement the analysis of bivariate relationships, however, with a somewhat more complex statistical analysis based on the estimation of nested sequences of multiple regression models. These models, largely inspired by a path-analysis logic, illuminate the results obtained through contingency tables and help interpret the observed raw associations. This chapter outlines the book's

30 When Willem met Laura?

main comparative strategy and examines the sample, focusing on the respondents' distribution along basic background variables like gender, age education, and nationality. It also analyzes the circumstances under which respondents met and started to live together with their partner. This background analysis sets the stage for the rest of the book by anticipating the scope for difference between the lifestyle, experiences, and worldviews of people in national and binational couples.

The sample[1]: comparative strategy

While Euro-couples sometimes live in countries different from both partners' country of nationality, the overwhelming majority reside in one of the partners' country of nationality. They constituted the *Eumarr*'s study research subject and structured the survey design itself (except in Switzerland, where the sampling frame targeted individuals in all kinds of binational couples, whether European or non-European). Studying European binational couples and comparing them to national couples entails the practical problem of determining what is one and what is the other. This is because in today's world many citizens have more than one nationality, acquired at different moments in the life cycle and for all kinds of idiosyncratic reasons. The *Eumarr* sample, for instance, included individuals who shared the country of residence's nationality with their national partner, but who also held another nationality, sometimes European and sometimes extra-European; it also included couples where one of the partners held the country of residence's nationality while the other partner held another European country's nationality, but where both held in common either the foreign partner's European nationality or another European or extra-European nationality. It would be interesting to know more about the reasons why people hold more than one nationality. If anything, this would help clarifying the meaning of weak or strong associations between nationality, identification, and worldviews. While the contingency of being born in a particular country or the need to deal with the practicalities connected to living in a foreign country are probably the main explanation for multiple nationalities, other factors also play a role. Special bilateral agreements between countries that automatically or semi-automatically entitle citizens from one country to hold the other country's nationality are one of these factors. Argentinians, for instance, depending on their family origins, can easily receive Spanish or Italian passports and enjoy all the benefits attached to being a European Union citizen. Another factor that can account for why people have more than one nationality is love for one's foreign partner or for one's foreign country of residence. Unfortunately, the *Eumarr* survey did not collect detailed enough information that would allow a categorization of respondents based on the reasons for why they hold multiple nationalities. Because of this, and in order to simplify the comparison between national and binational couples, I chose to just focus on individuals who belong to couples that one can unambiguously classify as national or European binational: individuals in national couples are those who hold the country of residence's nationality only and whose partner holds the country of residence's nationality only. Individuals in binational couples are those in couples where one of the partners holds the country of residence's nationality only and where the other partner holds one or more nationalities from other European countries only.[2]

Sixty-eight percent of the respondents in national or in binational couples formed by a national and a foreign partner can be classified into one of the two pure categories defined above and are the object of this book's analysis. Except for a small group of respondents who belong to couples where none of the partners has the country of residence's nationality (3%), those left out are respondents in couples where at least one of the partners has a second nationality that it shares with the other partner or where one of the partners has a non-European nationality. I thus compare individuals in a prototypical national couple to individuals, both national and foreign, in the most extreme form that a binational couple between Europeans can take. This comparative design maximizes the possibility of finding contrasts between the lifestyles, experiences, and worldviews of these two types of married and cohabiting couples.

The research team intentionally decided to only interview people who are between 30 and 46 years old. Two reasons underlie this decision: first, to circumscribe the inquiry to the first cohort of Europeans who became adults when the European single market and the Schengen passport-free space were created[3] and, second, in view of resource limitations, to control for life stage, a variable that strongly influences people's lifestyles, experiences, and worldviews, and at the same time secure a large enough sample size for this age group.

On average, respondents in this study have spent 11 years together with their current partner. This means that they are the survivors of those who started their relationship about a decade ago. Although the same applies to the partners in national couples, and although studies conducted in the Netherlands and Switzerland show that couple dissolution rates among European binational couples are only slightly higher than among national couples,[4] this study's sample somewhat overrepresents binational couples that have successfully negotiated intercultural differences in connection to both their partner and, in the case of foreign partners, the country of residence. One can nonetheless assume that the selection bias is small and that the sample under analysis still represents quite well the universe of Euro-couples in the four countries. As studies also show, divorce rates in general are not extremely high and about three-quarters of binational couples between Europeans remain intact after ten years.

The sample frames for this study were drawn from population registers in large cities of the four countries represented in the study (i.e. Madrid, Barcelona, Brussels, Antwerp, Amsterdam, The Hague, and Zurich). These registers included information on the nationality of household members, which made it possible to at least draw separate samples for potential national and binational couples. Households were selected randomly and so were respondents within households. Beyond this similarity, the sample design varied across countries,

32 When Willem met Laura?

as shown in the Appendix. Relevant contrasts between the countries' sampling designs concern the range of European nationalities that national research teams considered at the sample selection stage, the target sample sizes for individuals in national and binational couples, and stratification by education and foreign nationality. Whereas the Spanish and Belgian samples only targeted highly prevalent European nationalities, the Dutch and Swiss ones targeted all European nationalities; also, while the Spanish and Swiss sampling design aimed at equal representation of individuals in national and binational couples, the Belgian and Dutch sampling design aimed at a much higher sample of individuals in binational couples. Finally, whereas the Spanish sampling design aimed at balanced representation of less educated and more educated individuals in national couples and of European respondents from old and new European Union member states (i.e. more developed and less developed ones), the Belgian, Dutch, and Swiss sampling design did not differentiate by education or foreign nationality group.[5] The composition of the city samples by type of couple, education, and nationality are therefore not representative of the populations from which they are drawn. To account for this, most of the book's contingency tables control for education (less than University education; University education), type of couple (national, binational), and country of residence (Spain, Belgium, the Netherlands, Switzerland) whereas the more complex statistical analytical procedures (e.g. multiple regression) control for actual level of education, type of couple, and city of residence.[6] Drawing on the stratification and national identification literatures, I have also re-estimated relevant models so as to distinguish between respondents from relatively poor EU countries and respondents from relatively rich ones.[7]

Background

The respondents in this study are evenly split by gender (54% are women). They are also highly educated. About two-thirds of the respondents have studied beyond high school, regardless of whether they belong to a national or to a binational couple. As expected, because of the way the sample was designed, the Spanish sample includes almost as many less educated as more educated respondents (see Table 2.1). Educational homogamy is widespread in both national and binational couples, and only slightly higher among the former ($r = 0.55$ vs. $r = 0.51$).[8] Because of educational homogamy, and in order to simplify the narrative, throughout the book I describe couples as less or more educated based on the respondent's level of education.

The binational couples in the sample include individuals (respondents and partners) from 26 of the 27 European Union member states at the time of the survey as well as Swiss respondents (see Table 2.2). Again, the exact representation of different nationalities in the country samples partly reflects specific sampling choices made by the four research teams. In Spain, in particular, it overrepresents less educated individuals and married or cohabiting foreign partners from new

TABLE 2.1 Distribution of Respondents by Type of Couple, Education, and Country of Residence (%)

	Spanish Cities	Belgian Cities	Dutch Cities	Swiss City	Total
In National Couple					
No university education	48	35	24	25	32
	(159)	(33)	(38)	(236)	(466)
University education	52	65	76	75	68
	(171)	(61)	(121)	(285)	(638)
In Binational Couple (National Partner)					
No university education	47	32	20	19	27
	(71)	(71)	(56)	(90)	(288)
University education	53	68	80	80	73
	(79)	(148)	(230)	(149)	(606)
In Binational Couple (Foreign Partner)					
No university education	43	18	22	17	23
	(63)	(40)	(67)	(101)	(271)
University education	57	82	78	83	77
	(85)	(177)	(232)	(240)	(734)
N	(628)	(530)	(744)	(1100)	(3002)

() Number of respondents.

European Union member states. Still, the sample includes and represents the most important European nationality combinations that one finds in the four countries. If one divides the sample of foreign partners into nationals from relatively poor European Union states (i.e. Mediterranean and former Communist countries) and nationals from relatively rich European Union states, a distinction that becomes useful in the course of the book, about 32% of the foreign individuals in binational couples (respondents or partners), are nationals from the former, whereas 68% are nationals from the latter. Binational couples in which one of the partners is German, British, Dutch, Italians, Spanish, or Romanian are the most numerous ones. Germans, French, and Italian, in particular, are highly represented in the four samples. Romanian, on the other hand, are concentrated in the Spanish sample, as one would expect given that it is Spain's largest immigrant national group. Indeed, as shown in the *Population, Space, and Place* special issue referred to above, the European immigrants' group size is the most important factor determining the prevalence of specific nationality combinations in different European Union countries. Since the choice of migration destination is often driven by spatial and language proximity, one also sees that some of the most prevalent nationality combinations in the binational couples represented in the different countries involve partners who speak the same language: Belgian-Dutch and Belgian–French, Swiss–German. The lack of an exact overlap between national boundaries and language areas in the European Union

34 When Willem met Laura?

TABLE 2.2 Distribution of Foreign Individuals (Respondents or Partners) in Binational Couples, by Nationality (N)

	Spanish Cities	Belgian Cities	Dutch Cities	Swiss City	Total
Austria			11	39	50
Belgium			45	6	51
Bulgaria	24		3	4	31
Czech Rep.			5	8	13
Denmark			12	7	19
Estonia			3	3	6
Finland			13	1	14
France	53	152	59	34	298
Germany	40	26	108	306	480
Greece			8	9	17
Hungary	1		15	9	25
Ireland			25	1	26
Italy	53	36	40	26	155
Latvia			2	3	5
Lithuania			3	1	4
Luxembourg	1			5	6
Malta			1	2	3
Netherlands		157		14	171
Poland		21	26	15	62
Portugal	11		25	6	42
Romania	83		11	6	100
Slovakia			7	8	15
Slovenia			3	2	5
Spain		47	46	34	127
Sweden			8	16	24
United Kingdom	35		109	19	163
N	301	439	588	584	1912

is certainly a factor that facilitates mobility and the formation and stability of binational couples.

The sample of respondents reveals regularities across levels of education and countries revealing of contrasting patterns of family formation in national and binational couples. As mentioned above, respondents to the survey have been living together 11 years on average. Partners in national couples, however, started to live together about two to three years earlier than did partners in binational ones (see Table 2.3). Probably partly because of this they also have more children on average (see Table 2.4). Finally, the age gap between the partners is also about one year greater (see Table 2.5).[9] The *Eumarr* data are not suited to provide an explanation for these contrasts. The standard explanation in the literature is that people are generally endogamous and that entering a binational relationship is not people's first choice (Lichter, 1990; Oppenheimer, 1988). Other explanations are also plausible, however. The observed associations may perhaps reflect a population

TABLE 2.3 Average Age When Partners Started Life Together, by Type of Couple, Education, and Country

		Spanish Cities	Belgian Cities	Dutch Cities	Swiss City
No University Education	National	24	25	25	26
		(156)	(33)	(38)	(127)
	Binational	29	29	27	29
		(134)	(111)	(122)	(101)
University Education	National	25	26	26	27
		(170)	(60)	(120)	(389)
	Binational	29	28	27	29
		(159)	(325)	(460)	(572)

() Number of respondents.

TABLE 2.4 Average Number of Children with Current Partner, by Type of Couple, Education, and Country

		Spanish Cities	Belgian Cities	Dutch Cities	Swiss City
No University Education	National	1.2	1.2	1.5	1.4
		(159)	(33)	(38)	(125)
	Binational	1.0	0.8	1.3	0.9
		(134)	(111)	(123)	(101)
University Education	National	1.4	1.2	1.6	1.2
		(170)	(93)	(120)	(387)
	Binational	1.3	0.9	1.4	0.7
		(162)	(436)	(459)	(468)

() Number of respondents.

segment's greater propensity to disregard traditional social norms, including norms about marriage age, about the expected age gap between partners, and about exogamy (Fu, 2010). Also, one could speculate that they are the logical outcome of populations divided into endogamous and exogamous individuals, where, for sheer availability reasons, the latter have more trouble finding a suitable partner.

One of the *Eumarr* survey's original contribution is to have collected detailed information on how the partners in national and binational couples met. In particular, the questionnaire included questions regarding when and where they first met and when and where they started to live together. Recent work on the formation of binational couples has focused on mail-order brides and on marriages of convenience.[10] The onset of the internet age and the development of

36 When Willem met Laura?

TABLE 2.5 Mean Age Gap between Partners, by Type of Couple, Education, and Country

		Spanish Cities	Belgian Cities	Dutch Cities	Swiss City
No University Education	National	2.53	2.44	3.08	3.11
		(159)	(32)	(38)	(113)
	Binational	3.27	3.25	3.61	3.68
		(134)	(110)	(122)	(91)
University Education	National	2.35	2.28	2.20	2.54
		(171)	(60)	(121)	(375)
	Binational	3.27	3.33	2.98	3.22
		(164)	(322)	(462)	(431)

() Number of respondents.

social media have contributed significantly to the rise in these types of marriage and prompted preventive legal measures from governments keen on controlling migration flows. These types of marriages, however, should not be frequent among Europeans, mainly because of the freedom of movement in the Schengen space. The *Eumarr* survey results convey this. The percentage of respondents in binational couples who met their foreign partner through internet is certainly significant, especially in Belgium and Switzerland, where it reaches more than 10% among both less educated and more educated respondents. The very large majority of partners in binational couples between Europeans, however, met in the country where they currently live (Table 2.6) and tend to have lived several years in the country of residence before meeting their partner. This is particularly the case among less educated respondents. Whether one considers all

TABLE 2.6 Place of First Meeting for Individuals in Binational Couples, by Education, and Country (%)

		Spanish Cities	Belgian Cities	Dutch Cities	Swiss City
No University Education	Country of residence	81	64	51	58
	Another country	15	22	42	30
	Internet	4	14	7	12
	N	(134)	(111)	(123)	(103)
University Education	Country of residence	64	57	45	54
	Another country	33	32	51	37
	Internet	3	12	4	8
	N	(163)	(207)	(461)	(472)

( ) Number of respondents.

When Willem met Laura? **37**

TABLE 2.7 Average Number of Years Foreign Partner Spent in Country of Residence before Meeting Partner, by Education and Country (Information Provided by Foreign Partners to Binational Couples)

	Spanish Cities	Belgian Cities	Dutch Cities	Swiss City
No university education	3	9	8	7
	(44)	(23)	(35)	(12)
University education	2	4	4	3
	(50)	(84)	(114)	(103)

() Number of respondents.

TABLE 2.8 Average Number of Years Foreign Partner Spent in Country of Residence before Meeting Partner, by Education and Country (Foreign Partners Who Met in Country of Residence only; Information Provided by Foreign Respondent)

	Spanish Cities	Belgian Cities	Dutch Cities	Swiss City
No university education	3	11	9	8
	(42)	(15)	(24)	(10)
University education	2	5	4	4
	(41)	(52)	(73)	(74)

() Number of respondents.

foreign respondents (Table 2.7) or only those who met their national partner in the country of residence (Table 2.8), less educated ones had lived longer in the country of residence when they met their national partner. This is especially the case in Belgium, the Netherlands, and Switzerland with a considerably longer tradition of migration from low-income European countries than Spain's. As Table 2.9 also shows, the percentage of foreign nationals who already consider the host country as their own country is much greater among the less educated than among the more educated ones. Chapter 7, on identification, corroborates this finding, by showing that they also identify more strongly with the country of residence.

As other studies have shown, compared with less educated individuals, more educated individuals in relatively wealthy European Union states move more often, on holidays, to study abroad, or for professional reasons (Fligstein, 2008; Recchi, 2015). In contrast to the moves of less educated traditional migrants, these moves abroad generally reflect individual, not family, decisions and tend to be temporary or easily reversible. When more educated individuals start a relationship with a foreign European, they need to negotiate at some point where they want to settle on a more or less permanent basis. Cohabitation and marriage thus factor in as a reason to move to another country more among more educated partners than among less educated partners in binational couples, which explains

38 When Willem met Laura?

TABLE 2.9 Reasons for Coming to Country, by Nationality of Reporting Respondent, Place Where Partners Met, and Education (Partners in Binational Couples Only) (%)

		Met in Country of Residence: Reasons Why Foreign Partner Was There	Met in Another Country: Reasons why Partners Were There	
		Information provided by Foreign Respondent in Binational Couple	National Respondent	Foreign Respondent
No university education	Her/His own country	32	5	44
	Studying purposes	5	13	
	Professional reasons	37	28	14
	On holidays	9	43	29
	Something else	17	12	14
	N	(139)	(61)	(66)
University education	Her/His own country	18	4	41
	Studying purposes	26	28	22
	Professional reasons	44	28	16
	On holidays	6	31	15
	Something else	7	9	6
	N	(411)	(265)	(298)

( ) Number of respondents.

why only 28% of less educated nationals in binational couples met their foreign partner abroad, whereas 44% of the more educated ones did. Also because of this, highly educated foreign nationals have lived less time in the host country on average than have less educated ones. As I show later in the book, this has interesting and counterintuitive implications for the relative social integration of less educated and more educated foreign partners in their host countries.

In-depth interviews that I conducted with respondents in the Spanish sample illustrate the variety of circumstances under which partners in binational couples met. In some cases, the foreign partner was studying in the country where they now live. For instance, the Italian respondent who moved to Spain as an Erasmus student, settled there, and then, three years later, met his current partner. Or the French respondent who, after several career changes, and stays in different countries, landed in Spain to study for a degree in Tourism and then met her future husband. Or yet the Portuguese woman who moved to Spain to study economics, graduated, found a well-paying job, and eventually met her current partner. In other instances, it is the national partner who was studying abroad, met his or her current partner, and finally negotiated that they both move to Spain, the national partner's country of nationality. These stories are somewhat more complicated because more often than not it is not just one partner but the two of them who must find a suitable professional fit in the national partner's country of nationality. The second quote at the beginning of the chapter illustrates this: the partners first met in [Western European country], where one of them was completing a PhD, and the other was on a post-doc. Then they were able to find a provisional joint appointment in [Northern European country]. Finally, after a short separation in which the Spanish partner won a senior research position and moved back alone to Spain, his Romanian wife was awarded a post-doc position in Spain that allowed her to join him. Another complicated story involved a German consultant and a Spanish researcher. They first met in Switzerland, where both were studying different subjects. Upon graduation, they received job offers in different countries, which forced them into a long-distance relationship. Eventually, after 15 years of commuting, as both pursued successful careers, he experienced burn-out as a consultant, took a sabbatical year, and settled in Spain to try his chances in the Spanish labor market. Yet another complex story features a Spanish woman and another German man. The German partner came to Spain as a student, so as to be with his Spanish girlfriend. This relationship ended but months later he met his current wife. He tried to find a job in Spain for a while but since he did not find what he was looking for he returned to Germany and tried his luck there. She, in turn, quit her rather unfulfilling job and moved with him to Germany. She also found work there but was unhappy because of Germany's "bad weather" and could not wait for an opportunity to come up that would allow both she and her husband to move back to Spain. Eventually, her dream came true. Her German partner got a job at the Spanish branch of the bank for which he was working. They thus moved back to Spain and she resumed her former career (Interview # 13).

Professional appointments abroad offer another occasion for people with different European nationality to meet and start a relationship. This was the case with an English woman who I interviewed in a village near Barcelona. She first came to Spain as part of an M.A. program jointly managed by an international Consortium of universities and firms located in Britain, in Spain, and in some other countries:

"One of the companies was a design consultancy in Barcelona. And for my thesis project, what I wanted to do, 'cause I had a design background, what I would do is to come over and introduce the idea of sustainable design into the design consultancy that was here. So that's what I did. I was supposed to be here for an internship to do my thesis project and then go back to finish my thesis, and that would be it. But I finished my thesis and then the company said "why don't you come back?" So, it was because of that really, and so I came back afterwards and I continued working for them for eight years" (Interview # 5).

Eventually, she met her current husband, started a family, and became a freelance consultant working from her current suburban home.

Other stories involving a professional stay abroad are that of an English language teacher who moved to Spain with the idea of just spending some time in the country and then met and married one of his Spanish students (Interview # 10), or the story of the Spanish musician who toured in Belgium, met and started a relationship with an Italian woman who was making the transition from academia to the job market but had no clear job prospects either in Belgium or back in Italy, and convinced her to move to Spain with him (Interview # 9).

Finally, holidays and fate play a role in these stories too. There is the story of the Spanish man who travels to Italy on vacation with a female friend; once in Italy, the female friend introduces him to her and they fall in love. They start a long-distance relationship and eventually she moves with him to Spain (Partner of R in interview # 11). Similarly, there is the story of the German man who travels to Spain with a female friend of his, who then introduces him to her Spanish friend, with whom he falls in love (Partner of R in interview # 1). They also start a commuting relationship, but in this case, they both get a job for the same company in Italy, where they move together. They live in Italy for a while and then the German partner gets a job offer in Spain, which prompts them to move back to Spain, he to the new company that has made him an offer, she to the Spanish branch of the international travel company in which they were both employed in Italy.

In the stories above, the man sometimes moves to the woman's country of nationality and some other times it is the woman who moves to the man's country of nationality. One may be interested in the question of whether partners in binational couples tend to settle more often in the male or the female partner's country of nationality. Adrian Favell at some point refers to the "heavily gendered path of women who move to settle with their foreign partners" (Favell, 2008). Otherwise, no study has systematically studied this issue with respect to binational couples between Europeans. The data from this survey do not allow for a direct answer either. By looking at the gender distribution of nationals in national and binational couples, however, one can surmise that they indeed tend to settle in the male partner's country of residence, especially if the partners are less educated. Table 2.10 shows that whereas respondents in national couples tend to be female, regardless of the respondent's level of education, national respondents

TABLE 2.10 Gender Distribution, by Type of Couple, and Education (% Women)

	National Couples	Nationals in Binational Couples	Nationals in Binational Couples	Nationals in Binational Couples
	All	All	Met in Country	Met Abroad
No university education	62	41	43	45
	(358)	(244)	(159)	(62)
University education	52	44	47	42
	(746)	(650)	(336)	(265)

() Number of respondents.

in binational couples tend to be male, and this regardless of the respondent's level of education and of whether the partners met in the home country or abroad. Since respondents within households were chosen at random, since the number of binational marriages between Europeans involving national men or national women more or less balance each other in the countries in this study,[11] since there is no reason why national women in binational couples would be more reluctant than are national women in national couples to participate in the survey, and since the transnational mobility of women is not greater than that of men, a slightly greater propensity to settle in the male partner's country of nationality seems like the most plausible explanation for this puzzling finding. This, of course, may be a function of the countries and of the predominant nationality combinations in the binational couples between Europeans included in this study.[12]

Europe in Love examines differences in lifestyles, experiences, and worldviews of partners in national and binational couples in order to evaluate the extent to which binational couples between Europeans are or are not carriers of change. Occasionally, if data allow and with all the caution required when one analyzes cross-sectional data, I discuss the causal contribution of being in a binational couple to behavior, experience, or worldview that I am exploring. In such instances, it is important to rule out alternative, correlated factors that may underlie the observed associations. Although chance encounters between Europeans of different nationalities, driven primarily by the relative presence of foreign Europeans in the different countries of the European Union, are the main explanation for entering a binational couple, individual background variables may also play a role and may simultaneously impact on the behavior, experiences, and worldviews that I am analyzing.

Demographic research has demonstrated that more educated individuals have a greater propensity to marry or cohabit with foreign Europeans than do less educated ones (see de Valk and Díez Medrano, 2014). Education can stand for many variables, however, including greater openness or more economic resources. Potential confounding and intervening variables underlying the effect of education and observed associations between being in a binational couple and the practices and views of participants in the *Eumarr* study are their transnational family background, skills, and experience. In the *Eumarr* sample, these variables do not clearly differentiate partners in binational and national couples once one controls for education. Just like partners in national couples, partners in binational couples overwhelmingly come from families where both parents have the same nationality (see Table 2.11). Also, regardless of whether they live with a co-national or a European foreigner, national respondents visited approximately the same number of foreign countries before their seventeenth birthday (see Table 2.12) and between their seventeenth birthday and the year when they met their current partner (Table 2.13). Finally, the *Eumarr* data show that partners in national and binational couples do not differ much in the number of languages that they spoke before meeting their partner (Table 2.14).[13] Tables 2.13 and 2.14 also show, however, that university education is slightly correlated with having

42 When Willem met Laura?

traveled to more countries between the seventeenth birthday and the year when respondents met their current partner and with knowing more languages when they met their current partner. The correlations are actually equal to 0.33 and 0.27, respectively. Because of this, and since education correlates with being in a binational couple, partners in binational couples (especially nationals in these couples) have on average traveled to a slightly more diverse set of countries in late

TABLE 2.11 Parents Born in Different Countries, by Type of Couple, Education, and Country (%)

		Spanish Cities	Belgian Cities	Dutch Cities	Swiss City
	National	1	6	13	19
		(159)	(33)	(33)	(128)
No university education	Binational (national partner)	3	17	2	13
		(71)	(71)	(56)	(46)
	Binational (foreign partner)	2	10	15	10
		(63)	(40)	(67)	(58)
	National	1	15	5	12
		(171)	(61)	(121)	(393)
University education	Binational (national partner)	4	13	–	20
		(79)	(148)	(230)	(193)
	Binational (foreign partner)	6	8	15	14
		(85)	(177)	(232)	(282)

() Number of respondents.

TABLE 2.12 Average Number of Countries Visited Before Turning 17, by Type of Couple, Education, and Country

		Spanish Cities	Belgian Cities	Dutch Cities	Swiss City
	National	1	5	4	4
		(159)	(33)	(38)	(128)
No university education	Binational (national partner)	<1	5	5	4
		(71)	(71)	(56)	(46)
	Binational (foreign partner)	1	4	3	4
		(63)	(40)	(67)	(58)
	National	2	5	7	5
		(171)	(61)	(121)	(393)
University education	Binational (national partner)	1	6	6	5
		(79)	(148)	(230)	(193)
	Binational (foreign partner)	3	5	4	5
		(85)	(177)	(232)	282)

( ) Number of respondents.

When Willem met Laura? **43**

TABLE 2.13 Average Number of Countries Visited Between the Age of 17 and the Age When Met Partner, by Type of Couple, Education, and Country

		Spanish Cities	Belgian Cities	Dutch Cities	Swiss City
	National	2	7	5	8
		(159)	(33)	(38)	(128)
No university education	Binational (national partner)	3	8	9	9
		(71)	(71)	(56)	(46)
	Binational (foreign partner)	3	7	6	7
		(63)	(40)	(67)	(58)
	National	5	9	9	11
		(171)	(61)	(121)	(393)
University education	Binational (national partner)	7	9	11	11
		(79)	(148)	(230)	(193)
	Binational (foreign partner)	6	9	9	10
		(85)	(177)	(232)	(282)

( ) Number of respondents.

TABLE 2.14 Average Number of Languages Known before Meeting Partner, by Type of Couple, Education, and Country

		Spanish Cities	Belgian Cities	Dutch Cities	Swiss City
	National	2	3	2	3
		(159)	(33)	(38)	(128)
No University education	Binational (national partner)	2	3	3	3
		(71)	(71)	(56)	(46)
	Binational (foreign partner)	3	3	2	2
		(63)	(40)	(67)	(58)
	National	2	3	3	3
		(171)	(61)	(121)	(393)
University education	Binational (national partner)	3	3	3	3
		(79)	(148)	(230)	(193)
	Binational (foreign partner)	3	3	3	3
		(85)	(177)	(232)	(282)

( ) Number of respondents.

adolescence and early adulthood and know a slightly higher number of languages than do partners in national couples (Schroedter et al., 2015). These contrasts, together with other variables associated to education, may in turn translate into differences in life outlook and behavior.

In sum, *Europe in Love* rests on a sample of more than three thousand 30- to 40-year-old male and female residents in seven cities of four European countries, some of them in national couples and others in binational European couples or

44 When Willem met Laura?

"Euro-couples." The latter include citizens of most countries in the European Union. The description above shows that compared with respondents in national couples, those in binational couples began their life together later and on average have fewer children. As I show in the book, the lives, experiences, and world-views of respondents in the two types of couples display interesting contrasts, some of which owe to the couple's national or binational composition and to the nationality composition of binational couples. Being in a binational couple is associated among others with a greater propensity to identify as European, with distinct national and transnational networks, with distinct activities and coor-dination problems during holidays, with learning foreign languages, and with distinct careers.

In general, partners in binational couples met in the country where they now live, as students, professionals, tourists, or simply as people who for one reason or another had migrated there. In relative terms, foreign partners in less educated binational couples had resided longer in the country of residence before they started the relationship than had the foreign partners in more educated ones. A disproportionate number of the less educated foreign partners actually describe their country of residence as their home country. This contrast between the foreign partners in less educated and more educated binational couples reflects the fact that a higher proportion of those in the latter category originally met abroad (in the foreign respondent's country of residence or in a third country) and agreed to move to the national partner's country of residence. Data on the gender distribution of national respondents indirectly suggests that women tend to follow men more often to the latter's country of residence than the other way around. These initial comparisons already show that it is useful to distin-guish between binational couples formed by less educated (essentially, lower or lower-middle class) segments of the population and those formed by more edu-cated ones. Although the histories and experiences of these two types of couples overlap to a great extent, ideo-typically the former include nationals who meet and start living together with long established foreign migrants while the latter include nationals who meet post-graduate foreign students or professionals dur-ing the latter's open-ended stays in the country of residence or settle in the coun-try of residence after having met and started a relationship while on study stays or professional appointments abroad. As I show in coming chapters, this slightly different starting point is consequential for the social and professional lives of the partners in these couples, especially for the foreign ones.

Notes

1 Additional details about the survey design are provided in the Appendix.
2 An alternative to my approach would have been to categorize individuals as national or foreign based on their place of birth as many authors do. The registers for the cities in this study, however, generally provide information on the nationality of household members only. Consequently, this information was the basis for the sampling selec-tion procedure. One may also dispute whether birth place is a better proxy for the

cultural influences to which an individual has been subject than is nationality. Rights and obligations tied to citizenship, for instance, are based on nationality instead of birth place and the latter is not always the basis for citizenship. Also, many people are born in one place and grow up in another. Finally, I will not hide that my choice also rests on a certain discomfort with the "ethnic" bias that in my view prevails in academia and the public sphere.

3 The European Union and the Schengen space do not coincide. Some European Union states are not part of Schengen (i.e. the United Kingdom, Ireland, Bulgaria, Romania, Cyprus, and Croatia) whereas some members of the Schengen space are not European Union members (i.e. Switzerland, Iceland, Lichtenstein, Norway).

4 See Kalmijn et al. (2005), Van Huis and Steenhof (2003), Potarca and Bernardi (2018), Milewski and Kulu, (2014), Irastorza (2016), Feng et al. (2012). The last two studies find no differences in divorce rates between binational and co-national couples.

5 Also, whereas the Spanish, Dutch, and Swiss couples only include heterosexual couples, the Belgian one also targeted same-sex ones. Since they only represent 6% of the respondents in the Belgian working sample (51 respondents), I do not make distinctions between the two types of couples in the analysis.

6 Winship and Radbill argue that biased samples do not necessarily lead to biased regression coefficients as long as one controls for the variables that account for unequal selection (in our case, mainly education) (Winship and Radbill, 1994).

7 As a further robustness check for some of the statistical models in chapter 4, I have used register and census data for the study's seven cities in order to create a set of sample weights, with which I have re-estimated these models (details available from the author).

8 This finding is also consistent with the literature. See for instance, Choi et al. (2012). The *Eumarr* data, however, do not show foreign European men displaying a greater propensity to marry down than do native European men.

9 The Zurich and Belgium samples departed from the Spanish and Dutch ones in including respondents whose partners were below or above the 30- to 46-year-old range. This, however, hardly impacts on the averages for the cities in these countries. The observed contrasts are also consistent with those found for the US, Canada, and France in Irastorza (2016). See also Kang Fu (2010).

10 See Lu and Yang (2010), Schaeffer (2013), Balistreri, Joyner, and Kao (2017) and Haandrikman (2014, 2014).

11 See de Valk and Díez Medrano (eds.) (2014) for a whole set of articles on trends in Euromarriages in Belgium, the Netherlands, Spain, Sweden, and Switzerland.

12 This tendency to settle in the husband's country of nationality seems to be the case also in the UK, at least in the 1990–1991 period (Smith and Bailey, 2006).

13 Multiple regression analysis reveals a statistically significant contrast between national partners in binational couples and national partners in national couples. The magnitude of the contrast (b = 0.18), however, is trivial.

References

Balistreri, Kelly, Kara Joyner, and Grace Kao. 2017. "Trading Youth for Citizenship? The Spousal Age Gap in Cross-Border Marriages: The Spousal Age Gap in Cross-Border Marriages." *Population and Development Review* 43(3): 443–466.

Choi, Kate, Marta Tienda, Deborah Cobb-Clark, and Mathias Sinning. 2012. "Immigration and Status Exchange in Australia and the United States." *Research in Social Stratification and Mobility* 30(1): 49–62.

Díez Medrano, Juan, Clara Cortina, Ana Safranoff, and Teresa Castro-Martín. 2014. "Euromarriages in Spain: Recent Trends and Patterns in the Context of European Integration." *Population, Space, and Place* 20(2): 157–176.

Favell, Adrian. 2008. *Eurostars and Eurocities*. Oxford, UK: Blackwell.

Feng, Zhiquiang, Paul Boyle, Maarten van Ham, and Gillian M. Raab. 2012. "Are Mixed-Ethnic Unions More Likely to Dissolve Than Co-Ethnic Unions? New Evidence from Britain." *European Journal of Population / Revue Européenne de Démographie* 28(2): 159–176.

Fligstein, Neil. 2008. *Euro-clash*. Oxford, UK: Oxford University Press.

Fligstein, Neil and Frédéric Mérand. 2002. "Globalization or Europeanization? Evidence on the European Economy since 1980." *Acta Sociologica* 45: 7–22.

Haandrikman, Karen. 2014. "Binational Marriages in Sweden: Is there an EU Effect?" *Population, Space, and Place* 20(2): 177–199.

Irastorza, Nahikari. 2016. "Sustainable Marriages? Divorce Patterns of Binational Couples in Europe versus North America." *Ethnicities* 16(4): 649–683.

Kalmijn, Matthijs, Paul de Graaf, and Jacques Janssen. 2005. "Intermarriage and the Risk of Divorce in the Netherlands: The Effects of Differences in Religion and in Nationality, 1974–92." *Population Studies* 59(1): 71–85.

Kang Fu, Vincent. 2010. "Remarriage, Delayed Marriage, and Black/White Intermarriage, 1968–1995." *Population Research Policy Review* 29: 687–713.

Lichter, Daniel. 1990. "Delayed Marriage, Marital Homogamy, and the Mate Selection Process among White Women." *Social Science Quarterly* 71: 802–811.

Lu, Melody and Wen-Shan Yang. 2010. "Introduction." In Wen-Shan Yang and Melody Chia-Wen Lu (eds.), *Asian Cross-Border Marriage Migration*. Amsterdam: Amsterdam University Press, 15–30.

Milewski, Nadia and Hil Kulu. 2014. "Mixed Marriages in Germany: A High Risk of Divorce for Immigrant-Native Couples." *European Journal of Population* 30(1): 89–113.

Oppenheimer, Valerie. 1988. "A Theory of Marriage Timing." *American Journal of Sociology*, 94: 563–591.

Potarca, Gina and Laura Bernardi. 2018. "Mixed Marriages in Switzerland: A Test of the Segmented Assimilation Hypothesis." *Demographic Research* 38(48): 1457–1494.

Recchi, Ettore. 2015. *Mobile Europe: The Theory and Practice of Mobility in the EU*. Basingstoke, UK: Palgrave MacMillan.

Schaeffer, Felicity. 2013. *Love and Empire: Cybermarriage and Citizenship across the Americas*. New York: New York University Press.

Schroedter, Julia, Tom De Winter, and Suzana Koelet. 2015. "Beyond l'Auberge Espagnole: The Effect of Individual Mobility on the Formation of Intra-European Couples." *European Journal of Population* 31(2):181–206.

Smith, Darren P. and Adrian J. Bailey. 2006. "International Family Migration and Differential Labour-Market Participation in Great Britain: Is There a 'Gender Gap'?" *Environment and Planning A* 38(7):1327–1343.

Valk, Helga de and Juan Díez Medrano (eds.). 2014. "Meeting and Mating Across Borders: In the European Union: Union Formation in the European Union Single Market." Special Issue of *Population, Space, and Place* 20(2): 157–176.

Van Huis, Milas and Liesbeth Steenhof. 2003. "Divorce Risks for Foreigners in the Netherlands." *Statistics Netherlands*, 1–16.

Winship, Christopher and Larry Radbill. 1994. "Sampling Weights and Regression Analysis." *Sociological Methods and Research* 23(2): 230–157.

3

SOCIABILITY

Cross-European migration and binational couples will one day turn nationals of European member states into Europeans. A European society will emerge that is more than the sum of its constituent parts. In a world region as prosperous and secure as the European Union, however, permanent mobility to other countries and long-term relationships between Europeans will not become prevalent enough unless movers feel at home in European countries other than their own. Networks of friends and relatives that help them cope with everyday challenges, thrive professionally, and meet their sociability and emotional needs are essential in this respect. The literature has generally focused on traditional migrants, individuals who move in search of a better future and as part of family or even community strategies (van Tubergen, 2014). Social networks enter this research as a relevant explanatory factor (Boyd, 1989; Massey and Espinosa, 1997; Portes and Sensenbrenner, 1993) when the focus is on mixed marriages (De Miguel Luken et al., 2015; Rodríguez-García, 2006; Scott and Cartledge, 2009), the migrants' social mobility (Berman et al., 2003; Chiswick and Miller, 2009; Stöhr, 2015), family re-unification strategies, integration in and cultural assimilation to the host society (Bleakley and Chin, 2010), and the migrants' ties, especially economic ones, to their country of origin (Adams and Page, 2005; Zontini, 2004). The analysis of social networks also features in the literature on new types of mobility propitiated by cheaper transportation and the elimination of borders (Kearney, 1995; Recchi, 2015). Here, the focus tends to be on the life and professional trajectories of *free-movers*. These are highly educated professionals who generally move alone and not always for economic reasons.[1] Favell, in particular, speculates about the reasons why, in Europe, this type of mobility has fallen short of expectations. He argues that this is partly because *free-movers* often find it hard to live as comfortably and secure as they expected. When it comes to solving ordinary problems, for instance, like finding a nice house, a

48 Sociability

competent doctor, a good school for the children, and adequate childcare, *free movers* lack precious information that only circulates within the thick walls of local bourgeois networks. Marrying a local is, according to Favell, a sure way toward living the life to which *free-movers* aspire, but at the cost of sacrificing the de-nationalized project that inspired the *free-movers'* decision to move to another country.

This chapter tests Favell's hypothesis and provides rich empirical information on the social networks of Europeans who cohabit or are married to Europeans from countries other than their own. Building on previous work by Koelet et al., it focuses on contrasts between national and binational couples, between foreign and national partners in binational couples, and between less educated and more educated foreign partners in binational couples (Koelet et al., 2017). The chapter examines structural and systemic aspects of people's social networks that have received attention in the past. It connects to the literature by exploring the size of social networks, their composition, the settings where they develop, and the support that they provide to individuals. When compared with this literature, the analysis is unique in paying as much attention to the native as to the foreign partners and in comparing binational couples not to endogamous couples formed by foreign Europeans but to national couples instead. As the pages that follow make clear, the binational couples' social networks are less family- and more work-centered at the national level, and significantly more transnational. Also, in line with the book's general argument, the chapter reveals that the social networks of binational couples formed by partners with less education differ from those of binational couples formed by partners with more education. Because of the different migration logic that underlies the international mobility of less educated and more educated Europeans, less educated foreign partners in binational couples more frequently have relatives in the country of residence than do more educated ones. Partly because of this and also, as I will argue, because of different cultural predispositions, in turn anchored in different moral economies, less educated partners in binational couples receive more help with ordinary everyday tasks than do more educated partners in binational couples. These findings confirm Favell's gloomy appraisal of the lives of *Eurostars*. At the same time, however, they show that, contrary to Favell's claims, a certain helplessness also affects highly educated *Eurostars* who marry or cohabit with nationals. Finally, the findings below complement Favell's analysis by revealing that when confronted with everyday problems and chores, less educated Euro-couples benefit from a greater amount of social capital than do more educated ones.

The chapter is structured as follows. I first examine the social networks of national couples. I focus on local ties and then on transnational ones. In the second part of the chapter, I examine the social networks of binational couples, both local and transnational, and systematically analyze contrasts with the national couples' social networks and contrasts between the social networks of binational couples formed by partners with less education and those formed by partners with more education.

The social networks of national couples

The European citizens' lives are doubly insured, at least in Europe's wealthiest states: by a strong welfare state and by dense social networks of family and friends. The enduring significance of family and friends contradicts early modernization theory expectations that the welfare state would replace family and friends and that friends and freely chosen acquaintances would replace family as providers of emotional gratification and social support.[2]

Local family and friends

Network structure: size, history, national composition

National couples in the cities included in this study live surrounded by friends and relatives[3] (Table 3.1). Almost all of them claim more than eleven relatives in the country and a majority claims five or more friends. To these relatives one must add close friends, which number at least five for more than one in two respondents. Because of the Europeans' deep attachment to place and very little migration for most of the post-WWII period, nationals generally live close to relatives (Andreotti et al., 2015) and many of their friends are long-time friends. In particular, people's best friends are co-workers and friends from the school or university days, people whom they met in late adolescence and early adulthood (Table 3.2). To this core group of friends, new ones have been added later on in life either through one's spouse or cohabiting partner or through one's children.[4]

TABLE 3.1 Relatives, In–Laws, and Friends *in Country of Residence*, by Type of Couple and Education (Unweighted Average % across the Four Countries)

	National Couples	*Binational Couples*	
		National	*Foreign*
Has Close Relatives in CoR			
Less than university	94	96	30
University or more	94	95	15
Has In–Laws in CoR			
Less than university	85	31	84
University or more	84	24	84
Has Friends in CoR			
Less than university	89	92	88
University or more	90	92	91
N (Less than university)	(466)	(288)	(271)
N (University or more)	(638)	(606)	(734)

( ) Number of respondents.

50 Sociability

TABLE 3.2 Origin of Respondent's Friends in *Country of Residence*, by Type of Couple and Education (Unweighted Average % across the Four Countries)

	National Couples	Binational Couples	
		National	Foreign
Children's Schools			
Less than university	36	27	18
University or more	34	28	19
Work			
Less than university	60	61	62
University or more	65	63	65
Partners' Work			
Less than university	20	19	22
University or more	21	15	21
Neighborhood			
Less than university	43	36	35
University or more	33	28	30
School/University			
Less than university	57	58	19
University or more	78	83	32
Partner's Friends			
Less than university	50	37	41
University or more	52	36	50
Clubs/Assoc.			
Less than university	25	23	27
University or more	33	28	23
N (< than university)	(466)	(288)	(271)
N (university or >)	(638)	(606)	(734)

() Number of respondents.

Close friendships also stem from the children's school or the neighborhood. In fact, since people generally take their children to the local public school, friendships from the children's school and from the neighborhood often overlap (Munch et al., 1997). Having children and making friends in the neighborhood also often results from meeting people when parents take their children to nearby parks or playgrounds. The persistence of a gender division of labor means that this overlap is more common among women than among men (Moore, 1990).

The national populations' friendship network is often circumscribed to a fairly small residential radius. In this small residential radius, friends from school, from the children's school, and from the neighborhood converge. Only friends from work may live in more distant parts of the city. The more educated individuals' friendship network, however, tends to be less tied to the neighborhood, the city, and the country of residence than is the less educated individuals' (Table 3.2).

Maloutas and Andreotti et al. show that more educated individuals discriminate more socially when making friends, that they are more selective in their choice of a school for their children and are thus more predisposed to take them to schools in different parts of the city (Andreotti et al., 2015; Maloutas, 2007).

One could also point out that highly educated individuals more often reside in isolated suburban areas, where contact with neighbors is more infrequent, than do less educated ones. People's friendship networks are not only highly concentrated in space; they are also quite homogenous in their national composition. Immigration has made Europe more diverse than it ever was. Yet, even in cosmopolitan cities like the ones in this study, people's lives largely unfold within endogamous national social networks. This observation applies particularly to those who marry or cohabit with other nationals. They often live in the same neighborhoods as foreigners, buy in grocery stores or in commercial outlets run by foreigners, and increasingly work alongside foreign employees. The relatives and closest friends of partners in national couples, however, remain predominantly national. In the *Eumarr* study, only Zurich residents display some propensity to count foreigners among their inner circle of friends (Table 3.3), although these tend to be German, from a neighboring country with which they share a language and a long history of economic, social, and cultural exchanges.

Another interesting finding, given the literature's emphasis on the greater cosmopolitanism of the well-educated, is the absence of relevant contrasts between the national composition of the less educated and the more educated closest friends' networks. In fact, I could show that not even cosmopolitan experience and skills (i.e. travel abroad before age 17, number of languages spoken) help explain whether individuals in national couples count a foreign person in their circle of best friends. This is consistent with Andreotti et al.'s finding that in Paris, Milan, Lyon, and Madrid, even highly educated and transnational executives tend to socialize with other nationals, individuals whom they befriended while growing up (Andreotti et al., 2015).

Interaction and support

National couples communicate quite frequently with their friends and relatives in the country of residence. They meet, talk on the phone, and interact over the internet, especially with friends. On a scale from 1 to 8, where 1 means 'never,' and 8 means 'daily,' individuals reported meeting them on average 'once a month' (4 = 'once a month') (Tables 3.4 and 3.5). Also, more educated individuals have less contact with friends than have less educated ones, perhaps because, comparatively speaking, fewer among the former's friends live in the same neighborhood.[5] Family and friends in the country of residence are a significant source of assistance to national couples (Höllinger and Haller, 1990). When asked how much help they can count on when dealing with the smaller and bigger decisions and tasks they confront on an everyday basis (health problems, finding a school, finding a job, renting or buying a house, doing small

TABLE 3.3 A Close Friend among the Respondent's Five Closest Ones in the Country of Residence Has a Different Nationality from the Country of Residence's, by Type of Couple, Education, and Country (%)

	Spanish Cities			Belgian Cities			Dutch Cities			Swiss City		
	Purely National Couples	Binational Couples		Purely National Couples	Binational Couples		Purely National Couples	Binational Couples		Purely National Couples	Binational Couples	
		Nat	For		Nat	For		Nat	For		Nat	For
Less than Uni.	14	42	73	18	39	80	24	39	84	34	47	85
Uni. or more	14	27	82	26	39	88	17	37	81	35	48	82
N (< Uni.)	(159)	(71)	(63)	(33)	(71)	(40)	(38)	(56)	(67)	(236)	(90)	(101)
N (Uni. or >)	(171)	(79)	(85)	(61)	(148)	(177)	(121)	(230)	(232)	(285)	(149)	(240)

( ) Number of respondents

Sociability   53

TABLE 3.4 Average Frequency of Contact with Relatives and In-Laws who live *in Country of Residence*, by Type of Couple and Education (Average of the Country Means)

	Purely National Couples	*Binational Couples*	
		National	*Foreign*
Meet Them			
Less than university	4.83	4.31	4.20
University or more	4.60	4.33	3.90
Talk to Them on the Phone			
Less than university	5.15	4.92	4.24
University or more	5.13	5.01	3.87
Communicate through Internet			
Less than university	4.82	4.18	3.46
University or more	4.59	4.49	3.19
N (< university)	(466)	(288)	(271)
N (university or >)	(638)	(606)	(734)

( ) Number of respondents.

TABLE 3.5 Average Frequency of Contact with Friends who live *in Country of Residence*, by Type of Couple and Education (Average of the Country Means)

	Purely National Couples	*Binational Couples*	
		National	*Foreign*
Meet Them			
Less than university	4.55	4.31	4.66
University or more	4.23	4.32	4.60
Talk to Them on the Phone			
Less than university	4.55	4.39	4.65
University or more	4.26	4.34	4.46
Communicate through Internet			
Less than University	4.86	4.52	4.68
University or more	4.69	4.76	4.91
N (< university)	(466)	(288)	(271)
N (university or >)	(638)	(606)	(734)

( ) Number of respondents.

repairs, finding childcare, and filing taxes) (Table 3.6), the average answer on a scale from one to seven lies on the high end, ranging between 4 and 5 across items. Statistical analysis also reveals that the more frequently people meet with family and friends, the more help they get (Table 3.7). This is especially true for health issues, conducting minor repairs, and childcare (see R-square coefficients

54 Sociability

TABLE 3.6 Mean Perceived Degree of Help (1–7) Received by Respondents When Conducting Specific Tasks, by Type of Couple and Education (Average of the Country Means)

	National Couples	Binational Couples	
		National	Foreign
Health			
Less than university	5.67	5.69	5.73
University or more	5.71	5.58	5.55
School			
Less than university	4.90	4.74	5.04
University or more	4.96	4.85	4.82
Job			
Less than university	4.87	4.87	4.96
University or more	4.91	5.00	4.74
Rent/Buying House			
Less than university	4.96	4.82	4.99
University or more	4.91	4.92	4.80
Repairs			
Less than university	5.23	5.19	5.28
University or more	5.07	5.01	4.85
Childcare			
Less than university	4.95	4.80	4.91
University or more	5.10	4.80	4.71
Taxes			
Less than university	4.66	4.36	4.72
University or more	4.46	4.30	4.33
N (< university)	(466)	(288)	(271)
N (university or >)	(638)	(606)	(734)

( ) Number of respondents.

in Table 3.7). Last but not least, when it comes to getting a job, only contact with friends matters, which is consistent with the role of weak ties in Granovetter's early work (Granovetter, 1974).

Transnational ties

Europeans tend to live in close proximity to their relatives and closest friends. This contributes to make European cities cozy for those who enjoy this proximity and relatively cold for people coming from other countries or even other cities in the same country. Proximity to relatives and friends is particularly prevalent among those who cohabit or are married to co-nationals, the majority of the population. I have shown, however, that more educated individuals draw their closest friends from the neighborhood less often than less educated ones do. This greater

Sociability **55**

TABLE 3.7 Association between Having Family and Friends in Country of Residence and Meeting Frequency with Family and Friends, and Amount of Help received, Controlling for City of Residence and Education (National Couples Only) (OLS)

	R-square	Has Relatives in CoR	Has In-Laws In CoR	Has Friends In CoR	Frequency Meets (Relatives/ In-Laws)	Frequency Meets (Friends)
Health	11.4	+	ns	ns	★	★
School help	6.4	+	ns	ns	★	★
Jobs	7.7	ns	ns	ns	ns	★
Rent/buy house	5.4	ns	ns	ns	★	★
Small repairs	6.4	ns	★	★	★	★
Child care	11.2	ns	ns	ns	★	★
Taxes	6.3	ns	ns	ns	★	★

N= 917.
+: Significant at 0.10 level, two-tailed; ★: Significant at 0.05 level, two-tailed.
ns: Not significant at 0.05 level, two-tailed.

propensity for more educated individuals to have a network of friends and relatives that reaches beyond the immediate neighborhood resurfaces when one focuses on transnational ties. It partly reflects that more educated individuals are generally more open and wealthier. While most partners in national couples have no relatives abroad, and only a minority has friends abroad, this is less typical of more educated individuals than of less educated ones (Table 3.8).[6] The fact that one out of

TABLE 3.8 Relatives, In-Laws, and Friends *in the European Union*, by Type of Couple and Education (Unweighted Average % across the Four Countries)

	National Couples	Binational Couples	
		National	Foreign
Has Close Relatives in EU			
Less than university	25	29	90
University or more	32	28	90
Has In-Laws in EU			
Less than university	16	87	26
University or more	23	87	22
Has Friends in EU			
Less than university	31	60	77
University or more	52	73	89
N (< university)	(466)	(288)	(271)
N (university or >)	(638)	(606)	(734)

( ) Number of respondents.

56 Sociability

two university educated respondents claims to have a friend in another European Union country testifies to the intensification of short-term mobility in Europe in recent decades. Direct contact with friends abroad, however, even among highly educated individuals, remains a once a year event. When communication takes place, it tends to be through phone calls or via the internet (Table 3.9).

To conclude: the lives of nationals in this study's European cities (i.e. partners in national couples) are embedded in large and dense networks of co-national family members and friends. Except for in-laws and for friends made during their professional careers, these networks remain unchanged for most of people's lives and provide a modicum of emotional and practical security. Technology, mainly telephone and increasingly the internet, ensures a great deal of communication with friends and relatives which, especially in the case of friends, contributes to the reproduction of social networks over time. The life-cycle structures to some extent the density of flows within the network. Within the age span considered in this study, family takes a growing share of the couples' time and energy. It is mainly highly educated individuals who step beyond the "coziness" of these life-long networks. Not only do they depend less on friends from the neighborhood, but they travel abroad more often. This gives them the opportunity to make friends with people from other nationalities. Although communication with friends abroad is infrequent and mainly virtual, these friendships abroad situate them in a world in-between that of less cosmopolitan partners in national couples and that of co-nationals who are married or cohabit with foreign Europeans.

TABLE 3.9 Average Frequency of Contact with Friends who live *in the European Union*, by Type of Couple, Education, and Country

	Purely National Couples	*Binational Couples*	
		National	*Foreign*
Visit Them			
Less than university	0.48	1.23	1.61
University or more	0.86	1.49	2.04
Receive Visits From Them			
Less than university	0.51	1.14	1.34
University or more	0.98	1.47	1.81
Talk to Them on the Phone			
Less than university	0.78	1.88	2.69
University or more	1.30	2.00	3.02
Communicate through Internet			
Less than university	1.07	2.22	3.23
University or more	1.70	2.55	3.77
N (< university)	(466)	(288)	(271)
N (university or >)	(638)	(606)	(734)

( ) Number of respondents.

The social networks of binational couples

Compared with those of national couples, the binational couples' social networks are more work-centered and more international. Also, while the social networks of the two partners in national couples are structurally very similar, those of the two partners in binational couples are structurally different. This structural difference leads to different worlds of experience for the foreign and national partner in these couples at the same time as it imposes significant constraints on how the couple organizes and coordinates its social life during the year. Finally, more so than is the case for national couples, the structure and interaction dynamics of the binational couples' social networks differ dependent on the partners' level of education.

Local family and friends

Network structure: size, history, national composition

The binational couples' family networks in the country of residence are small compared with the national couples' ones. This is because close relatives of the foreign partner usually live abroad (see Table 3.1). Socio-economic status matters, however, for the proportion of those who have a relative who lives in the country of residence is higher among less educated than among more educated foreign respondents (30% versus 15%).

The contrast between less educated and more educated foreign partners in binational couples reflects two different migration logics. The first one, the more traditional one, is that of families that migrate to escape material and physical insecurity. Less educated foreign partners in binational couples are often individuals who migrated with their families or who moved first and were then joined by their blood relatives. The second one, the more contemporary one, is the *free movers'*, highly qualified professionals who do not so much escape poverty as explore new opportunities, look for adventure, or join the person they love (see Favell, 2008; Kennedy, 2004; Ryan, 2011). The statistical results in Table 3.10, column 2, support this interpretation, for they reveal that the probability of having a relative in the country of residence for foreign partners from poorer countries is the same as that for nationals (b = −0.12, not statistically significant) whereas the probability for those coming from relatively richer countries is smaller (b = −0.64, significant at 0.05, two-tailed). Also, whether they come from poorer or richer countries, more educated foreign partners benefit less from the presence of relatives in the country of residence than do less educated ones (see b = −0.09 and b = −0.02, significant at 0.05 level).

National and binational couples also differ in the composition of their friendship networks in the country of residence. Like people in national couples, a large percentage of partners in binational ones draw their best friends from work (Table 3.2), but only national partners draw their best local friends from school

TABLE 3.10 Association between Being in a Binational Couple and Having Relatives, In-Laws, and Friends *in Country of Residence, EU, and outside the EU,* Controlling for City of Residence and for Country of Nationality, Socio-Demographic and Transnational Experience and Skills Variables (OLS)

	Has Relatives in CoR (1)	Has Relatives in CoR (2)	Has In-Laws in CoR (3)	Has Friends in CoR (4)	Has Relatives in another EU country (5)	Has In-Laws in another EU country (6)	Has Friends in another EU country (7)
-Foreign in binational couple	−0.40 ★		0.04 ★	8.0E-03 ★	0.78 ★	0.26 ★	0.75 ★
-National in binational couple	0.01	0.01	−0.54 ★	0.02 +	−0.02	0.81 ★	0.49 ★
-Poor country		−0.12					
-Not poor country		−0.64 ★					
-Gender (1=Woman)	-0.02 +	−0.02	0.05 ★	0.01	0.02	−0.01	−0.04 ★
-Age	0.00	1.0E-03	2.0E-03	0.00	2.0E-03	2.0E-03	3.0E-03
-Education	−2.0E-03 +	−1.0E-03	-0.01 +	−2.0E-03	2.0E-03	0.02	0.06 ★
-Parents' education	−4.0E-03	−3.0E-03	1.0E-03	−1.0E-03	7.0E-03	3.0E-05	0.01 ★
-Countries visited before 17	9.0E-03 ★	9.0E-03 ★	4.0E-03	6.0E-03 ★	5.0E-03 +	2.0E-03	6.0E-03 ★
-Languages known	−5.0E-03	−7.0E-03	−0.01	0.00	9.0E-03	8.0E-03	0.09 ★
-Foreign★Ed.	−0.05 ★		0.01		−0.02	−0.04 ★	−0.05 ★
-National in binational couple★Ed.			−6.0E-03			−0.02 +	−0.04 ★
-Poor country ★ Ed.		−0.09 ★					
-Not poor country ★ Ed.		−0.02 ★					
-Constant	0.97 ★	0.96 ★	0.82 ★	0.87 ★	0.17	0.04	−0.30
R-square (%)	67.0	67.4	37.0	3.1	34.6	41.4	21.2
N				2232			

Controls for city of residence. +. Significant at 0.10 level, two-tailed; ★: Significant at 0.05 level, two-tailed.

and university. For foreign partners in these couples, far away from their child-hood and school friends, work is actually the main vehicle through which they independently forge new friendships.

The contrast between the nationals' and the foreigners' circle of friends is well captured in this statement from a Portuguese woman, an employee at a major multinational financial institution: "I tend to go out with my female friends from *work*, Josep with his *old-time friends*" (Interview # 6). In another interview, this time to a Spanish musician who lives with an Italian woman, my respondent describes his partner's relative isolation and expresses concern that she depends too much on acquaintances from work:

> Although she is very sociable, she does not have a very active social life. Her friends are basically from the school where she teaches, people with whom she works and with whom she became friends the first year here; they are like satellites from school. The truth is that she misses not having a couple of good male and female friends.
>
> *(Interview # 9)*

Nationals are also less likely to draw their friends from their partner's social network when their partner is a foreign European than when he or she is a national (Table 3.3). The respective friendship networks of foreign and national partners in binational couples are thus more distinct than are those of partners in national ones, as illustrated by the following quote from my interview with a female Italian researcher:

> R.: I obviously consider Roger's friends my friends, but they are still primarily his friends; even if they love me, that's not the issue. But, how should I put it? It is their history, his history; and I very much like that he has this past with them, just as I have mine with my women friends, and although he feels at ease with them and although they adore him, they are still my friends.
>
> *(Interview # 6)*

Foreign partners are as likely as national ones to have friends that were introduced to them by their spouse or partner. The significance that these friends have for foreign partners, however, is much greater. European cities, despite their cosmopolitan *façade,* remain quite closed socially, as Favell describes in *Eurostars and Eurocities* (2008). This applies whether foreigners are poor or rich and even when they are fluent in the local language (Kennedy, 2008). In this closed context, to have a national partner can be an entry ticket to an otherwise exclusive world. This was well conveyed to me by a successful German consultant married to an also highly successful university researcher:

> R: As a foreigner one must always be alert, like at bars or restaurants: 'Hey, why do you charge me four times what you are charging this other person?'

60 Sociability

> The reason for this is that I am a foreigner and locals, verbally or through their behavior, are constantly telling you 'you are a foreigner'. How many times do I ask something in Spanish and the person whom I am addressing answers in English? Things change once you know a local, and this is my advantage here, which is that I have [Wife's name] She is from here, she has her friends, the friends' boyfriends and girlfriends, and this makes it much easier for me to meet people.
>
> *(Interview # 14)*

National partners in binational couples facilitate the foreign partners' social integration by introducing them to their friends, who formally become own friends and are the bridge to independently meeting new people.

Foreign partners in binational couples thus have more recent and contingent friendships in their country of residence than have their national partners and other nationals. In addition to this, foreign partners tend to have foreign friends (Domínguez and Maya-Jariego, 2009; Gill and Bialsky, 2011). Although lack of space prevents me from elaborating on this, data from *Eumarr* show that of the five closest friends that foreign respondents have in the country of residence on average only two or three are nationals. The other two or three are either co-nationals or other foreign residents. A relatively high presence of foreigners in the foreign partners' circle of friends probably reflects the relatively closed character of local society in even the most cosmopolitan of European cities. This closedness forces foreign partners in binational couples to socialize and make friends with nationals from their own nationality or from other nationalities, immigrants or expats like themselves. Of course, a mix of national and foreign friends, however, is not necessarily a problem and can in fact contribute to better integrate in the host society. Co-nationals and other foreigners help foreign partners to share experiences, insights about their new country of residence, and advice with others in the same situation. International ties can also satisfy a pre-existing liking of diversity. Some of this transpired in my interview with an English freelance professional in a small village, about thirty kilometers away from Barcelona:

> R: I know more people now and I feel more integrated in the community. I quite like that when I go walking, I meet people I know. I find this very nice because I also come from a small village, where we used to know more or less everybody. This place is somewhat bigger, but everyone knows who I am, perhaps because I am fairly distinctive. I like that I am not with my peers all the time. I can relate really well and I have very good friends here. Very often, however, I really want to get to Barcelona, where I feel that I am with other people who are more international, sometimes from other countries, and who have a different mentality. I often feel the need to be in Barcelona, to be in a place where new things are happening, art galleries, things like that... Int.: Do you keep friends in Barcelona from the time you used to live there? R.: Many of them, because they are from

different countries, have gone. It's a bit sad, that many of my good friends are no longer there, but we interact through email, skype, whatever. Int.: Were they British mainly? R.: I think that I am a bit unusual. I only got to know a British person since I came here. I am not part of the clans of British people who live here. I think that I am unusual, because other people tend to kind of make friends from their group, from their culture; I know that Dutch people are that kind. I, on the other hand, have friends from Germany, Ireland, some from here...I have a group of friends that is related to my life here and my children's life here; but I also have other friends who are completely separate from them. I feel I need a balance of both groups because, as I said before, I feel very different sometimes from the people here, so I need to keep a balance, a sort of international view, a different perspective.

(Interview # 5)

The last sentences of the quote above call attention to the tendency for the foreign networks of migrants to include an increasing share of natives as time in the host country goes by (see b = 0.04, significant at 0.05 level in Table 3.11) (Domínguez and Maya-Jariego, 2009; Kennedy; 2004; Lubbers et al., 2010).

TABLE 3.11 Association between Socio-Demographic Variables and Availability of Family in Country of Residence and How Many Native Close Friends Foreign Partners in Binational Couples have (OLS)

	Number of Native Friends (Out of Five Best) (1)	
–Gender (1=Woman)	−0.13	
–Age	−3.0E-03	
–Years of residence in CoR	0.04	⋆
–Years in relationship	0.03	+
–Education	−0.06	
–Parents' education	0.09	⋆
–Countries visited before 17	0.03	+
–Languages known	0.09	
–Has relatives in CoR	0.30	
–Constant	1.43	+
R-square (%)	11.8	
N	594	

Controls for city of residence. +: Significant at 0.10 level, two-tailed; ⋆: Significant at 0.05 level, two-tailed.

62 Sociability

While the literature stresses the role of native partners and their relatives, and of increasing proficiency in the host country's language, in propitiating this change (e.g. De Miguel Luken et al., 2015), the British respondent's comments above highlight another important but rarely mentioned factor, which is that many foreign acquaintances and friends are in the country only for the short run. This was also emphasized by the Portuguese respondent above: "I have to be flexible because living abroad means new friendships, people come and go, look for other places. I thus must be flexible and adapt" (Interview # 6). And this flexibility and adaptation, together with gradual integration in local society, sooner or later draws foreigners into longstanding friendships with natives.

The national partner in binational couples

From the analysis above one would be tempted to conclude that the only relevant contrast between national and binational couples involves foreign partners, whose social world differs significantly from that of nationals in both national and binational couples. This is only partially true. Although nationals in binational couples have lived longer in the country of residence and usually retain friendships from school or university, the contrasts between them and their partners should not be overstated. One can in fact say that their social world stands somewhere in between that of more rooted individuals in national couples and that of their foreign partner. Also, although national partners in binational couples benefit from the presence of many long-term friends in the country of residence, their propensity to lead more itinerant lives than are those of nationals in national couples can sometimes make them feel somewhat isolated, as the Spanish musician above remarked:

> It is certainly worse for her [his Italian partner] than for me, because, well, I have acquaintances whom I have known all my life; but, my experience is not all that different from hers: I often feel that I do not find people with whom to talk and whose cultural competence is high enough...with the friends I have here I entertain a very casual and relaxed relationship, we share laughs and so on, but I miss being with people who share my interests. In Belgium [where he lived for a while and still goes often] it was much easier.

The void that both foreign Europeans in binational couples and their itinerant partners sometimes feel is not always filled through visits to those abroad, even in the age of low-cost travel:

> R.: My friends come seldom to visit...I do travel and visit my best friend, who lives in Brussels. I see him regularly...but it is not the same. I, for one, because of my frequent travelling obligations, find it difficult to then step on yet another plane to go visit him, plus we [he and his Italian girlfriend]

must travel often to Italy to visit family, and, then, when all this is done, I rather go to the countryside to visit my father and spend some settled time.[7]

(Interview # 9)

Nationals in binational couples are also more likely to have foreign friends in the country of residence than are nationals in national couples (Table 3.4 above). This is in part because although national partners in these binational couples more seldom draw their close friends from their partner's network, when they do, these tend to be foreign too. One-fourth of the national respondents in binational couples in the *Eumarr* study met at least one of their foreign friends through their foreign partner, and 13% of the foreign friends that nationals in binational couples have were introduced to them by their foreign partner. Being with a foreign partner thus somewhat contributes to detach the national partners in binational couples from their local context. This detachment is re-enforced, as I show below, by the significance of their transnational social networks. Before I examine these, however, I focus on the practical implications of the binational couples' distinctive social networks in the country of residence.

Interaction and support

Because relatives of foreign partners in binational couples rarely live in the country of residence, the binational couples' social life is less centered on the family (Table 3.4). They socialize as much with friends as national couples do, but they do not meet with family as often. This is particularly the case for those who are highly educated, in part because they are less likely to have relatives in the country than are foreign partners with less education (Table 3.1). Although the percentages in Tables 3.1 and 3.4 already hint at this explanation, multiple regression analysis conveys this more precisely, while controlling for potential confounding variables (Table 3.12).

The story for national partners in binational couples is easy to tell: whether they are less or more educated, they meet family less often partly because they do not have in-laws living in the country. A change from −0.21 in column 1 to 0.47 in column 2 in the value of the regression coefficient for being a national partner in a binational couple after controlling for whether the national partner has in-laws in the country of residence is consistent with this interpretation.

The story for foreign partners in binational couples is more complex, for it is different for less and more educated ones. While foreign partners with no education meet family as often as nationals do, the more educated foreign partners are, the less frequently they meet family. Column 1 in Table 3.12 provides the relevant statistical coefficients on which this conclusion rests. The first relevant coefficient is 0.36, which measures how frequently foreign partners with no education meet family, compared with nationals with no education. The second one is −0.12, which measures the effect that the foreign partners' level of education has on how often they meet family (see line for "Foreign in a Binational Couple"

64 Sociability

TABLE 3.12 Association between Being in a Binational Couple and the Frequency of Contact *with Relatives/In-Laws*, Controlling for City of Residence, for Socio-Demographic Variables, and for the Presence of Relatives and In-Laws in CoR (OLS)

	Meet (Relatives/ In-Laws) (1)		Meet (Relatives/ In-Laws) (2)	
-Foreign in binational couple	0.36		1.31	★
-National in binational couple	−0.21	★	0.47	★
-Gender (1=Woman)	0.23	★	0.22	★
-Age	−0.04	★	−0.04	★
-Has child	0.62	★	0.53	★
-Duration of relationship	0.02	★	0.01	+
-Education	−0.02		−3.0E-03	
-Foreign in binational couple ★ education	−0.12	★	−0.03	
-Has relatives in CoR			2.18	★
-Has in-laws in CoR			1.26	★
-Constant	5.39	★	2.04	★
R-square (%)	7.2		23.3	
N		2232		

Controls for city of residence; +: Significant at 0.10 level, two-tailed; ★: Significant at 0.05 level, two-tailed.

★ Education). The first regression coefficient (0.36) is not statistically significant. This means that one cannot rule out that less educated foreign partners interact with family as frequently as do national partners in national couples. The second regression coefficient (−0.12), on the other hand, is statistically significant at the 0.05 level. The negative sign for the interaction coefficient means that the more educated foreign partners are, the less frequently they meet with family in the country of residence.

To verify that more educated foreign partners in binational couples meet family less often than do less educated ones because they are less likely to have relatives in the country one needs to move to column 2. The coefficients displayed in this column control for whether respondents have relatives in the country. Moving down to the line for the interaction between foreign status and education, one sees that the regression coefficient (−0.03) for the interaction between education and foreign status is no longer statistically significant.

In his well-known book, Favell emphasizes that relative to the national population, *free movers* find themselves at a disadvantage when dealing with the practical problems and decisions of daily life. He also stresses that *free movers* become increasingly aware of this disadvantage as they get older and form families. This study does not exclusively focus on *free-movers*, for it also includes less educated, lower class, binational couples. It also examines individuals at a slightly later stage in the life-cycle than were those whom Favell observed and interviewed. They are in some ways the survivors of the group that he studied, a group of individuals perhaps self-selected for their ability to overcome the problems that he discusses, whether finding a suitable home, a good school for the children, or competent and trustworthy doctors for them and their families. Furthermore, the fact that the "migrants" in the *Eumarr* study cohabit or are married to nationals is already a sign of success in integrating in the host society. The analysis above, however, highlights features of the binational couples' social networks that could hinder their ability to successfully address problems and decisions arising as they move through life: smaller family and friendship networks, and ties to foreign residents who perhaps are not able to provide much help. The fact is that whereas less educated foreign partners receive at least as much help as do less educated national partners, highly educated foreign partners receive less help than do highly educated nationals (Table 3.6).

Multiple regression models in Table 3.13 provide supporting empirical evidence for the claim that the availability of family impacts on how well individuals address ordinary problems and explains why highly educated foreign partners are particularly disadvantaged in this respect. For each of the tasks listed above, from Health to Taxes, it displays the multiple regression estimates for two models, with the second one controlling for how often individuals meet family and friends. I focus on the amount of help individuals obtain when addressing health issues because it captures quite well the results for all the tasks. The coefficients in line 1 ('Foreign in Binational Couple'), in lines 4, 5, and 6 ('Foreign ★ Education'; 'Frequency meets Family'; 'Frequency meets Friends') are particularly relevant to the interpretation. The coefficient 1.39 in line 1, column 1 of Table 3.17 shows that the degree of help foreign partners with no education claim to get when confronted with health issues is 1.39 points higher on average than it is for national partners in national couples with no education. Then, the negative interaction coefficient −0.20 for the combined effect of foreign status and education means that this contrast decreases as the respondents' level of education increases. Simple calculations would show that university-educated foreign partners receive less help than do university-educated national partners in national couples. This is in fact what the percentages in Table 3.6 convey.

One can then move to column 2, which controls for how frequently individuals meet family and friends. The contrast between foreign partners and nationals (line 1) and the interaction coefficient for the effect of education among foreign partners (line 4) are now smaller (1.29 and −0.19, respectively) but still statistically significant. Meanwhile, the regression coefficients in lines 5 and 6 show that meeting family and friends is associated with getting more help in solving health issues (0.06 and 0.13, respectively). These findings can be made extensive, in lesser or greater measure, to the rest of the tasks examined in Table 3.13. The reduction in the size of the coefficients between column 1 and column 2 (extensive to other tasks) mean that highly educated foreign respondents get less help than do less educated ones (relative to the contrasts between highly educated

TABLE 3.13 Association between Being in a Binational Couple and the Amount of Help Received When Solving Problems or Conducting Specific Tasks, Controlling for City of Residence, Socio-Demographic Variables, and Social Networks in the Country of Residence (OLS)

	Health (1)		School (2)		Job (3)		Rent/Buy (4)		Small Repairs (5)		Childcare (6)		Taxes (7)	
-Foreign in binational couple	1.39 ★	1.29 ★	1.16 ★	1.08 ★	0.92 ★	0.82 ★	1.23 ★	1.14 ★	0.95 ★	0.85 ★	0.74 +	0.65 +	0.74 ★	0.66
-National in binational couple	−0.05	−0.02	−0.09	−0.05	0.01	0.03	−0.02	2.0E-03	−0.09	−0.06	−0.32 ★	−0.26 ★	−0.22 ★	−0.20 +
-Education	0.04	0.02	0.02	0.04	0.03	0.02	0.02	0.03	−0.05 ★	−0.03	2.0E-03	0.03	−0.05	−0.02
-Foreign★ education	−0.20 ★	−0.19 ★	−0.16 ★	−0.15 ★	−0.14 ★	−0.14 ★	−0.18 ★	−0.17 ★	−0.16 ★	−0.15 ★	−0.14 ★	−0.13 ★	−0.12 +	−0.10 +
-Frequency meets family		0.06 ★		0.10 ★		0.05 +		0.06 ★		0.09 ★		0.15 ★		0.07 ★
-Frequency meets friends		0.13 ★		0.08 ★		0.14 ★		0.13 ★		0.12 ★		0.08 ★		0.09 ★
-Constant	5.96 ★	4.95 ★	4.63 ★	3.73 ★	5.22 ★	4.26 ★	5.07 ★	4.09 ★	5.51 ★	4.42 ★	5.24 ★	4.12 ★	5.07 ★	4.27 ★
R-square (%)	3.2	6.9	2.0	4.9	2.4	5.6	1.6	4.8	2.0	5.6	2.8	7.2	1.8	3.4
N							2232							

Controls for city of residence. +: Significant at 0.10 level, two-tailed; ★: Significant at 0.05 level, two-tailed.

and less educated nationals) in part because they have less contact with relatives and friends. I could show that this in turn reflects that highly educated foreign partners are less likely to have blood relatives in the country of residence than are less educated ones.

The contrast in the amount of help that less educated and more educated foreign partners receive does not disappear, however, after controlling for contact with family and friends. It remains statistically significant and similar in magnitude. To further explain this contrast, I would draw on the literature on individualism and class-based moral economies, which suggests that the propensity to help others is more prevalent among the lower classes than among the middle and upper classes. Whereas Euro-couples in which the partners are more educated can use their greater economic resources to pay for solutions to their everyday problems and more often come from social environments that emphasize self-reliance, less educated foreign partners have more limited economic resources and are used to assisting and being helped, usually in kind, from people in their same circumstances.

One of my respondents, a female Italian researcher with a small child, illustrates the problems faced by highly educated foreigners when trying to solve child care problems. In her particular case, this had forced her into a part-time job:

> R.: It is not that I do not want [to work full-time]; it is simply that I cannot. My family is in Italy, and this means that they cannot help. As for his family, well, what can I say, it's only his mother, who is quite old even though she does not look that way; but, you see, my son is quite active, quite active, and she, on the other hand, is almost eighty. I really cannot expect her to be chasing behind a two-and-a-half-year-old little child...I can have her with him two, three hours max, no more. It's not that she does not want or that she cannot; it is simply that I have sometimes been told by other mothers that, when in the park, they have sometimes seen my son suddenly starting to chase a pigeon and there is Ladia [R's mother-in-law] running after him.
>
> *(Interview # 11)*

In order to make it easier for relatives to help with child care, and just like national couples do, many binational couples often strategize to live close to family, in this case the national partner's family. Such strategies are common in Europe, as Andreotti et al. demonstrate in their comparative study of the lives of transnational professionals in Milan, Madrid, Paris, and Lyon (2015). One of my middle-class respondents, an English freelance professional who worked mainly from home in a small village located about thirty kilometers away from Barcelona, illustrated this quite nicely:

> Int.: You came to live in this village because of your husband, for family reasons? R.: Yes. The house was his mother's and this is why we came here. He was living in Sabadell before; I was living in Barcelona.

68 Sociability

For this respondent, the proximity of the mother-in-law was a sort of blessing:

> R.: My two children attend a school and a nursery, between 9 am and 4:30 pm. Before, I used to have them here for lunch, but I got really tired of the four journeys a day to school and back. I could not get much done, really. It was cutting out on my day. I thus decided that they would stay two days at school for lunch and then two days with their grandmother who lives just five minutes away.
>
> *(Interview # 5)*

Transnational ties

By far, what makes the binational couples' social network distinctive and consequential for the lives of their members is that it extends beyond national borders (see Tables 3.8–3.10). Having children leads to more frequent contact with relatives and to relatively less frequent contact with friends (Koelet et al., 2017) (Table 3.14). The mutual desire by relatives to get to know one another and establish lasting emotional bonds as well as the explicit or implicit strategic goal of making the children become familiar with another culture, which may benefit them in the future, perhaps contribute to this empirical association (Levrau et al., 2014; Rodríguez and Egea, 2006).

Whereas having children impacts on the frequency of communication with relatives abroad only, income intervenes in the explanation of contact with both relatives and friends abroad. Wealthier people are more likely to live in flats or houses with enough space to host visitors and spare them hotel costs, as conveyed by the answers to my questions offered by an Italian whom I interviewed in Barcelona:

> Int.: I see that you maintain pretty close ties with family and friends abroad: R: Yes, certainly… In the past, they came more often; nowadays, some are already tired of coming to Barcelona but people still come. And my parents too. Ryan Air makes it easy. Int.: Yes, I know from the survey that they come visit you. Where do they stay? R: since I live with my partner they stay here, because we have a room for guests. Before they rented a hotel room and that was it.
>
> *(Interview # 4)*

For less educated and poorer partners in binational couples, who usually lack the economic resources to travel abroad frequently or to host people for long periods of time, the internet revolution has radically changed the quantity and quality of interaction with relatives and friends in faraway places, as put by an Italian married to a Spanish woman:

> R.: Contact with my parents takes place mainly via Internet. The possibility of communicating with them has changed dramatically in the past ten years

and now we interact almost daily...through skype. My son, for instance, as soon as he hears my parents' voice, he rushes toward the computer.

(Interview # 15)

Another factor that impacts on the regularity of contact with family and friends abroad is the passage of time. As Koelet et al.'s work demonstrates for Belgium and the Netherlands, the *Eumarr* data indeed show that contact between respondents and their families and friends abroad is less frequent the longer respondents have lived in the country of residence (Koelet et al., 2017).[8] Some of the people with whom I conducted in-depth interviews conveyed this to me very clearly. First, a British respondent, an English teacher who lives in Madrid: R.:

I have lost contact with almost everybody there [in Scotland, where he comes from]. I have a friend, that's all. The rest of my friends at university it's just like me. They live around the world. I have a woman friend whom we met last Christmas, but she currently lives in New York, just as other friends live in many other countries. But there, in Scotland, just one friend. I have few friends there and more friends here.

(Interview # 10)

Then, a lower middle-class Italian married to a Spanish woman, a resident of a small industrial town near Barcelona:

Yes, I really do not have many friends left in Italy. Before I moved here I had more, but then I lost track of them and now there is only one couple whom I would describe as friends. Interestingly, before I met them, they only were friends with my older brother, but due to the vagaries of life they have become closer friends of mine than of my brother.

(Interview # 15)

Consistent with the quotes above, the regression coefficients for the effect of the number of years in the country of residence on mutual visits with friends and relatives abroad reported in Table 3.14 show that time has a slightly greater impact on contact with friends than it does on contact with relatives (Eve, 2008; Mollenhorst et al., 2014; Viry, 2012).

The greater presence of family and friends abroad explains that partners in binational couples travel more frequently to European destinations (Table 3.15). Sometimes, it is only the foreign partner who travels more. The obvious explanation for this is relative emotional closeness. One of my two Spanish female respondents married to a German citizen, a professional with four children who had previously lived in Germany, explained this to me this way:

Int.: How often do you meet your friends from Germany? R.: Well, to tell the truth less and less. [Husband interrupts]: When we both go, yes you do!

TABLE 3.14 Association between Being a *Foreign Partner* in a Binational Couple and the Frequency of Contact *with Relatives/In-Laws* and Friends *in other EU States*, Controlling for City of Residence and for Socio-Demographic, and Transnational Experience and Skills Variables (OLS)

	Visit (Relatives/In-Laws) (1)		Visit (Friends) (2)		Get Visited (Relatives/In-Laws (3)		Get Visited (Friends) (4)		Telephone (Relatives/In-Laws) (5)		Telephone (Friends) (6)		Internet (Relatives/In-Laws) (7)		Internet (Friends) (8)	
-Gender (1=Woman)	0.04		−5.0E-03		0.15		0.07		0.44	★	0.17		0.67	★	0.27	
-Age	−0.02	+	0.02	+	−0.02	+	0.02		−0.05	★	0.03		−0.07	★	9.0E-03	
-Years in CoR	−0.02	★	−0.04	★	−8.0E-03		−0.03	★	−0.04	★	−0.05	★	−0.03	★	−0.06	★
-Duration of relationship	0.02	+	−6.0E-03		4.0E-03		0.0E-03		0.05	★	−0.03	+	0.04	★	1.0E-03	
-Has a child	0.21	★	6.0E-03		0.52	★	0.06		0.53	★	0.27	+	0.55	★	0.30	
-Education	0.05		0.03		−0.02		0.02		0.09		−0.07		−0.03		−0.01	
-Parents' education	−0.01		2.0E-03		0.03		0.02		−0.06		−6.0E-03		0.03		−0.07	
-Countries visited before 17	0.02	★	0.04	★	0.05	★	0.05	★	−0.03		0.05	★	−0.01		0.05	★
-Languages known	0.01		0.08		1.0E-03		0.04		0.24	★	0.20	★	0.19	+	0.30	★
-Income (PPS)	2.0E-03		3.0E-03		6.0E-03	★	5.0E-03	★	2.0E-03		4.0E-03		5.0E-03		7.0E-03	
-Constant	2.86	★	0.94	+	2.21	★	0.51		5.82	★	1.71	+	5.81	★	2.50	★
R-square (%)	14.2		19.2		14.8		14.4		9.6		7.7		9.4		9.5	
N							594									

Controls for city of residence. +: Significant at 0.10 level, two-tailed; ★: Significant at 0.05 level, two-tailed.

TABLE 3.15 Association between Being in a Binational Couple and the Number of States Visited Since with Partner, the Number of Trips to Border Countries, and the Number of Trips to other European Union Countries in the 12 months before the Interview, Controlling for City of Residence and for Socio-Demographic Variables and Transnational Experience and Skills Variables (OLS)

	Number of States Visited since with Partner (1)		Number of Trips to Neighboring EU Countries in last 12 Months (2)		Number of Trips to Other EU Countries in last 12 Months (3)	
-Foreign in binational couple	0.25	3.0E-03	1.35 ★	1.03 ★	0.73 ★	0.49 ★
-National in binational couple	0.13	-0.46 +	0.86 ★	0.84 ★	0.48	0.24
-Gender (1=Woman)	-0.80 ★	-0.76 ★	-0.51 ★	-0.50 ★	-0.69 ★	0.66 ★
-Age	-9.0E-03	-0.02	0.02	0.02 ★	0.01	0.01
-Education	0.67 ★	0.65 ★	0.21 ★	0.20 ★	0.17 ★	0.16 ★
-Parents' education	-0.08	-0.09 +	0.01	7.0E-03	-0.03	-0.03
-Years in relationship	0.23 ★	0.23 ★	-0.01	-0.01	-7.0E-03	-4.0E-03
-Countries visited before 17	0.28 ★	0.27 ★	0.12 ★	0.12 ★	0.08 ★	0.08 ★
-Languages known	0.44 ★	0.35 ★	0.27 ★	0.23 ★	0.39 ★	0.32 ★
-Close relatives in EU		-0.12		0.28 ★		0.08
-In-laws in EU		0.63 ★		-0.08		0.21 +
-Close friends in EU		0.88 ★		0.38 ★		0.51 ★
-Constant	-0.18	-0.11	-0.72	-0.69	-1.46 ★	-1.42 ★
R-square (%)	30.2	31.1	22.6	23.0	19.3	20.2
N			2332			

Controls for city of residence. +: Significant at 0.10 level, two-tailed; ★: Significant at 0.05 level, two-tailed.

72 Sociability

R.: Yes, of course, what happens is that [R's husband's name] has another group of friends. [Husband]: Yes, the friends from childhood, the soccer team, with whom I went together to school. R.:

Yes, of course, your friends from adolescence, with whom you went to discos and so on. I have my own group of friends, whom my husband knows, but they are my friends, and I also try to keep in touch with them. I have a friend from Hawaii, who now lives in Dortmund. We met in Darmstadt as we both worked there for Berlitz, then she moved to Lilienthal, near Bremen, and then her husband, a university Professor was posted in Dortmund and they moved there. I have visited her and she has come to visit us; I also keep in touch with her through Skype, letters that we send one another, telephone conversations. I also have a friend in Frankfurt, a German woman who used to be our neighbor. I do as much as I can to visit her. Int.: So, you do travel frequently to Germany to visit your friends? [Husband]: Yes, yes. R.: He does it more often. [Husband] I do, and I do it more often because I still have family there. R: He does it more often, and I try to see if I can also travel along…What happens is that [Husband's name] has more vacations at work than I do. So, it is in part because he is on vacation at times when I still have work and also because he feels more the need to visit his family and so on, to visit his land. But, of course, I also like to go. Whenever I can, I do.

(Interview # 13)

Information that I collected through the in-depth interviews also suggests another reason why the foreign partner in binational couples often travels on his or her own to visit family and friends, which is that her or his national partner does not speak foreign languages. The number of languages that people know is indeed systematically associated with the frequency of mutual visits between couples and their families and friends abroad and also plays a role in the explanation of the frequency of international travel. The following excerpt illustrates this with respect to a Spanish-French couple with residence in Madrid. The respondent is a French citizen who works for the administration of a bus company and is married to a Spanish bartender:

R: I have not visited my family often, and when I have done it, alone and with my son. [Husband] generally does not join in, basically because his holidays are very short and he prefers to spend this time with his own family. On top of this, he does not speak foreign languages. So, the interaction between him and my family is cordial--they are kind to each other, it can even be fun when my parents come visit--but there is not the closeness that I have developed with his family. I would not label it distant- too strong, I do not know how to describe it.

(Interview # 12)

Far away from half of their family, binational couples, more so than national ones, must carefully partition their holidays between time spent on their own and time spent with their respective families, as one British respondent told me when I asked her about the summer holidays:

> R.: Every summer we travel about ten to fifteen days to England. Then starts the tour of family visits around Spain: grandparents in Málaga, family in Bilbao, visit to my brother in Murcia. We struggle to square it all as well as we can.
>
> *(Interview # 7)*

Another of my respondents, a middle-class English professional, described a very similar routine:

> Int.: What do you generally look forward to when you plan your holidays? R.: A bit of everything, really, because the children are young we spend lots of time visiting my family. This is something that we would like to start to change because we would like an actual holiday. This is why we tried Menorca this year, for five days. The rest of the holidays we split between the families. My parents visit me twice a year and I would like that the children spend more time there and see life in England as well, that they spend as much time there as possible.
>
> *(Interview # 5)*

Yet another of my binational couples, formed by an Italian male and a Spanish woman, illustrate the complications that juggling holidays with family obligations introduces, complications that increase even more when the national partner's family does not live in the city of residence and when economic resources are limited:

> "R: Beach, quiet, and good food. These are my main priorities when I travel to Mediterranean countries. Last summer we traveled to Greece; then, on our way back, we stopped in Italy, at my home; then, when, after coming back, she (the partner) proceeded to Majorca, with her family, while I stayed here. Int.:
>
> I see that you do not have much contact with her family, which, as you just mentioned, lives in Majorca. R.: Let's see, much contact, certainly not. We meet when the occasion arises. She [partner] travels there frequently. I don't join her always because I do not benefit from the travel discount that benefits residents of the Balearic Islands, but I do sometimes and we have a good relationship."
>
> *(Interview # 4)*

As stated above, it is not only having more family abroad that distinguishes people in binational couples. It is also having friends abroad. These friends abroad

74 Sociability

provide a good excuse to travel abroad, drive the choice of travel destinations, and, very often, make trips affordable. This is, for instance, what a Portuguese respondent, employed by a major international banking institution, told me about her and her boyfriend's recent travel experiences:

> R.: Lately, we have travelled guided by where people we know are. We attended, for instance, several weddings in different places. We went to Japan to a cousin's wedding; then, to New York, to a friend's home; from there to Berlin, to stay at a friend's flat, who had exchanged it for ours in Barcelona. To the Netherlands, to visit some other friends. Int.: When you travel to these places, do you stay at your friends' place or you book a hotel? R.'s Spanish partner: If there is enough space we stay at our friends'. R.: Except for Japan. Int.: On a typical summer, what do you do? Do you have a routine? Do you go to Portugal every summer? R.: No, it is not comfortable. It is ok when we can kill two birds at once, that is, see my family and my friends. I still have many friends there. But apart from Porto I have friends in many other places and we like to meet them. There are always weddings. It is the season.
>
> *(Interview # 6)*

Social networks are a fundamental aspect of a person's quality of life, behavior, worldviews, and identities. This chapter has shown that binational couples are part of thick transnational networks, encompassing the partners' countries of origin. In terms of cosmopolitan competence, they differentiate themselves clearly from national couples. The chapter has also shown that the foreign partners' social networks in the country of residence are more contingent and have shallower roots than those of nationals in both national and binational couples. Whereas the nationals' social networks generally include both blood relatives and in-laws and friends made in late adolescence or early adulthood, those of foreign Europeans generally include only in-laws and friends from work or mediated by their national partner. The chapter has also revealed an interesting contrast between the social networks of less educated and more educated foreign partners to binational couples that confirms and throws light on Favell's seminal contribution to the study of the *free-movers* intra-European mobility. Whereas the former can and do rely quite frequently on other people to solve everyday chores and problems, the latter can and do so less frequently. This is in part because less educated foreign partners more often benefit from a relative's presence in the country of residence than do more educated ones. It also probably reflects a different culture and a different set of dispositions distinguishing two types of binational couples. Less educated foreign Europeans in binational couples often share in a traditional migration—and also lower-class—culture where lack of resources, foremost economic and social, encourages greater reliance on others in the same situation to address and solve problems. The following chapter shows, in fact, that less educated foreign partners in binational couples, especially when

Sociability **75**

coming from poorer countries, actually confront considerable barriers in the labor market that make reliance on others ever more pressing. More educated foreign Europeans, on the other hand, Favell's *Eurostars*, share in an individualistic culture that emphasizes self-reliance. This culture of self-reliance, since it is propitiated in part by greater economic and social resources, works relatively well most of the time. Under exceptional circumstances, however, it can be a disadvantage. Just as one is not used and does not know how to ask for help, those on whom one would naturally lean when needed are also not used to be asked for assistance and are often "too busy" to provide it. Finally, this chapter has shown that the national and binational couples' social networks differ in geographical reach. This difference in reach makes the lives of binational couples more complex and demands more planning, especially when it comes to holidays.

Notes

1 Ryan (2007), Favell (2008), Van Mol and Michielsen (2015), Recchi (2015).
2 For these pessimistic predictions, see Parsons, 1949. For predictions to the contrary and empirical studies that confirm them (see Bruckner et al., 1993; Höllinger and Haller, 1990; Litwak and Szelenyi, 1969; Zapf, 1991).
3 The *Eumarr* survey questionnaire defined the concept "family" as including the respondent's and the partner's brothers, sisters, parents, grandparents, uncles, aunts, cousins, nephews, and nieces. Also, in this and other chapters I only report country percentages when the contrasts are statistically significant and meaningful. These tables, however, are available upon request from the author.
4 In contrast, the partner's workmates very seldom figure as a person's closest friends. A simple interpretation for this is probably that respondents only get to meet those partners' workmates whom the partner considers his or her friends, in which case respondents list them as a partner's friend instead of a partner's work friends.
5 Additional tables would also confirm previous studies, which show that, compared with men, women interact more frequently with family and friends who live in the country of residence and that they communicate relatively more so over the phone and internet. See Fischer and Oliker, 1983, Wellman, 1984. These tables would also show that communication with family and friends becomes less frequent, the older respondents are and that contact with relatives and in-laws is more frequent among individuals who have been longer with their partner and, especially so, if they have children.
6 The percentages are even smaller when one asks about relatives, in-laws, and friends outside the European Union.
7 In *Eurostars and Eurocities*, Favell also discusses globetrotting nationals, whose itinerant lives make them feel "out of the loop" in their own country and who often end up socializing with mobile Europeans (Favell, 2008).
8 See also Eve (2008), Hedberg and Kepsu (2008), Morosanu (2013), Levrau et al. (2014), Viry (2012).

References

Adams, Richard and John Page. 2005. "Do International Migration and Remittances Reduce Poverty in Developing Countries?" *World Development* 33(10): 1645–1669.
Andreotti, Alberta, Patrick Le Galès, and Francisco Javier Moreno-Fuentes. 2015. *Globalized Minds, Roots in the City.* Oxford, UK: Wiley Blackwell.

76 Sociability

Berman, Eli, Kelly Lang, and Erez Siniver. 2003. "Language Skill Complementarity: Returns to Immigrant Language Acquisition." *Labour Economics* 10(3): 265–290.

Bleakley, Hoyt and Aimee Chin. 2010. "Age at Arrival, English Proficiency, and Social Assimilation among US Immigrants." *American Economic Journal: Applied Economics* 2(1): 165–192.

Boyd, Monica. 1989. "Family and Personal Networks in International Migration: Recent Developments and New Agendas." *International Migration Review* 23(3): 638–670.

Bruckner, Elke, Karin Knaup, and Walter Müller. 1993. "Soziale Beziehungen und Hilfeleistungen in Modernen Gesellschaften." *Working Papers AB 1/ Nr. 1*, Mannheim Centre for European Social Research.

Chiswick, Barry R. and Paul. W. Miller. 2009. Earnings and Occupational Attainment among Immigrants. *Industrial Relations* 48(39): 454–465.

De Miguel Luken, Verónica, Miranda Lubbers, Miguel Solana, and Dan Rodríguez-García. 2015. "Evaluación de la Integración Relacional de los Inmigrantes en Uniones Mixtas a Partir del Análisis de Redes Personales." *Revista Española de Investigaciones Sociológicas* 150: 151–172.

Domínguez, Silvia and Isidro Maya-Jariego. 2009. "Acculturation of Host Individuals: Immigrants and Personal Networks." *American Journal of Community Psychology* 44(3–4): 309–327.

Eve, Michael. 2008. "Some Sociological Bases of Transnational Practices in Italy." *Revue Européenne des Migrations Internationales* 24(2): 67–90.

Favell, Adrian. 2008. *Eurostars and Eurocities*. Oxford, UK: Blackwell.

Fischer, Claude and Stacey Oliker. 1983. "A Research Note on Friendship, Gender, and the Life Cycle." *Social Forces* 62(1): 124–133.

Gill, Nick and Paula Bialski. 2011. "New Friends in New Places: Network Formation during the Migration Process among Poles in the UK." *Geoforum* 42(2): 241–249.

Granovetter, Mark. 1974. *Getting a Job*. Chicago, IL: University of Chicago Press.

Höllinger, Franz and Max Haller. 1990. "Kinship and Social Networks in Modern Societies: A Cross-Cultural Comparison among Seven Nations." *European Sociological Review* 6(2): 103–124.

Kearney, Michael. 1995. "The Local and the Global: The Anthropology of Globalization and Transnationalism." *Annual Review of Anthropology* 24: 547–565.

Kennedy, Paul. 2004. "Making Global Society: Friendship Networks among Trans-national Professionals in the Building Design Industry." *Global Networks* 4(2): 157–179.

Kennedy, Paul. 2008. "The Construction of Trans-Social European Networks and the Neutralisation of Borders: Skilled EU Migrants in Manchester—Reconstituting Social and National Belonging." *Space and Polity* 12(1): 119–133.

Koelet, Suzana, Christof Van Mol, and Helga A. G. De Valk. 2017. "Social Embeddedness in a Harmonized Europe: The Social Networks of European Migrants with a Native Partner in Belgium and the Netherlands." *Global Networks* 17(3): 441–459.

Levrau, François, Edith Piqueray, Idesbald Goddeeris, and Christiane Timmerman. 2014. "Polish Immigration in Belgium since 2004: New Dynamics of Migration and Integration?" *Ethnicities* 14(2): 303–323.

Litwak, Eugen and Ivan Szelenyi. 1969. "Primary Group Structures and their Functions: Kin, Neighbors and Friends." *American Society Review* 34, 465–481.

Lubbers, Miranda, José Luis Molina, Jürgen Lerner, Ulrik Brandes, Javier Avíla, and Christopher McCarty. 2010. "Longitudinal Analysis of Personal Networks. The Case of Argentinean Migrants in Spain." *Social Networks* 32(1): 91–104.

Maloutas, Thomas. 2007. "Middle Class Education Strategies and Residential Segregation in Athens." *Journal of Education Policy* 22(1): 49–68.

Massey, Douglass and Kristin E. Espinosa. 1997. "What's Driving Mexico-U.S. Migration? A Theoretical, Empirical, and Policy Analysis." *American Journal of Sociology* 102(4): 939–999.

Mollenhorst, Gerald, Beate Volker, and Henk Flap. 2014. "Changes in Personal Relationships: How Social Contexts Affect the Emergence and Discontinuation of Relationships." *Social Networks* 37: 65–80.

Moore, Gwen. 1990. "Structural Determinants of Men's and Women's Personal Networks." *American Sociological Review* 55(5): 726–735.

Munch, Allison, Miller McPherson, and Lynn Smith-Lovin. 1997. "Gender, Children, and Social Contact: The Effects of Childrearing for Men and Women." *American Sociological Review* 62(4): 509–520.

Parsons, Talcott. 1949. "The Social Structure of the Family." In Ruth N. Anshen (ed.), *The Family: Its Function and Destiny*. New York: Harper, pp. 173–201.

Portes, Alejandro and Julia Sensenbrenner. 1993. "Embeddedness and Immigration: Notes on the Social Determinants of Economic Action." *American Journal of Sociology* 98(6): 1320–1350.

Recchi, Ettore. 2015. *Mobile Europe: The Theory and Practice of Mobility in the EU*. Basingstoke, UK: Palgrave MacMillan.

Rodríguez, Vicente and Carmen Egea. 2006. "Return and the Social Environment of Andalusian Emigrants in Europe." *Journal of Ethnic and Migration Studies* 32(8): 1377–1393.

Rodríguez-García, Dan. 2006. "Mixed Marriages and Transnational Families in the Intercultural Context: A Case Study of African–Spanish Couples in Catalonia." *Journal of Ethnic and Migration Studies* 32(3): 403–433.

Ryan, Louise. 2007. "Migrant Women, Social Networks and Motherhood: The Experiences of Irish Nurses in Britain." *Sociology* 41(2): 295–312.

Ryan, Louise. 2011. "Migrants' Social Networks and Weak Ties: Accessing Resources and Constructing Relationships Post-Migration." *The Sociological Review* 59(4): 707–724.

Scott, Sam and Kim Cartledge. 2009. "Migrant Assimilation in Europe: A Transnational Family Affair." *International Migration Review* 43(1): 60–89.

Stöhr, Tobias. 2015. "The Returns to Occupational Foreign Language Use: Evidence from Germany." *Labour Economics* 32: 86–98.

Tubergen, Frank van. 2014. "Size and Socio-Economic Resources of Core Discussion Networks in the Netherlands: Differences by National-Origin Group and Immigrant Generation." *Ethnic and Racial Studies* 37(6):1020–1042.

Van Mol, Christof and Joris Michielsen. 2015. "The Reconstruction of a Social Network Abroad. An Analysis of the Interaction Patterns of Erasmus Students." *Mobilities* 10(3): 423–444.

Viry, Gil. 2012. "Residential Mobility and the Spatial Dispersion of Personal Networks: Effects on Social Support." *Social Networks* 34(1): 59–72.

Wellman, Barry. 1984. "Domestic Work, Paid Work, and Network." *Research Paper* 49. University of Toronto. Center for Urban and Community Studies.

78 Sociability

Zapf, Wolfgang. 1991. "Modernisierung und Modernisierungstheorien." In Zapf, Wolfgang (ed.), *Die Modernisierung Moderner Gesellschaften. Verhandlungen des 25. Deutschen Soziologentages in Frankfurt am Main 1990*. Frankfurt: Campus, pp. 23–39.

Zontini, Elizabetta. 2004. *Italian Families and Social Capital: Rituals and the Provision of Care in British-Italian Transnational Families*. London, UK: London South Bank University.

4

MAKING A LIVING

Material circumstances shape how people think and behave. It is thus fitting to explore the binational couples' material circumstances. How economically successful they are relative to national couples may impact on their civil and political engagement, their consumer taste, and their identity and more or less differentiate them as a social group. At the same time, the study of the binational couples' material circumstances speaks to the question of whether Europe is already a society, a group of inter-connected and exchanging individuals whose members live and work across Europe under the same conditions as locals.

The chapter's primary focus is on the foreign partners in binational couples, for they are the ones who have changed geographical location and must adapt to new social and cultural circumstances. At the same time, however, I examine whether national partners in binational couples differ from other married or cohabiting nationals in terms of employment, occupational status, earnings, and subjective social position. The chapter shows that binational couples are not a homogeneous group. In general, binational couples where the foreign partner comes from a poor European country are less well-off than those where the foreign partner comes from a wealthy European country. The analysis of self-assessments of where one stands on the social scale indirectly suggests, however, that while foreign partners from rich countries perceive their decision to settle in another European country as taxing, the latter, especially if less educated, perceive it as a step up.

Immigration and socio-economic status in the literature

The sociology and economics literature on the stratification of immigrant populations in Europe has primarily focused on employment and earnings and, then, secondarily, on access to different positions in the employment hierarchy. Over

80 Making a living

the years, it has shown interest in three major comparisons: first-generation with second-generation migrants, migrants with stayers,[1] and migrants with natives (Barrett and Duffy, 2008; Gorodzeisky and Semyonov, 2017; Green, 1999). These comparisons generally differentiate immigrants based on gender and origin (Gorodzeisky and Semyonov, 2017; Luthra et al., 2016). They also explore variation across destinations (Adserà and Chiswick, 2007; Gorodzeisky and Semyonov, 2017; Luthra et al., 2016). Theoretical and descriptive concerns guide scholarly publications in this area. Firstly, a scientific desire to explain differences in the relative performance of different groups in different destinations and then, secondly, political and policy concerns about the prevalence of economic and social inequality in society. The accumulation of research on the topic has revealed that the economic success of migrants depends on a long list of individual and social factors. These factors determine who migrates and how well immigrants integrate in the destination labor markets. An underlying theme in the literature is the extent to which immigrants are subject to discrimination.

Since the book focuses on European couples, it is relevant to examine what the literature says about the European migrants' performance in European markets relative to other groups. Most publications cover the period since 1980. During this period Europe, especially the West, experienced sustained immigration, which prompted national and international agencies to collect suitable data for the study of stratification outcomes among immigrant populations. When one compares natives and migrants at a given moment in time, three descriptive findings stand-out: first, Europeans are often better off than other migrant groups and sometimes even over-perform natives in terms of both employment and earnings; second, relative to natives of the same gender, European male migrants tend to perform better than do European female migrants; and third, Northern European migrants exhibit higher employment rates and higher earnings than do other European migrants. The latter suggests that migrants from more developed European countries are more successful than migrants from less developed ones.

Explanations for why immigrants experience higher unemployment rates and earn less than natives invoke numerous individual and social variables, the latter referring to the immediate household and personal networks, to the country of origin, and to the country of destination. They extend and refine Classic Assimilation and Segmented Assimilation theories, as formulated and developed by authors like Becker, Schultz, Chiswick, Piore, or Portes.[2] Human capital (e.g. educational credentials, linguistic and other type of skills, talent), motivation (García Polavieja et al., 2018), sensitivity to economic incentives (Lanzona, 1998; Nakosteen et al., 2008), and economic constraints and opportunities (e.g. the impact of having children on men and women)[3] are the focus of individual-level explanations of the decision to move and of labor market performance at destination. Relative economic opportunity and power relations within the household enter household level explanations of both the decision to move and labor market outcomes at destination.[4] Economic development (absolute or relative to the country of destination), economic inequality (also absolute or relative to the country of destination), political factors, and migration policy both at origin and destination dominate explanations of the process through which migrants are selected at the country of origin (Borjas, 1987; Rodríguez-Pose et al., 2010; van Tubergen et al., 2004). Finally, social capital (e.g. friends, relatives, size of the migrant group at destination) (Brooks and Waters, 2010; Portes and Bach, 1985; Portes and Rumbaut, 1996), occupational structures (e.g. relative demand for high or low skill labor; the extent of labor market segmentation), wage structures, and labor and welfare state regimes,[5] policies concerning the recognition of foreign educational credentials (Favell, 2008; Nivalainen, 2005), and socio-cultural distance between migrants and natives and related discrimination[6] inform contextual explanations of labor market outcomes at destination.

Foreign partners in binational couples between Europeans are a special type of family migrant. They do not fit neatly in existing classifications of family migration, for these usually refer to families in which both members are from the same nationality[7]. One peculiarity of binational couples is that the vast majority of the foreign partners were already in the country when they met their future spouse or partner, and only few of them were just on holidays. They were there for exclusively individual reasons (work, education, holidays) or as part of family migration strategies. Therefore, the situation of European foreign partners in binational couples is generally unlike that of "tied" or "trailing" individuals who follow or come to join their spouse and who often sacrifice a more promising career in their country of origin.[8] In most cases, their move to the country preceded their chance encounter with their future spouse or companion. Couples who met in one country, one of the partners' country of origin or a third country, and then moved from that country in order to settle in the other partners' country of origin are more the exception than the rule. In those cases, the "tied" mover may pay a price in terms of career and earnings opportunities.

One should also qualify the generalization made for foreign partners who were already in the country of residence when they met their current national spouse or partner. While their original move may have been unrelated to their current marriage or cohabitation arrangement, the fact that they are now married or in a cohabitation relationship can be an obstacle to the foreign partners' careers if it constrains their freedom to go back to their country of origin in search of better economic opportunities. This constrain may be felt more acutely by foreign partners who come from richer countries than by those who come from poorer ones, simply because richer countries generally offer greater economic opportunity to those among their nationals who may want or need to come back than do poorer ones. Quite often, nationals from poorer countries simply do not have the option to go back home.

If the experience of foreign partners in Euro-couples mirrors that of European migrants in general, their socio-economic status (e.g. employment, earnings,

82 Making a living

occupational status) should be the same or just slightly worse than that of nationals. In fact, there is reason to believe that it may even be better. First of all, empirical data show that more educated Europeans intermarry with other Europeans more frequently than do less educated ones (de Valk and Díez Medrano, 2014). The average level of education among the foreign European population in binational couples is therefore higher than that among the foreign European population in general. Since higher educational levels are associated with greater employment chances, higher occupational status, and higher earnings, one would expect that the small gap that exists between the labor market opportunities of natives and foreign Europeans in general may shrink or disappear when the focus is on foreign Europeans in binational couples only. Second, the same factors that positively select European foreigners for migration and then success in the labor market (e.g. individuals with low levels of education and individuals from poorer or lower status countries but with higher than average talent, resilience, or motivation) may also select them for marrying or cohabiting with a national partner in the country of destination. Again, this would impact on the amount of human capital in the group of foreign Europeans in binational couples relative to foreign Europeans in general. Third, foreign European partners in binational couples benefit from greater integration in the national community, which improves their social capital and their level of information, and thus increases their opportunities in the labor market relative to those of foreign Europeans in general. Finally, household externalities derived from the national partner's education and earnings may also contribute to higher employment rates, higher occupational status, and higher earnings among foreign European partners than among foreign Europeans in general. This is because employment rates, average occupational status, and earnings are on average somewhat higher among nationals than among European immigrants.

Whether factors improving the economic prospects of foreign Europeans in binational couples relative to nationals and to the European foreign population do so in a significant way is an empirical issue. One would be inclined to predict that they do, if only because of the paramount role that education plays in determining a person's opportunities in the labor market and the empirically strong effect of education in selecting individuals into Euro-couples. The *Eumarr* data do not allow for an optimal analysis of this question for the seven cities included in the study because the obtained sample strongly over-represents more educated individuals, whether national or foreign European. The strength of the analysis, however, and my main focus, is on the net contrasts that obtain after controlling for education and other variables. Here, the statistical results can be safely compared to those obtained in stratification studies focused on foreign Europeans in general, with the caveat that they pertain to seven large cosmopolitan cities in just four European states.

The story this chapter tells is quite simple. By and large, employment, occupational status, and earnings among partners in binational couples, including the foreign one, mirror those of partners in national couples in the countries where binational couples reside. On closer look, however, one discovers that foreign partners from poor European countries are at a disadvantage with respect to those from richer ones and do not enjoy the same opportunities as nationals. Furthermore, both foreign partners in binational couples who are either highly educated or come from rich countries place themselves in a lower social position than do nationals with the same education, with the same employment and occupational status, and with the same earnings. Their perceptions contrast with those of foreign partners in binational couples with low education and who are nationals from poorer countries, who tend to place themselves on a higher social position than do nationals with the same employment, the same occupational status, and the same earnings.

Employment and occupational status

Foreign partners in binational couples, with or without university education, display somewhat lower employment rates than do nationals with the same education (Table 4.1) and they are less likely to be employed in managerial, professional, or technical occupations (Table 4.4). Also, when compared with nationals of the same gender, foreign women fare better than foreign men both with respect to their likelihood of being employed and their likelihood of being employed in managerial, professional, or technical occupations (Tables 4.2 and 4.3 and Tables 4.5 and 4.6). In regression analysis, controlling for city of residence, these contrasts, although small, are statistically significant. The foreign men's relative disadvantage is unexpected, for the literature highlights that female immigrants suffer greater penalties than do male ones. One plausible interpretation of this seeming contradiction is that binational couples include "trailing wives" but also many "trailing husbands," foreign men whose main motivation to follow their partner to another country is love instead of economic calculus, whereas migration in general includes vastly more women who follow men (i.e. co-nationals) than men who follow women. Why are "trailing" husbands in binational couples more penalized than are "trailing" wives is a question that one cannot answer with the data at hand.

TABLE 4.1 Employment Status, by Type of Couple and Education (Employed–Unweighted Average % across the Four Countries)

No university education	National	81	(433)
	Binational (national partner)	79	(278)
	Binational (foreign partner)	77	(260)
University education	National	88	(599)
	Binational (national partner)	87	(575)
	Binational (foreign partner)	83	(700)

( ) Number of respondents.

TABLE 4.2 Employment Status, by Type of Couple and Education (Employed–Unweighted Average % across the Four Countries) (Women)

No university education	National	70	(278)
	Binational (national partner)	68	(117)
	Binational (foreign partner)	68	(164)
University education	National	80	(300)
	Binational (national partner)	81	(251)
	Binational (foreign partner)	77	(448)

( ) Number of respondents.

TABLE 4.3 Employment Status, by Type of Couple and Education (Employed–Unweighted Average % across the Four Countries) (Men)

No university education	National	92	(155)
	Binational (national partner)	89	(161)
	Binational (foreign partner)	85	(96)
University education	National	96	(299)
	Binational (national partner)	93	(324)
	Binational (foreign partner)	88	(252)

( ) Number of respondents.

TABLE 4.4 Employed in Managerial, Professional, or Technical Occupations (Unweighted Average % across the Four Countries) (Currently Employed)

No university education	National	48	(316)
	Binational (national partner)	50	(223)
	Binational (foreign partner)	48	(187)
University education	National	88	(516)
	Binational (national partner)	84	(504)
	Binational (foreign partner)	79	(569)

( ) Number of respondents.

TABLE 4.5 Employed in Managerial, Professional, or Technical Occupations (Unweighted Average % across the Four Countries) (Currently Employed-Women)

No university education	National	42	(176)
	Binational (national partner)	44	(79)
	Binational (foreign partner)	48	(106)
University education	National	86	(231)
	Binational (national partner)	82	(201)
	Binational (foreign partner)	78	(345)

( ) Number of respondents.

TABLE 4.6 Employed in Managerial, Professional, or Technical Occupations (Unweighted Average % across the Four Countries) (Currently Employed Men)

No university education	National	54	(140)
	Binational (national partner)	56	(144)
	Binational (foreign partner)	47	(81)
University education	National	90	(285)
	Binational (national partner)	85	(303)
	Binational (foreign partner)	81	(224)

( ) Number of respondents.

Work for multinationals

The literature on globalization emphasizes that individuals with transnational experiences and skills benefit in a world formed by culturally diverse national states (Gerhards et al., 2015; Grosse, 1998). It focuses on the economic rewards to knowing various languages, to study abroad and to being acquainted with other cultures, either because of travel or because one lives amidst diversity in huge global cities.[9] Data that allow for a rigorous test of these hypothesis are scarce, however. I have argued elsewhere that the benefits of transnational skills and experiences have been overblown (Díez Medrano, 2016). When one considers the labor market in general, it is largely populated by firms where those skills are not a pre-requisite. Then, firms and sectors of the economy where these skills are in high demand are not necessarily those that guarantee better employment conditions (e.g. waiters who work in bars and restaurants in tourist areas). In the article to which I am referring here, I show empirically that the association between fluency in foreign languages and employment status is most likely spurious, that is, that it stands for other factors that determine a person's employability. I suggest that, more than enhancing the economic prospects of workers, transnational skills channel workers into areas of the economy where these skills are needed.

Individuals with transnational skills and experiences enjoy some competitive advantage in transnational or multinational firms. National and foreign partners in binational couples share in common that they are generally fluent in various languages, that they have traveled and travel more on average than ordinary citizens, and that they are familiar with at least two cultures. They should therefore seek more often and be especially attractive to transnational firms. No study that I know of has examined the absolute and relative propensities of nationals and foreigners in binational couples to work for multinationals and the mediating effect of transnational skills and experience on the likelihood of working for a multinational. The *Eumarr* survey, however, queried respondents on the type of company or organization for which they work, including work for multinationals, and thus allows for such analysis. Across levels of education and across countries, both national and foreign partners in binational couples display a higher propensity to work for multinationals (Table 4.7).

86 Making a living

TABLE 4.7 Works for a Multinational, by Type of Couple and Education (Currently Employed)

	National	22
		(316)
No university education	Binational	23
	(national partner)	(223)
	Binational	27
	(foreign partner)	(187)
	National	23
		(516)
University education	Binational	27
	(national partner)	(504)
	Binational	32
	(foreign partner)	(569)

( ) Number of respondents.

Multiple regression analysis allows for a more rigorous comparison between partners in national and binational couples and at the same time provides insights into the role of transnational skills and experiences (Table 4.8). It shows that both foreign and national partners in binational couples, especially the former, display a greater propensity to work for multinationals than do nationals in national couples (column 1). Fluency in English is also associated to work for multinationals (column 2). The contrast between nationals and foreign partners in binational couples results in fact from a much stronger association between speaking English and work for multinationals among foreign partners. An interaction coefficient between foreign status and the ability to speak English ("Foreign in a Binational Couple" ★ Speaks English) equal to 0.14 (column 4) means that, holding other factors constant, the probability that a foreign partner in a binational couple works for a multinational is fourteen percentage points higher if he or she speaks English. It also means that, holding other factors constant, the probability that a person who speaks English work for a multinational is fourteen percentage points higher if she or he is a foreign partner in a binational couple instead of a national in a national couple and eleven percentage points higher if she or he is a foreign partner in a binational couple instead of a national partner in a binational couple (0.14−0.03 = 0.11). This could in turn reflect that employers prefer foreign to national speakers of English, that foreigners speak English better than nationals, or that foreigners are drawn to work for multinationals more often than are nationals.

Table 4.8 offers insights into other factors that are associated with working for a multinational. For instance, holding other variables constant, including the ability to speak English, people who speak the local language at home show less propensity to work for multinationals than do those who do not (column 5). One can speculate that people who speak the local language at home do not practice

TABLE 4.8 Association between Being in a Binational Couple and Work for a Multinational, Controlling for City of Residence, Gender, Education, and Specific Nationality (OLS) (Employed respondents only)

	Works for Multinational (1)		Works for Multinational (2)		Works for Multinational (3)		Works for Multinational (4)		Works for Multinational (5)		Works for Multinational (6)		Works for Multinational (7)	
-Foreign in a binational couple	0.09	★	0.09	★	0.10	★	−0.03		−0.06		−0.06		−0.06	
-National in binational couple	0.05	+	0.04	+	0.03		0.03		0.02		0.02		5.0E−03	
-Education	0.02	★	0.01		0.01		0.01		0.01		9.0E−03		4.0E_03	
-Speaks English			0.13	★	0.13	★	0.09	★	0.10	★	0.10	★	0.08	★
-Gender (1=Female)					−0.10	★	−0.11	★	−0.11	★	−0.11	★	−0.10	★
-Foreign in a binational couple ★ speaks English							0.14	+	0.16	★	0.16	★	0.16	+
-Uses local language with partner									−0.06	★	−0.06	★	−0.06	★
-Parents' average level of education											−1.0E−03		−3.0E−03	
-Number of states visited before 16											3.0E−03	★	1.0E−03	
-Number of states visited between 17 and meet partner													9.0E−03	★
-Constant	0.07		0.01		0.06		0.09		0.14	★	0.14	★	0.12	+
R-square (%)	1.7		2.3		3.7		3.9		4.2		4.2		5.1	
N	1929		1929		1929		1929		1929		1929		1929	

Controls for city of residence; +: Significant at 0.10 level, two-tailed ★: Significant at 0.05 level, two-tailed.

88 Making a living

foreign languages, especially English, which multinationals prioritize. How often people traveled abroad in late adolescence and early adulthood, as measured by the number of states visited between the seventeenth birthday and the year respondents met their current partner, is also associated with a slightly higher propensity to work for multinationals (column 7). This conveys perhaps that multinationals reward transnational experience or that people with transnational experience are more attracted to multinationals. The association is anyway very small compared with the relationship between speaking English and work for multinationals.

In sum, foreign partners in binational couples, especially if male, must overcome greater barriers than nationals in securing a job and getting access to prestigious and well-paid occupations, but they benefit from greater work opportunities in multinationals. One way to determine whether this is enough compensation is to examine the earnings of individuals in national and binational couples.

Earnings

Just as I showed for employment and access to high-status, high-income, occupations, while female foreign partners earn as much as female national partners do, male foreign partners earn less than male national partners do (Table 4.9, column 1). Because of this, Table 4.9 focuses mainly on men. The statistical results are consistent with those of previous analyses: they convey that foreign men earn less than national men, partly because they are more often unemployed, partly because they have less access to managerial, professional, and technical positions (columns 2 and 3), and in spite of working more often for multinationals (column 4). Surprisingly, however, these variables' overall contribution to the explanation of the income gap between foreign and national men is very small (i.e. the regression coefficient for the effect of being foreign only changes from -0.13 to -0.12 when one moves from column 1 to column 4). Furthermore, incomes among foreign partners are far from homogeneous and actually vary strongly across nationalities. When one controls for the foreign respondents' nationality, the estimate for the average income among foreign male respondents is actually higher than that for national male respondents (i.e. coefficient 0.16 in column 5).

Table 4.10 allows us to explore the effect of nationality further. Building on previous findings in this chapter, the statistical models in this table treat male and female foreign partners separately. Also, because the literature shows that country of origin [10] impacts on people's chances of being employed in Europe, I use information on GDP/capita to differentiate between foreign partners from relatively poor European countries and foreign partners from relatively rich European countries. The first category includes nationals from Eastern and Southern Europe whereas the second one includes nationals from Northern and Western Europe.

TABLE 4.9 Association between Being in a Binational Couple and Personal Income, Controlling for City of Residence, Gender, Education, Nationality, Work for a Multinational, and English Knowledge (OLS)

	Ln(Income)		Ln(Income) (Men)		Ln(Income) (Men)		Ln(Income) (Men)		Ln(Income) (Men) (Controlling for Nationality)	
	(1)		(2)		(3)		(4)		(5)	
-Foreign in a binational couple	-0.13	★	-0.10	★	-0.09	★	-0.12	★	0.16	+
-National in binational couple	-0.03		-0.01		-3.0E-03		-0.02		-0.02	
-Gender (1=Female)	-0.32	★								
-Foreign in a binational couple ★ gender	0.11	★								
-Education	0.11	★	0.09	★	0.08	★	0.08	★	0.08	★
-Other occupational status			-0.28	★	-0.22	★	-0.20	+	0.21	★
-Unemployed			-0.15	+	-0.11		-0.05		-0.03	
-Student			0.03		0.09		0.21		0.18	
-Housework			-0.70	★	-0.64	★	-0.64	★	-0.65	★
-In managerial, professional, technical occupations					0.09	+	0.05		0.04	
-Low Service occupations					-0.11		-0.10		-0.10	
-Age							0.02	★	0.02	★
-Works for a multinational							0.27	★	0.27	★
-Speaks English							0.10	+	0.09	
-Constant	3.18	★	3.31	★	3.34	★	2.45	★	2.53	★
-R-square (%)	28.2		35.7		36.4		41.9		44.3	
N	2307		1086		1086		1086		1086	

Note: Reference category for occupation (skilled and unskilled industrial occupation).
Controls for city of residence; +: Significant at 0.10 level, two-tailed; ★: Significant at 0.05 level, two-tailed.

90 Making a living

TABLE 4.10 Association between Being in a Binational Couple and Personal Income, Controlling for City of Residence, Gender, Education, Specific Nationality, Work for a Multinational, and English Knowledge (OLS)

	Ln(Income) (Men) (1)		Ln(Income) (Men) (2)		Ln(Income) (Women) (3)		Ln(Income) (Women) (4)	
–Foreign from poor country in binational couple	−0.20	★	−0.39	★	−0.07		0.01	
–Foreign from not poor country in binational couple	−0.09	★	−0.08		−0.03		−0.02	
–National in binational couple	−0.02		−0.03		−0.05		−0.05	
–Education	0.08	★	0.08	★	0.09	★	0.08	★
–Other occupational status	0.20	+	−0.20	+	0.14		0.15	
–Unemployed	−0.04		−0.02		−0.12		−0.12	
–Student	0.21		0.18		−0.33	★	−0.33	★
–Housework	−0.63	★	−0.62	★	−0.07		−0.07	
–In managerial, professional, technical occupations	0.04		0.04		0.06		0.06	
–Low service occupations	−0.10		−0.10		−0.07		−0.06	
–Age	0.02	★	0.02	★	0.00		0.00	
–Works for a multinational	0.26	★	0.27	★	0.29	★	0.29	★
–Speaks English	0.10	+	0.11	+	0.05		0.05	
–Partner's employed status			0.02				0.05	
–Partner's education			−2.0E−03				0.01	
–Uses local language with partner			−0.05				0.02	
–Uses local language with partner ★ foreign in a binational couple (poor country)			0.28	★			−0.13	
–Uses Local Language with Partner ★ Foreign in a Binational Couple (Not Poor Country)			−0.03				−7.0E−03	
–Constant	2.46	★	2.52	★	2.88	★	2.76	
R-square (%)	42.0		42.3		23.8		24.0	
N	1086		1086		1221		1221	

Note: Reference category for occupation (skilled and unskilled industrial occupation).
Controls for city of residence +: Significant at 0.10 level, two-tailed.
★: Significant at 0.05 level, two-tailed.

The statistical estimates confirm that female foreign partners do not earn less than their national counterparts (columns 3 and 4). At the same time, they show that the relative earnings disadvantage experienced by foreign male partners is mainly born by those from poorer European countries and is quite substantial. It is estimated at 20% less and 39% less than what nationals in national couples earn, depending on what control variables are included in the model (columns 1 and 2). This disadvantage remains even when individuals know and use the local language (column 2). In fact, foreign male partners from poorer countries pay a much greater price for not using the local language than do foreign male partners from richer ones (i.e. coefficients -0.39 and -0.08 in column 2). One can only speculate about the mechanisms that mediate this contrast.

Confronted with similar findings regarding immigrants in general, scholars have generally interpreted them as resulting from discrimination, in turn based on perceived social and cultural distance (van Tubergen et al., 2004). This conclusion is plausible and rests on abundant and consistent empirical research. It is unclear, however, whether it is entirely applicable to comparisons between Europeans. For instance, recent research suggests that migrants from countries with weak welfare states into countries with generous welfare states (e.g. Romanian immigrants) may actually be negatively selected in terms of motivation (García Polavieja et al., 2018). Also, a discrimination explanation does not account for the sources of the relatively high earnings of foreign partners from richer countries who cannot speak the local language. Other factors must also be at play. In the context of the single market, for instance, where numerous firms have opened branches across the European Union, it is conceivable that movers from wealthier countries benefit from greater employment opportunities in branches from firms from their home country, in which command of the local language is perhaps secondary to command of the foreign firm's national language, than do those who moved from poorer ones. The inclusion of a variable that taps on whether the respondent works for a multinational captures part of this, but some small foreign firms from wealthier European countries can be significant sources of employment for natives from these countries and still not be perceived as multinationals by the respondents.

The literature has focused on the role of length of residence in explaining earnings differentials between groups of immigrants. This is a hotly debated issue, for as Borjas pointed out many years ago, only panel data collected for a long period of time can provide conclusive evidence (Borjas, 1987). Some studies find an effect and others do not. Those that find an effect claim that after about fifteen years of residence in the country, the migrants' average earnings match those of natives (Chiswick, 1978; Chiswick et al., 2005). The *Eumarr* sample includes foreign Europeans who were not born in the country of residence and who have lived nine to ten years on average in the country of residence, thus close to the fifteen-year threshold highlighted in the literature. The absence of great contrasts between the foreign partners' earnings and those of national partners observed above is therefore consistent with this prediction.

The *Eumarr*'s design is far from fulfilling the requirements for testing the effect of length of residence on the earnings of foreign partners. Also, the *Eumarr* survey did not ask respondents when they settled in the country of residence for the first time. One can only infer this from information that the survey collected on the places where they had resided in the past and on the dates when

92 Making a living

these stays took place. The following analysis must therefore be treated with caution, as just an effort to at least provide a descriptive analysis of earnings differences between foreign partners who have lived different amounts of time in the country of residence, and between them and national partners in national and binational couples.

Table 4.11 examines the association between length of residence and earnings from various angles. The model in column 1 is the baseline model to which the other models can be compared. It is the full multiple regression model presented in Table 4.9, estimated for men only and based on the subset of respondents for which one can establish their date of settlement in the country of residence with

TABLE 4.11 Association between Being in a Binational Couple and Personal Income, Controlling for Years of Residence, City of Residence, Gender, Education, Specific Nationality, Work for a Multinational, and English Knowledge (OLS) (Subsample of Male Respondents with known years of residence in Country of Residence)

	Income (All Respondents)		Income (Foreign Respondents with More Than 12 Years of Residence vs. Nationals)		Income (Foreign Respondents with Fewer Than 12 Years of Residence vs. National Respondents)		Income (Only Foreigners in Binational Couples)	
	(1)		(2)		(3)		(4)	
–Foreign in a binational couple	−0.10	★	−0.05		−0.12	★		
–National in binational couple	−0.02		−0.03		−0.02			
–Years of Residence							9.0E–03	
–Education	0.08	★	0.08	★	0.07	★	0.10	★
–Other occupational status	−0.23	★	−0.23	+	−0.24	★	−0.07	
–Unemployed	−0.05		−0.14		−0.05		0.22	
–Student	0.20		0.24		0.19		0.23	
–Housework	−0.61	★	−0.62	★	−0.56	★	−0.64	★
–In managerial, professional, or technical occupations	0.04		0.01		0.04		0.20	★
–Low service occupations	−0.08		−0.13	+	−0.09		0.22	
–Age	0.02	★	0.02	★	0.02	★	0.04	★
–Works for a multinational	0.25	★	0.23	★	0.25	★	0.34	★
–Speaks English	0.11	★	0.14	★	0.14	★	0.14	
–Constant	2.42	★	2.56	★	2.46	★	1.51	★
R-square (%)	42.0		43.2		42.1		43.3	
N	1015		866		953		211	

Controls for city of residence; +: Significant at 0.10 level, two-tailed; ★: Significant at 0.05 level, two-tailed.

Making a living **93**

some confidence. The estimates obtained for this model show that, holding other factors constant, the yearly earnings of male foreign partners in binational couples are about ten percent lower than those of nationals. The rest of the table shows that foreign partners who have lived twelve or more years in the country of residence earn about the same as national partners in national and binational couples (column 2) while male foreign partners who have lived fewer than twelve years earn twelve percent less on average than do male national partners (column 3).

These results are consistent with the dominant view about the effect of length of residence but must be interpreted carefully. First, because a test for the statistical significance of the difference between the coefficients for foreign status in columns 2 and 3 is not statistically significant at the 0.05 level. Second, because an additional model displayed in column 4 and restricted to male foreign partners shows that the effect of length of residence is extremely small and not statistically significant. Third, because most recent migrants come from Central and Eastern Europe, which means that one cannot disentangle the effect of years of residence from the effect of coming from this part of Europe. In sum, this analysis raises more questions than it answers but it provides a reference for future research on the effect of years of residence on the earnings of foreign partners in binational couples.

The results presented in this section show that the economic fortunes of foreign partners in binational couples vary by gender and by origin. The experiences and lives of foreign men and women differ from one another, just as those of foreign partners from poorer countries and foreign partners from wealthier ones. The sections above highlight that, when compared with nationals, male foreign partners from poorer European countries do not fare as well economically as do female foreign partners or male foreign partners from wealthier countries[11].

Social position

Does material well-being, as measured through earnings and other measures of wealth, predict where people place themselves on the stratification system? Does it predict it as well for partners in binational couples as for partners in national ones? The relationship between objective and subjective material well-being has occupied social thinkers since at least Tocqueville's treatise on the French revolution.[12] This interest is well-justified: while objective material conditions constrain and create opportunities for action, while they impact in complex ways on how people see and behave in the world, the immediate motivations underlying behavior rest on perceptions that not always match objective conditions. A focus on the immigrants' perceptions of their social position is largely missing in the literature, especially the more quantitative one. The closest one gets to this question is recent research on subjective well-being. This work underlines that immigrants pay a price in terms of life satisfaction, no matter how well they do in the material sense (see Bartram, 2010; Safi, 2009; Stillman et al., 2012). This is also the impression conveyed by the participants in Favell's book *Eurostars and*

94 Making a living

Eurocities. Even when objectively successful, many among them expressed frustration about the effort needed to satisfy major needs, such as finding a decent place to live, good doctors, or a suitable school for their children. The previous chapter has indeed confirmed that highly educated foreign partners do not benefit from as much assistance in addressing these issues as do nationals and less educated foreign partners.

People tend to measure themselves through periodic comparisons with others with similar background and qualifications, what is known as one's reference group. Favell's *Eurostars,* however, seemed especially sensitive to how they compared with those like them in their country of residence and to those like them in their country of origin. This is perhaps because the decision to move to another country is such an important one and because in their case, *free-movers (thus "accountable only to themselves"*), it was not forced upon them by economic need. Their evaluations were often tainted with some measure of regret. Is there an objective basis for this? One could interpret Favell's participants' seething dissatisfaction as reflecting too much counterfactual thinking (what if...?) on their part; perhaps also, as resulting from that pernicious human tendency to think that the grass is always greener on the other side of the fence. One could argue too, however, that their sense of regret is perhaps justified, that there is an unmeasured objective basis for why immigrants who have succeeded in many ways, also material, feel relatively deprived when they compare themselves with locals and with their reference group in their country of origin. As the previous chapter shows, it is not only that a relative lack of social capital forces migrants to invest a lot of time, effort, and money into tasks that locals solve easily and often at no cost; it is also that living abroad generally entails more expenditures than living in one's country, some of them extending beyond the initial period of settlement (e.g. the cost of regularly visiting relatives and friends abroad or the cost of paying for a private school if parents want that their children become fluent both in the local and in their home country's language).

The *Eumarr* survey included a question that allows for an examination of the participants' perceptions of economic status. The question read as follows:

> On the following scale, step 0 corresponds to 'the lowest level in the society of [Country of Residence]', step 10 corresponds to 'the highest level in the society of [Country of Residence]'. When you consider your household income from all sources and the wealth you and your partner may have accumulated, could you tell me on which step you would place yourself?

A comparison of perceptions of social position between partners in national couples and partners in binational ones, both national and foreign, complements the analysis of objective material contrasts and at the same time provides quantitative evidence that helps extend and deepen the discussion that Favell started in *Eurostars and Eurocities*.

Partners in binational couples, especially the foreign partners, rank themselves lower in the stratification system than do partners in national couples. This is well conveyed by Table 4.12. Table 4.12 also shows that the contrast is less clear among the less educated than among the more educated ones. These results are confirmed and become clearer through multiple regression analysis, as in Table 4.13. Holding education and city of residence constant, foreign partners place themselves at a lower social position than do national partners in both national and binational couples (see coefficient -0.36 in column 1). The contrast, however, is significantly greater among the more educated foreign respondents, precisely those who are better off and whose employment and individual earnings are more similar to those of equally educated national respondents (column 2). In fact, foreign partners with low levels of education on average rank themselves higher socially than do national partners with the same level of education (i.e. the positive regression coefficient, 0.80, in line 2 of column 2). Although differences in earnings and in occupational status contribute somewhat to explain these contrasts, they are far from accounting for them (columns 3 and 4). Highly educated foreign partners perceive themselves on a lower ladder in the social scale than do highly educated national partners, even when they have the same occupational status, earn the same, and contribute the same amount to the overall household earnings. Controlling for additional variables, such as the partner's education and employment status, does not change the picture (column 5).

Since the analysis above has shown that the economic circumstances of foreign partners from poorer countries are bleaker than those of foreign partners from richer ones, I distinguished the two groups of foreign partners in the analysis (columns 6 and 7). The results are quite unambiguous: foreign partners from richer countries, regardless of their level of education and other economic variables, place themselves on a lower social position than do national partners with

TABLE 4.12 Mean Level in Society, by Type of Couple and Education (Unweighted Average of Country Means)

No university education	National	5.54
		(424)
	Binational	5.34
	(national partner)	(261)
	Binational	5.42
	(foreign partner)	(253)
University education	National	6.41
		(588)
	Binational	6.27
	(national partner)	(563)
	Binational	6.23
	(foreign partner)	(859)

( ) Number of respondents.

TABLE 4.13 Association between Being in a Binational Couple and Perceived Social Position, Controlling for City of Residence, Gender, Education, Specific Nationality, Work for a Multinational, and English Knowledge (OLS)

	Social Position (1)	Social Position (2)	Social Position (3)	Social Position (4)	Social Position (5)	Social Position (6)	Social Position (7)
-Foreign in a binational couple	−0.36 ★	0.80 ★	0.70 ★	0.67 ★	0.65 ★		
-Foreign from poor country in binational couple						1.52 ★	1.52 ★
-Foreign from not poor country in binational couple						−0.24 ★	−0.08
-National in binational couple	−0.11	−0.12	−0.10	−0.09	−0.12 +	−0.12	−0.13 +
-Education	0.26 ★	0.32 ★	0.23 ★	0.21 ★	0.15 ★	0.32 ★	0.15 ★
-Foreign in binational couple ★ Education		−0.16 ★	−0.14 ★	−0.14 ★	−0.14 ★		
-Foreign from poor country in binational couple ★ Education						−0.28 ★	−0.26 ★
-Foreign from not poor Country in binational couple ★ Education						−0.08	−0.04
-Income (PPS)			0.03 ★	0.03 ★	0.03 ★		0.03 ★
-Individual contribution to household income			−0.54 ★	−0.68 ★	−0.37 ★		−0.39 ★
-Other occupational status				0.10	0,16		0.17
-Unemployed				−0.22	−0.15		−0.16
-Student				−0.35	−0.31		−0.32
-Housework				−0.10	−0.05		−0.03
-In managerial, professional, Technical occupations				0.18 +	0.16 +		0.18 +
-Low service occupations				0.04	0.05		0.08
-Age					0.02 ★		0.02 ★
-Gender (1 = Female)					0.04		0.05
-Partner employed					0.26 ★		0.26 ★
-Partner's education					0.12 ★		0.12 ★
-Constant	3.74 ★	3.39 ★	2.85 ★	3.01 ★	1.63 ★	3.38 ★	1.57 ★
R-square (%)	19.4	19.9	30.9	31.3	32.8	20.2	33.1
N	2307	2307	2307	2307	2307	2307	2307

Note: Reference category for occupation (skilled and unskilled industrial occupation).
Controls for city of residence. +: Significant at 0.10 level, two-tailed; ★: Significant at 0.05 level, two-tailed.

similar education and in similar economic circumstances. Meanwhile, foreign partners from poor countries divide into two groups: those with low education see themselves as higher in the social scale than do national partners with the same level of education, whereas those with higher levels of education tend to place themselves on a lower position of the social scale than do highly educated national partners. I estimated additional models, to control for whether respondents own their home and for the number of children respondents have. The results are robust to the inclusion of these additional variables. They support Favell's contention that many highly educated migrant Europeans do not quite feel like their gamble paid-off and they suggest at the same time that underprivileged European migrants, less educated migrants from poor European countries, evaluate their social and economic circumstances much more positively. They actually rank themselves higher on the social scale than do nationals in comparable circumstances. This last finding is congruent with Barbulescu's et al.'s finding regarding the life satisfaction of Romanian migrants compared with that of stayers and returnees (Barbulescu et al., 2019).

It is difficult to find measures that fully capture the objective factors that Favell emphasizes as causes for the *Eurostars*' malaise. I estimated statistical models with variables that, based on the literature and the analysis of networks in the previous chapter, should have contributed to explain why married and cohabiting *Eurostars* underestimate their social rank when compared with nationals in the same material circumstances. I controlled for the degree to which they are inserted in local social networks. I also controlled for whether or not relatives of theirs live in the country, since *Eurostars* are less likely to have close relatives in the country where they have settled than do less educated foreign partners from poorer countries. I controlled for the extent to which foreign partners feel that they can count on others for help in dealing and solving up to seven recurrent problems in daily life, such as finding a doctor, getting childcare, or even filling out taxes. None of these variables impact on the contrasts outlined above. I also tested for the possibility described above that binational couples incur into more expenditures connected, among others, with maintaining ties with their country of origin. I thus controlled for a variable that measures how often they travel to visit relatives abroad. Again, the inclusion of this variable in statistical models does not alter at all the contrasts already described. These findings do not necessarily contradict Favell's argument. Perhaps other, better measures, would help account for these contrasts. Also, Favell is dealing with a more diverse group of *Eurostars* than I do, a group that often includes foreign couples in which both partners come from the same country. The social barriers these couples are faced against are probably greater than those of binational couples and they contribute more to their relative "anomie."

In order to account for the contrasts described above it is worth noticing that the perceptions that nationals in binational couples have of their social position do not greatly differ from those of nationals in national couples. Regardless of the model one fits the coefficient fluctuates between -0.10 and -0.13 on a scale

98 Making a living

from 0 to 10, and it is statistically significant at the 0.10 level only. Models that are not displayed in Table 4.13 show in fact that their perceptions do not vary with their level of education, as do those of foreign partners in binational couples. The inference that one can draw from this finding is that, whatever the cause of the foreign partners' tendency to place themselves in a lower social position than do national ones, it is largely unrelated to the material circumstances of the couple itself. Otherwise, national partners in binational couples would share these perceptions with their spouses or companions.

Highly educated foreign partners and less educated foreign partners from wealthier countries share in common that their lives in their country of origin were relatively comfortable and secure, either because of what they could obtain for themselves or because they benefitted from high levels of collective wealth in the country of residence: a strong welfare state, relatively modern infrastructure, collective amenities, a relatively clean environment, a rich cultural life, and so on. From this comfort and security derives a certain sense of status and entitlement, both social and national, which they carry to their country of destination and that leads them to take the standard of living that they enjoy for granted. In these circumstances, the fact that, as foreigners, they may have to invest more effort into achieving and obtaining what locals like them achieve and obtain, the awareness that their social capital is not commensurate in quality to that of people with deeper roots in the community, may bear on their perceptions of where they stand in the social scale. These considerations are especially applicable to highly educated foreign nationals from poor countries, for as shown above, their educational credentials do not get the same recognition as those from nationals or from foreigners from richer countries, which hampers their chances of finding jobs commensurate to their level of education.

The Romanian researcher whom I interviewed and whom I introduced in the previous chapter perfectly illustrates the situation and perceptions of highly educated individuals, especially if they come from poorer European countries. She and her husband are a paradigm of success in Spanish society: both are established researchers, who have a secure job and work in the same department, twenty to twenty-five minutes away from home, joint earnings that place them at the top 10% of all Spanish households. For most of our conversation, however, she dwelled on the huge bureaucratic difficulties she had had to overcome in order to get a post like her Spanish husband, whose career progression had been much smoother. She complained about the many struggles of everyday life, like saving enough in order to pay the installments of the couple's huge mortgage, reconciling work and family, making sure that her children's school provided the "right" education, fighting against Spain's idiosyncrasy. Although not unhappy, she seemed genuinely overburdened by life in this foreign and "strange" country—as she described it—and part of this may reflect that, the way she sees it, she is into a David versus Goliath struggle against the system, where her only help is her husband and his family, both a blessing and a curse, for she would rather depend on other people.

The following remark perfectly captures the mindset of many highly educated partners in binational couples once they reach a certain stage in their life: "...I know that Romania offered me greater opportunities; perhaps I would not have benefitted from that many professional resources, but viewed from a Romanian perspective, my prospects were excellent. My CV was very good. In [year], I was honored by [Romanian Institution] with one of the most prestigious awards while I was still working on my PhD Thesis" (Interview # 8).

In truth, the other five highly educated foreign partners in binational couples whom I interviewed (three women and two men) did not voice this message in these or similar terms. Based on the full model presented in Table 4.13, the perceptions of all but one of the persons whom I interviewed were within one standard deviation of the estimated value for the dependent variable; all of them, however, placed themselves higher in the social scale than the model predicts, so one would not expect them to express much frustration about their economic and social circumstances. The Romanian respondent featured here is, precisely, the one whose predicted value best aligns with her perceived social position (Standardized residual = 0.22), which, one may speculate, perhaps accounts for why she expressed more frustration. Counterfactual thinking as to what life would have brought had they stayed in their country, probably explains why, on average, highly educated foreign partners in binational couples place themselves on a lower social level than do highly educated nationals.

Less educated foreign partners from poor countries differ radically from the other two groups, and probably for good reason. Many of them moved in search of economic opportunity. As shown above, they fare worse that nationals with similar qualifications, in part, perhaps, because of discrimination. And yet, they tend to place themselves higher in the social scale than do nationals. While one can read this as an act of self-assertion in the face of adversity, perhaps it also reflects that despite the question's wording, which calls them to compare themselves with nationals living in their country of residence, they cannot avoid thinking about their hypothetical life prospects in their country of origin. Many among them probably earn considerably more than they would have earned at home, a fact actualized whenever they go back to their country to visit family and friends. In addition to this, their perceptions are probably shaped by the collective wealth in their host country, a collective wealth that contrasts with relative poverty in their countries of origin. For some, living or having married a local may feel like success, especially if their reference group are other migrants from the same country who remain single or live with a co-national. More research is needed to determine the role of these or other factors, but Barbulescu's et al.'s recent findings with survey data from Romanian movers, stayers, and returnees are consistent with this interpretation (Barbulescu et al., 2019).

I have situated national and binational couples in the stratification system of the countries in which they reside. Seen from the literature on immigration and intermarriage, this is the first systematic study of the location of both national and European partners in the stratification system. In connection to these literatures,

100 Making a living

its main contributions are to highlight that in the cities and countries examined, and with the exception of males from poor European countries (whose employment opportunities and earnings are lower than those of national workers with similar qualifications), the foreign European population in binational couples displays similar employment levels, occupational status, and earnings as does the national population. This is what one would expect given previous findings concerning Europeans who live in other European countries. In contrast to this literature, however, which shows that foreign women generally fare worse than foreign men, this chapter shows that it is male married or cohabiting foreigners in binational couples, not female ones, who do not do as well as nationals in finding employment, reaching high status positions in firms, or earning in consonance with their educational qualifications.

This chapter is unique because of examining both actual and perceived economic attainment among foreign Europeans. The most interesting finding is that members of the social segments of the foreign population in binational couples who do objectively better in terms of employment, occupational status, and earnings on average tend to place themselves in a lower level of the stratification scale than do nationals with same qualifications and objective indicators of material wealth. Meanwhile, foreign partners with low education and from poorer European countries, precisely those most disadvantaged relative to nationals in the labor market, on average tend to place themselves in a higher level of the stratification scale than do nationals with the same qualifications and objective indicators of material wealth. I have relied on the literature, mainly on Favell's book *Eurostars and Eurocities*, and on in-depth interviews conducted with a number of participants in the survey, to speculate that the main explanation for this is that whereas *Eurostars* have to struggle hard, and often with little social capital, to reproduce the standards of living that they would have attained in their country of origin, less educated individuals from poorer European countries generally win if they compare their current achievements with their prospects in their country of origin.

Another of this chapter's contributions is the analysis of employment opportunities, occupational status, earnings, and perceived social position of nationals in binational couples. It is conceivable that the same special personality or background characteristics that selected them into to marrying or cohabiting with a foreigner, like a greater fluency in foreign languages, correlate with personality and background characteristics that lead to economic success. The statistical analysis, however, has revealed that nationals in binational couples are not different from other nationals.

The next chapters follow from this preliminary sketch of the stratification of binational couples. They explore social and political participation, consumer taste, and identification. This chapter suggests that since the position in the stratification system of partners in Euro-couples does not differ from that of partners in national ones, the contrasts result from background characteristics and internal dynamics within the couples themselves more than from material circumstances.

Notes

1 Simón et al. (2014), Redstone Akresh (2008), Chiswick et al. (2005), Zimmermann and Bauer (1999), Rooth and Ekberg (2006).
2 Schultz (1961), Becker (1962), Chiswick (1978), Piore (1979), Portes (1993).
3 Waite (1980), Gomulka and Stern (1990), Yu et al. (1993), Booth et al. (1997), Hämäläinen and Pehkonen (2001).
4 On trailing spouses: Mincer (1978), Hardill and MacDonald (1998), Nivalainen (2005), González Ferrer (2013), van Bochove and Engbersen (2015), Rodríguez-Pose and Tselios (2010).
5 Borjas (1987), Kogan (2006), Adserà and Chiswick (2007), Gorodzeisky and Semyonov (2017).
6 Becker (1962), Phelps (1972), Bergmann (1974), Model and Lapido (1996), Portes and Rumbaut (1996), van Tubergen et al. (2004).
7 Kofman (2004), Lauth Bacas (2002), Smith and Bailey (2006), Luthra et al. (2016).
8 Mincer (1978), Hardill and MacDonald (1998), van Bochove and Engbersen (2015).
9 On language: Di Paolo and Tansel (2015), Ginsburgh and Prieto-Rodríguez J. (2011), Saiz and Zoido (2005), Stöhr (2015). On study abroad: Igarashi and Saito (2014), Di Pietro (2013). On transnational social networks: Igarashi and Saito (2014).
10 Berman et al. (2003), Bleakley and Chin (2010), Chiswick and Miller (1995), Chiswick and Miller (2007), Chiswick and Miller (2009), Dustmann and Van Soest (2002).
11 Selection processes affecting men's and women's decision to settle in one's country or in the partner's country and discrimination, rooted on social and cultural distance, probably play a role in explaining the findings above. In the absence of direct measures that would allow to substantiate this interpretation, one can only treat it as provisional.
12 de Tocqueville (1998 [1856]), Hodge and Treiman (1968), Hout (2008) Evans and Kelley (2004), Sosnaud et al. (2013).

References

Adserà, Alicia and Barry R. Chiswick. 2007. "Are There Gender and Country of Origin Differences in Immigrant Labor Market Outcomes across European Destinations?" *Journal of Population Economics* 20(3): 495–526.

Barbulescu, Roxana, Irina Ciornei, and Albert Varela. 2019. "Understanding Romanians' Cross-Border Mobility in Europe: Movers, Stayers, and Returnees." In Ettore Recchi et al.'s *Everyday Europe: Social Transnationalism in an Unsettled Continent*. Bristol, UK: Policy Press, pp. 195–225.

Barrett, Alan and David Duffy. 2008. "Are Ireland's Immigrants Integrating into Its Labor Market?" *International Migration Review* 42(3): 597–619.

Bartram, David. 2010. "International Migration, Open Borders Debates, and Happiness." *International Studies Review* 12(3): 339–361.

Becker, Gary S. 1962. "Investment in Human Capital: A Theoretical Analysis. Part 2: Investment in Human Beings." *Journal of Political Economy* 70(5): 9–49.

Bergmann, Barbara R. 1974. "Occupational Segregation, Wages and Profits When Employers Discriminate by Race or Sex." *Eastern Economic Journal* 1(2): 103–110.

Berman, Eli, Kelly Lang, and Erez Siniver. 2003. "Language Skill Complementarity: Returns to Immigrant Language Acquisition." *Labour Economics* 10(3): 265–290.

Bleakley, Hoyt and Aimee Chin. 2010. Age at Arrival, English Proficiency, and Social Assimilation among US Immigrants. *American Economic Journal: Applied Economics* 2(1): 165–192.

Bochove, Marianne van and Godfried Engbersen. 2015. "Beyond Cosmopolitanism and Expat Bubbles: Challenging Dominant Representations of Knowledge Workers and Trailing Spouses: Beyond Cosmopolitanism and Expat Bubbles." *Population, Space and Place* 21(4): 295–309.

Booth, Alan, Ann C. Crouter, and Nancy Landale (eds.). 1997. *Immigration and the Family: Research and Policy on U.S. Immigrants*. Hillsdale, NJ: Lawrence Erlbaum Associates.

Borjas, George J. 1987. "Self-selection and the Earnings of Immigrants." *The American Economic Review* 77(4): 531–553.

Brooks, Rachel and Johanna Waters. 2010. "Social Networks and Educational Mobility: The Experiences of UK Students." *Globalization, Societies and Education* 8(1): 143–157.

Chiswick, Barry R. 1978. "The Effect of Americanization on the Earnings of Foreign-Born Men." *Journal of Political Economy* 86(5): 897–921.

Chiswick, Barry R. and Paul W. Miller. 1995. "The Endogeneity between Language and Earnings: International Analyses." *Journal of Labor Economics* 13(2): 246–288.

Chiswick, Barry R. and Paul W. Miller. 2007. *The Economics of the Language: International Analyses*. New York: Routledge.

Chiswick, Barry R. and Paul. W. Miller. 2009. "Earnings and Occupational Attainment among Immigrants." *Industrial Relations* 48(39): 454–465.

Chiswick, Barry R., Yew Liang Lee, and Paul W. Miller. 2005. "A Longitudinal Analysis of Immigrant Occupational Mobility: A Test of the Immigrant Assimilation Hypothesis." *International Migration Review* 39(2): 332–353.

Díez Medrano, Juan. 2016. "Globalization, Transnational Human Capital, and Employment in the European Union." *International Journal of Comparative Sociology* 57(6): 449–470.

Di Paolo, Antonio and Aysit Tansel. 2015. "Returns to Foreign Language Skills in a Developing Country: The Case of Turkey." *Journal of Development Studies* 51(4): 407–421.

Di Pietro, Giorgio. 2013. *"Do Study Abroad Programs Enhance the Employability of Graduates?"* Discussion paper 7675. Bonn: IZA.

Dustmann, Christian and Arthur Van Soest. 2002. "Language and the Earnings of Immigrants." *Industrial and Labor Relations Review* 55(3): 473–492.

Evans, Mariah and Jonathan Kelley. 2004. "Subjective Social Locations: Data from 21 Nations." *International Journal of Public Opinion Research* 16(3): 3–38.

Favell, Adrian. 2008. *Eurostars and Eurocities*. Oxford, UK: Blackwell.

García Polavieja, Javier, Mariña Fernández-Reino, and María Ramos. 2018. "Are Migrants Selected on Motivational Orientations? Selectivity Patterns amongst International Migrants in Europe." *European Sociological Review* 34(5): 570–588.

Gerhards, Jürgen, Silke Hans, and Soren Carlson. 2015. "Die Globalisierung des Arbeitsmarktes. Die Veränderung der Nachfrage nach transnationalem Humankapital in Zeitverlauf 1960–2014) und in Ländervergleich auf der Grundlage einer Analyse von Stellenanzeigen." *Arbeitspapier* 35, *Berliner Studien zur Soziologie Europas*. Berlin: FU, 1–32.

Ginsburgh, Victor A. and Juan Prieto-Rodríguez J. 2011. "Returns to Foreign Languages of Native Workers in the European Union." *Industrial and Labor Relations Review* 64(3): 599–618.

Gomulka, Joanna and Nicholas Stern. 1990. "The Employment of Married Women in the United Kingdom 1970–83." *Economica* 57: 171–199.

González Ferrer, Amparo. 2013. "La Nueva Emigración Española. Lo Que Sabemos Y Lo Que No." *Colección Zoom Político* 18. Madrid: Fundación Alternativas.

Gorodzeisky, Anastasia and Moshe Semyonov. 2017. "Labor Force Participation, Unemployment and Occupational Attainment among Immigrants in West European Countries." *PLOS ONE* 12(5): e0176856.

Green, David A. 1999. "Immigrant Occupational Attainment." *Journal of Labor Economics* 17(2): 49–79.

Grosse, Christine. 1998. "Corporate Recruiter Demand for Foreign Language and Cultural Knowledge." *Global Business Languages* 3(2). West Lafayette, IN: Purdue Research Foundation.

Hämäläinen, Kari and Jaakko Pehkonen. 2001. "Gender, Labour Market Training and Employment," University of Jyväskylä, School of Business and Economics." *Working Paper No 243/2001.*

Hardill, Irene and Sandra MacDonald. 1998. "Choosing to Relocate." *Women's Studies International Forum* 21(1): 21–29.

Hodge, Robert W. and Donald J. Treiman, 1968. "Class Identification in the United States." *American Journal of Sociology* 73(5): 535–547.

Hout, Michael. 2008. "How Class Works in Popular Conception: Most Americans Identify with the Class their Income, Occupation, and Education Implies for Them." In Annette Lareau and Dalton Conley (eds.), *Social Class: How Does It Work?* New York: Russell Sage Foundation, pp. 25–65.

Igarashi, Hiroki and Hiro Saito. 2014. "Cosmopolitanism as Cultural Capital: Exploring the Intersection of Globalization, Education, and Stratification." *Cultural Sociology* 8(3): 222–239.

Kofman, Eleonore. 2004. "Gendered Global Migrations." *International Feminist Journal of Politics* 6(4): 643–665.

Kogan, Irena. 2006. "Labor Markets and Economic Incorporation among Recent Immigrants in Europe." *Social Forces* 85(2): 697–721.

Lanzona, Leonardo A. 1998. "Migration, Self-selection and Earnings in Philippine Rural Communities." *Journal of Development Economics* 56: 27–50.

Lauth Bacas, Jutta. 2002. "Cross-border Marriages and the Formation of Transnational Families: A Case Study of Greek-German Couples in Athens." *WPTC-02–10*, 1–12.

Luthra, Renee, Lucinda Platt, and Justyna Salamońska. 2016. "Types of Migration: The Motivations, Composition, and Early Integration Patterns of 'New Migrants' in Europe." *International Migration Review* 52: 1–36.

Mincer, Jacob. 1978. "Family Migration Decisions." *Journal of Political Economy* 86: 749–773.

Model, Suzanne and David Lapido. 1996. "Context and Opportunity: Minorities in London and New York." *Social Forces* 75: 485–510.

Nakosteen, Robert A., Olie Westerlund, and Michael Zimmer. 2008. "Migration and Self-Selection: Measured Earnings and Latent Characteristics." *Journal of Regional Science* 48: 769–788.

Nivalainen, Satu. 2005. "Interregional Migration and Post-move Employment in Two-earner Families: Evidence from Finland." *Regional Studies* 39(7): 891–907.

Phelps, Edmund. 1972. "The Statistical Theory of Racism and Sexism." *The American Economic Review* 62(4): 659–661.

Piore, Michael J. 1979. *Birds of Passage: Migrant Labor and Industrial Societies.* Cambridge, UK: Cambridge University Press.

Portes, Alejandro. 1993. "The New Second Generation: Segmented Assimilation and Its Variants Among Post-1965 Immigrant Youth." *The Annals of the American Academy of Political and Social Science* 530: 74–96.

104 Making a living

Portes, Alejandro and Rubén G. Rumbaut. 1996. *Immigrant America: A Portrait*, 2d edition. Berkeley: University of California Press.

Portes, Alejandro and Rubén. L. Bach. 1985. *Latin Journey: Cuban and Mexican Immigrants in the United States*. Berkeley: University of California Press.

Redstone Akresh, Iliana. 2008. "Occupational Trajectories of Legal US Immigrants: Downgrading and Recovery." *Population and Development Review* 34(3): 435–456.

Rodríguez-Pose, Andrés and Vassilis Tselios. 2010. "Returns to Migration, Education and Externalities in the European Union: Migration, Education and Externalities." *Papers in Regional Science* 89(2): 411–434.

Rooth, Dan-Olof and Jan Ekberg. 2006. "Occupational Mobility for Immigrants in Sweden." *International Migration* 44(2): 57–77.

Safi, Mira. 2009. "Immigrants' Life Satisfaction in Europe: Between Assimilation and Discrimination." *European Sociological Review* 26, 159–176.

Saiz, Albert and Elena Zoido. 2005. "Listening to What the World Says: Bilingualism and Earnings in the United States." *The Review of Economics and Statistics* 87(3): 523–553.

Schultz, Theodor W. 1961. "Investment in Human Capital." *The American Economic Review* 51(1): 1–17.

Simón, Hipólito, Raul Ramos, and Esteban Sanromá. 2014. "Immigrant Occupational Mobility: Longitudinal Evidence from Spain." *European Journal of Population* 30(2): 223–255.

Smith, Darren P. and Adrian J. Bailey. 2006. "International Family Migration and Differential Labour-Market Participation in Great Britain: Is There a 'Gender Gap'?" *Environment and Planning A* 38(7): 1327–1343.

Sosnaud, Benjamin, David Brady, and Steven M. Frenk. 2013. "Class in Name Only: Subjective Class Identity, Objective Class Position, and Vote Choice in American Presidential Elections." *Social Problems* 60(1): 81–99.

Stillman, Steven, John Gibson, David McKenzie, and Halhingano Rohorua. 2012. "Miserable Migrants? Natural Experiment Evidence on International Migration and Objective and Subjective Well-Being." *IZA DP 5871*.

Stöhr, Tobias. 2015. "The Returns to Occupational Foreign Language Use: Evidence from Germany." *Labour Economics* 32: 86–98.

Tocqueville, Alexis de. 1998 [1856]. *The Old Regime and the Revolution*. Chicago, IL: University of Chicago Press.

Tubergen, Frank van, Ineke Maas, and Henk Flap. 2004. "The Economic Incorporation of Immigrants in 18 Western Societies: Origin, Destination, and Community Effects." *American Sociological Review* 69(5): 704–727.

Valk, Helga de and Juan Díez Medrano (eds.). 2014. "Meeting and Mating Across Borders: in the European Union: Union Formation in the European Union Single Market." Special Issue of *Population, Space, and Place* 20(2): 157–176.

Waite, Linda J. 1980. "Working Wives and the Life Cycle." *American Journal of Sociology* 86: 272–294

Zimmermann, Klaus F., and Thomas K Bauer. 1999. "Occupational Mobility of Ethnic Migrants." *IZA Discussion Paper* No. 58.

Yu, Lucy C., Min Q. Wang, Lynne Kaltreider, and Ying-Ying Chien. 1993. "The Impact of Family Migration and Family-Life Cycle on the Employment Status of Married, College-Educated Women." *Work and Occupations* 20: 233–246.

5

CIVIL AND POLITICAL ENGAGEMENT

Unlike in other parts of the world, the emergence of a European society is simultaneous to and partly propitiated by the process of European economic and political integration. Europe's cohesion requires that its members judge the process legitimate and that they be interested in and informed about what transpires politically from the European Union's political institutions. The political science literature has questioned the European Union's democratic credentials. In so doing, scholars have echoed voices in the public sphere who blame an alleged "democratic deficit" for the European citizens' lukewarm feelings toward the European Union.[1] This chapter examines the extent to which binational couples provide a solid social foundation for the European Union's development and consolidation. It explores levels of local civil and political engagement among partners in national and binational couples. I borrow from the literatures on social capital and transnational processes. This perspective alerts us to the threat that transnational mobility and networks represent to the quantity and quality of social capital deemed necessary for democracy.

Ever since Putnam's seminal book, *Making Democracy Work*, social scientists have emphasized the role that collective social capital plays in sustaining democracy and the efficiency of democratic government (Putnam, 1994). Drawing from classics like Tocqueville and Durkheim, Putnam and Fukuyama, among others, have extolled the benefits of a dense network of civil and political associations and of the citizens' engagement in them. Participation in the life of civil and political associations teaches people to take control over their lives, promotes a culture of cooperation, of give and take, of mutually satisficing compromises, and contributes to the development of generalized trust. These are virtues and qualities that improve democracy and society's capacity to procure collective goods.

106 Civil and political engagement

Low participation in national elections and declining membership rates in political parties and trade unions observed across Western democracies have been interpreted as a warning sign that democracy is imperiled. Putnam's empirical analysis in *Bowling Alone* concludes that these trends are just the most visible aspects of a secular decline in the citizens' proclivity to create and participate in all kinds of associations (Putnam, 2000). Controversy breeds controversy and for almost two decades countless scholars have questioned and checked the validity of Putnam's conclusions, just as others, persuaded by his assertions, have ventured explanations. One popular interpretation of the alleged decline in social capital in Western societies links it to globalization. More specifically, authors connect this decline to international migration (and the resulting cultural diversification of receiving societies) and the proliferation of transnational associations and organizations. In particular, they stress that the transportation and communications revolutions have altered how individuals and organizations relate to place, by increasing the opportunity for transnational movement and the development of permanent transnational bonds. One can live in one place physically but have one's consciousness somewhere else. If this process has a significant impact on a large number of people, one reads, it may be detrimental to social cohesion and the quality of democracy. Authors who emphasize the impact of cultural diversification posit that it is inimical to association. The most conservative among them even blame immigrants for not making the effort to assimilate and to take an active part in local and national life (Huntington, 2004). Authors who focus on transnational organizations posit that transnational ties deviate the associations' attention away from local and national problems (Clifford, 2005; Mendelson and Glenn, 2002).

Although the theoretical arguments above sound plausible, the empirical record to date contradicts them. Recent increases in political participation in the United States and in some European countries, while linked to the rise of left and right populism, question the social capital explanation of low electoral participation in the 1990s and early 2000s. Also, research shows that the impact of transnational migration and transnational organizations on the vibrancy of local civil and political life is conditional on a myriad of factors. Research on the civil and political engagement of immigrants, for instance, reveals that those who nurture ties to their countries of origin, either directly or indirectly, through transnational organizations are also those who engage more in local and national affairs in their host countries (Itzigsohn and Giorguli Saucedo, 2002; Portes et al., 1999, 2009). Similarly, another strand of research shows that local and national organizations that establish transnational linkages tend to be more active and better connected to local and national life (Stark et al., 2007). These findings reveal major flaws in the theoretical assumptions and reasoning underlying the hypothesis of a zero-sum game between transnational and local engagement.

At the European Union level, Ettore Recchi's is one of the most comprehensive analysis of the impact of migration on political engagement (Recchi, 2015). In *Mobile Europe*, he examines non-institutional political mobilization and voting behavior among migrants, and compares migrants with co-nationals from the migrants' countries of origin. Recchi finds that migrants are actually more interested in politics than their co-nationals back home. At the practical level, however, and with minor exceptions, migrants appear to display less political engagement than do co-nationals back home. In particular, they are much less likely to vote in elections. Recchi's analysis focuses on the political and leaves out the civil dimension of social engagement. Furthermore, while he compares migrants to co-nationals in the country of origin, he does not compare them to nationals from the country in which they settle. Seen from the perspective of social integration, this is perhaps the most important comparison.

Rich and rigorous as it is, the literature on the impact of globalization on individuals' local and national political engagement has generally focused on immigrants. It has thus overlooked a major consequence of the transportation and telecommunications revolution, which is the opportunity it affords to locals to travel, study, work, and live abroad for short periods. It has also overlooked the emergence of new types of geographic mobility, whether seasonal, commuting, circular, and so on (e.g. Recchi, 2015). Finally, the literature has generally been blind to the fact that the diversification of societies connected to immigration and virtual distant communication also provide new opportunities for sedentary locals to develop frequent and deep transnational ties. The transnational ties that ensue from transient forms of actual and virtual geographic mobility may also impact on the local populations' levels of civil and political engagement with their local and national communities. This chapter contributes to fill this gap by examining whether the transnational tie represented by marrying or entering into cohabitation with a national from another European country has a significant effect on civil and political engagement.

It is easy to imagine individual and social mechanisms that would lead partners in a binational couple to be less engaged in civil and political life than are partners in a national one. One of them is a change in the role of the local in people's minds. Partners in a binational couple have more extensive ties with family and friends abroad (see Chapter 3). They thus invest a substantial amount of time in sustaining these ties, which may distract them from local issues and diminish their interest in the development and nurturing of local ties. Frequent communication with those abroad, conversations about these conversations within the binational couple, periodic visits by friends and relatives from abroad, followed or preceded by visits to the foreign partner's country of origin, may well be all that a family needs to feel socially connected. At the same time, watching foreign news on T.V., instead of local and national ones, reading foreign newspapers to keep up with what happens in other countries, and engaging in conversations with friends and relatives abroad may contribute to distance a binational couple's concerns and interests from what happens at the local or national levels.

The complexities and complications of all sorts that binational couples often face in their country of residence are another source of social and political disengagement. The most important of these is the cultural, social, and professional

108 Civil and political engagement

integration of a foreign partner. Chapter 4, in particular, has shown that male foreign partners from poorer countries must overcome serious obstacles to secure jobs and earnings commensurate with their educational credentials. At least at the beginning, foreign partners may not be fluent in the country's language, may have no social ties in the country of residence, may face bureaucratic hurdles related to residence in a foreign country, may find out that his or her academic credentials are not useful for obtaining a job, or may feel lost when confronted with routine household tasks (e.g. utility contracts, getting help to repair things, or doing simple things such as finding a doctor). Then, or later on, if the couple has children, the foreign partner, unfamiliar with the host country's school system and academic culture, may find it difficult to participate in the search and choice of a day care center or the right school. This problem gets compounded if the couple ponders whether to educate the child at a bilingual institution, as is often the case. One indirect consequence of the learning process that the foreign partner in a binational couple has to go through is a multiplication of the range of tasks that the national partner has to take upon her- or himself. At least for a while, this heavy burden may leave both partners in a binational couple with little time, energy, or inclination to engage in civil and political activity.

The scenario described above lists factors that can diminish involvement in civil and political activities by partners in binational couples. It does not justify predictions, however, as to the overall magnitude of this effect. Partners in a binational couple may after all be perfectly capable of juggling their transnational lives and interests with engagement with the local and national community. Also, the problems faced by foreign partners as they adapt to a new society may in the end not be so taxing and allow both partners to participate in civil and political life. Finally, one should not fall into the trap of thinking only about aspects in the lives of binational couples that lead to less civil and political involvement. It is indeed easy to imagine factors that lead in the opposite direction. For instance, partners in a binational couple may engage more in civil and political activity in order to facilitate the foreign partner's integration in the host society or to compensate for a less fulfilling social life. Also, if the foreign partner is a woman, the male partner may get more involved in civil activities that, at least in more traditional countries, are generally left to women, such as becoming a member and participating in the activities of parents' associations. Last but not least, unpleasant encounters with discrimination and bureaucracy experienced by the foreign partner in a binational couple and conflict between the foreign partner's cultural expectations and the realities of the country where she or he lives may stimulate civil and political mobilization above and beyond levels observed among nationals. It is conceivable, for instance, that partners in binational couples more frequently become involved with associations that assist immigrants and fight for their rights.

From the discussion above, it should have become clear that the extent of civil and political engagement of partners in binational couples relative to that of partners in national couples must be established at the empirical level. Some

Civil and political engagement **109**

factors speak in favor of more involvement and other factors speak in favor of less involvement. The sections that follow examine the net effect of these countervailing forces and the role of different mechanisms in promoting greater or lesser civil and political involvement. To determine the actual contribution of being part of a binational couple to explain contrasts in civil and political engagement, I consider other explanatory factors that the literature has found to be relevant. These factors can be classified into five categories: socio-demographic, socio-economic, relational, residential, and psychological.

With regard to the role of socio-demographic variables, the literature shows that older people participate more in social and political activities than do younger ones, although the evidence for political participation is more ambiguous and suggests that it may only apply to electoral behavior.[2] This literature also shows that women are more engaged in civil organizational life whereas men tend to express more interest in politics and be more politically engaged. One major exception to this contrast is voting behavior, where there is parity between men and women. Finally, the literature has shown that natives are more involved in civil and political life than are non-natives (Burns et al., 2001; Enns et al., 2008; Teney and Hanquinet, 2012).

With regard to the role of socio-economic variables, the literature shows that more educated individuals engage more in civil and political activity than do less educated ones. Brand has elaborated on the education-civil engagement nexus and found that the "civil" returns to education are greatest among those with lesser probability of reaching into the highest stages of formal education.[3] Other authors have shown that people with higher income are more likely to be recruited for participation in civil life (Bachmann et al., 2010). Finally, research consistently reveals that unemployed people volunteer less and join civil associations less often.[4]

The role of embeddedness in networks of social relations has also attracted the research community's interest. Social embeddedness, in particular, features prominently in explanations of civil and political engagement that explore the mechanisms that mediate the effects of structural variables like education, employment, local rootedness, and sociability. Social networks matter because they provide people with information about and incentives to participate in and join civil and political organizations and because they shape norms of participation in such activities (Brady et al., 1999; Freeman, 1996; Musick and Wilson, 2008).

While political engagement can relate to local, regional, national, and European issues, civil engagement takes place in and relates mainly to the locality where individuals live. Although there are many national or international human rights associations, most of them (e.g. sports and cultural associations) are local and work as a vehicle for social integration. Because of this, one may expect natives/nationals to display higher levels of civil engagement than do non-natives and one may also expect people who have deeper roots in the community to be more active in civil life than are other people. The literature shows, in particular that homeowners participate in civil life more than other people do. This is because home ownership

110 Civil and political engagement

reflects residential stability, which is related to people developing dense social networks and interpersonal relationships in their community.[5] Related to residential stability, as expressed through home ownership, is the degree of residential satisfaction. Grillo, Teixeira, and Wilson, for instance, show that the greater people's residential satisfaction is, the greater their engagement in civil activities (Grillo et al., 2010).

Finally, the literature allots significant space to the role of personality and psychological factors in the explanation of civil and political engagement. While depression and low self-esteem appear to be related to lesser engagement, extraversion and life satisfaction are associated to greater engagement (Gil de Zúñiga and Valenzuela, 2011; Harlow and Cantor, 1996; Helliwell and Putnam, 2004). Depression and self-esteem also seem to underlie the relatively lower levels of civil and political involvement displayed by the unemployed relative to those who have a job.[6]

Binational couples and civil engagement

People join clubs, associations, and other civil organizations for personal benefit, to meet other people, or to cooperate toward a collective goal. Participants in the *Eumarr* survey reported whether they are members of or volunteer in eight types of clubs or associations: (1) Sports Clubs/Outdoors Organizations; (2) Organizations for Cultural/Hobby Activities; (3) Religious Organizations; (4) Organizations for Peace, Humanitarian Aid, Human Rights, Minorities, and Immigrants; (5) Parents' Organizations in School; (6) Organizations for Environmental Protection; (7) Organizations for Animal Rights; and (8) Social Clubs, Clubs for the Young, Clubs for the Elderly, Women's Clubs, or Friendly Societies. On average they belong to about two types of organization or association (Unweighted Country Average = 1.7) (Table 5.1). They favor Sports Clubs and Outdoors Organizations (40.7%); Organizations for Peace, Humanitarian Aid, Human Rights, Minorities, and Immigrants (26.1%); and Parents' Organizations at Schools (25.4%), and are less likely to join Religious organizations (12.8%) and Social Clubs, Clubs for the Young, Clubs for the Elderly, Women's Clubs, and Friendly Societies (9.8%).

Partners in national couples join or volunteer in civil organizations more frequently than do partners in binational couples, and, in turn, nationals in binational couples join civil organizations and clubs or volunteer more frequently than do foreign partners in these couples. For most organizations, clubs, or associations, however, this contrast is of just a few percentage points. Multiple regression analysis, focused on the number of clubs, associations, and other organizations, shows that the contrast between the two types of couple is of just about half a unit (Table 5.2, column 1).

Various factors could help explain the contrast, even if small, between partners in binational and national couples. First of all, compared with national couples in the age group 30–46, binational couples were formed more recently. More of these couples still do not have children, and if they do, these tend to be younger.

Civil and political engagement **111**

TABLE 5.1 Participation in Civil Activities and Associations, by Type of Couple and Education (Unweighted Average of Country %)

	National Couple		Binational Couple (National)		Binational Couple (Foreign)	
Sports Club-Outdoors Organization						
Less than university	41	(423)	35	(275)	38	(256)
University or more	44	(608)	39	(578)	41	(712)
Organization for Cultural or Hobby Activities						
Less than university	19	(419)	21	(275)	13	(252)
University or more	25	(599)	27	(572)	24	(709)
Religious Organization						
Less than university	12	(423)	11	(273)	15	(256)
University or more	15	(600)	12	(574)	11	(709)
Organizations for Peace, Humanitarian Aid, Human Rights, Minorities, Immigrants						
Less than university	19	(426)	17	(273)	14	(252)
University or more	31	(600)	34	(573)	24	(709)
Parents' Organization in School						
Less than university	25	(420)	23	(275)	20	(250)
University or more	29	(604)	27	(573)	22	(712)
Organizations for Environmental Protection						
Less than university	14	(420)	15	(275)	11	(253)
University or more	21	(598)	18	(572)	15	(707)
Organization for Animal Rights						
Less than university	18	(423)	17	(275)	16	(253)
University or more	21	(504)	15	(576)	10	(709)
Club: Social, for the Young, for the Elderly, Women, A Friendly Society						
Less than university	10	(418)	9	(274)	10	(251)
University or more	11	(600)	10	(576)	8	(709)
Other Organizations						
Less than university	15	(414)	10	(275)	11	(249)
University or more	11	(601)	11	(572)	14	(708)

( ) Number of respondents.

Therefore, the time has not come for many of these couples to join parents' associations or sports clubs. Also, partners in binational couples have had relatively less time than have partners in national couples to develop a cohesive social network that provides them with information about or motivation to become member of clubs, organizations, and associations. Moreover, as Chapter 4 shows, foreign partners in binational couples are at some disadvantage in the labor market. This means that both partners in these couples probably need to invest more time and effort in meeting their immediate economic needs than do nationals. Last but

112 Civil and political engagement

TABLE 5.2 Association between Being in a Binational Couple and Participation in Civil Activities and Associations, Controlling for City of Residence, and for Socio-Demographic Variables, Transnational Skills and Experience, Social Support Network Embeddedness, Identification, and Socio-Psychological Variables (OLS)

	(1)		(2)		(3)	
Foreign in binational couple	−0.49	★	−0.26	★	−0.23	★
National in binational couple	−0.26	★	−0.10		−0.16	+
Duration relationship			0.05	★	0.04	★
Number of relatives and in-laws			0.03	+	0.03	+
Number of close friends			0.08	★	0.06	★
Age					0.03	★
Gender (Female=1)					0.14	+
Education	0.12	★	0.12	★	0.09	★
Income (PPS)					1.0E−03	
Household size					0.18	★
Homeowner					3.0E−03	
Unemployed					−0.04	
Housework					0.06	
Student					0.33	
Other occupational status					−0.27	
Partner employed					−0.17	+
Languages spoken					0.06	
Countries visited between 17 and meeting partner					0.04	★
Psychological well-being (+=Less)					−0.02	
Perception of help available					0.05	★
Satisfaction with relationship					−0.04	+
Identification with city					0.02	★
Identification with nation					−0.03	★
Identification with Europe					2.0E−03	
Constant	1.30	★	0.26		−1.52	★
R-Square %	4.9		9.5		15.5	
N	2078		2078		2078	

Controls for city of residence.
+: Significant at 0.10 level, two-tailed; ★: sig at 0.05 level, two-tailed.

not least, the logistics of organizing life in a binational couple are often more demanding than those in ordinary national couples. Finding a school for the children that meets the parents' expectations, organizing holidays, and mutual visits with relatives and friends abroad, as discussed in Chapter 3, are examples of this greater complexity, which may limit the time available for civil engagement.

One can thus expect that the longer a couple has been together, the more socially integrated the partners will be, the more time the foreign partner will have had to find his or her place in the job market, and the more skillful the partners will have become in coping with the complexity associated to accommodating their respective expectations and social worlds. Empirical data support this prediction (Table 5.2). In particular, they show that the contrasts between partners in binational and national couples diminish by half when one simply controls for the duration of the relationship and for the couples' degree of social embeddedness in family and friendship networks (column 2).

Age, household size, the amount of help that individuals secure in addressing or solving everyday tasks and problems, and the degree to which individuals identify with the city of residence also contribute, but much less, to explaining the empirical contrast between the civil engagement of partners in binational couples and partners in national ones (Table 5.2, column 3). Compared with partners in national couples, those in binational ones are younger, are less likely to have children, and secure less assistance in addressing ordinary problems. They also identify less with the city of residence, as I show in Chapter 7. These compositional characteristics detract from their joining clubs and other associations. Indeed, as Table 5.2 shows, older people (even in the 30–46 age range), families with children, people who benefit from assistance from friends and relatives with childcare, small repairs, advice on how to find a good doctor, and so on, and people who strongly identify with the city where they live join clubs or volunteer in civil associations more often than younger individuals, childless families, or people who must solve everyday tasks and problems on their own.

Demographic or social characteristics of binational couples that differentiate them from national couples thus explain their slightly lesser civil engagement. They complement other factors in explaining why some people volunteer or join clubs and associations more often than others (Table 5.2). Some of these characteristics, like being male, satisfaction with the relationship, partner's employment, detract from volunteering or joining associations and clubs, but are unrelated to being in a binational or a national couple. Other factors that are associated with civil engagement are related to being in a binational couple, but they do not explain why binational couples volunteer or join clubs and associations less often than do national couples. Travel experience in late adolescence-early adulthood, for instance, is associated to greater civil engagement (Recchi, 2015), but, on the whole, foreign partners in binational couples have slightly more travel experience at those stages of the life-cycle than have nationals. Also, while strong identification with the country of nationality is associated with less citizen involvement, foreign partners in binational couples identify less with their country of nationality than do nationals in national couples. Therefore, if only travel at a young age and national identification explained whether people join clubs or associations, binational couples would join these *more* instead of *less* often than do national couples.

Binational couples and political engagement

This section separately examines and compares levels of political interest and levels of political engagement. I thus depart from Muxel's and Recchi's analysis, which subsumes the two (Muxel, 2009; Recchi, 2015).

114 Civil and political engagement

Political interest

Political interest varies across geographical locations. One may be strongly interested in European politics but have no interest in city politics, or vice versa. So, although adding the amount of interest that the respondents in the city samples report for city, national, European, and world politics reveals moderate interest in politics (Unweighted Country Average = 53.0, on a scale from 0 to 100),[7] the fact is that people are primarily interested in national politics. In the *Eumarr* study, about 44% are very or extremely interested in the politics of the country, whereas no more than a third of all respondents are interested in city, European Union, and international politics. Swiss participants report more interest in politics than do participants from Spain, Belgium, and the Netherlands, especially when referred to the world outside Europe (Table 5.3).

Generally speaking, partners in binational couples are as interested in politics as their counterparts in national ones. Partners in binational couples, however, are somewhat less interested in city politics and somewhat more interested in European Union and world politics, as one would expect, and foreign partners in binational couples are less interested in politics in the country of residence. Because partners in national and binational couples display different and often opposite degrees of interest in local and international politics, it is worth analyzing these two dimensions separately.

Interest in national and local politics in the country of residence depends in part on how socially embedded individuals are (Table 5.4). The fact that when one controls for the number of relatives and friends that people have in the country of residence the contrast between nationals in national couples and both nationals and foreign partners in binational couples diminishes (column 2) supports this interpretation. Social embeddedness matters more for foreign than for national partners in binational couples, however (i.e. compare the drop in the regression coefficients for both groups when on moves from column 1 and column 2). Also, separate statistical models for foreign partners and national partners in binational couples not displayed here show that the family network plays a more important role than the friends' network.

When one turns to the explanation of interest in European and world politics, the most relevant finding is that socio-demographic and social embeddedness variables play no role in accounting for why partners in binational couples express more interest in European and world politics than do partners in national couples. In fact, the contrasts are bigger when one controls for those variables (rows 1 and 2 in columns 4 and 5). By elimination, this suggests that personality traits highlighted in the literature, such as greater openness, may enter in the explanation of the contrast. That is, the findings suggest that partners in binational couples express more interest in international politics because they are generally more open than partners in national couples are.

As highlighted in the theoretical review above, research on migration has focused on the social and political ties that migrants retain with their country of

TABLE 5.3 Interest in City, Country of Residence, European, World Politics, and Country of Nationality, by Type of Couple, Education, and Country (% Very and Extremely Interested)

	Spanish Cities			Belgian Cities			Dutch Cities			Swiss City		
	National Couple	Binational Couple (National)	Binational Couple (Foreign)	National Couple	Binational Couple (National)	Binational Couple (Foreign)	National Couple	Binational Couple (National)	Binational Couple (Foreign)	National Couple	Binational Couple (National)	Binational Couple (Foreign)
Interest in City Politics (% Very and Extremely Interested)												
Less than university	40	31	34	25	13	23	23	19	17	34	35	30
University or more	46	34	37	40	31	28	16	17	14	50	41	28
Interest in National Politics (% Very and Extremely Interested)												
Less than university	49	44	55	18	24	20	23	31	24	41	47	29
University or more	61	56	56	42	35	37	54	48	37	64	56	44
Interest in European Politics (% Very and Extremely Interested)												
Less than university	30	39	43	11	15	17	10	15	23	16	27	32
University or more	41	47	57	23	24	42	19	35	32	41	38	53

(Continued)

	Spanish Cities			Belgian Cities			Dutch Cities			Swiss City		
	National Couple	Binational Couple (National)	Binational Couple (Foreign)	National Couple	Binational Couple (National)	Binational Couple (Foreign)	National Couple	Binational Couple (National)	Binational Couple (Foreign)	National Couple	Binational Couple (National)	Binational Couple (Foreign)
Interest in World Politics (% Very and Extremely Interested)												
Less than university	18	23	26	7	14	17	6	12	18	20	29	32
University or more	30	35	46	26	24	36	18	28	29	46	44	49
Interest in Politics own Country (% Very and Extremely Interested)												
Less than university	49	44	54	18	24	43	23	31	17	41	47	45
University or more	61	56	63	42	35	54	54	48	38	64	56	54
N (< university)	(149)	(70)	(56)	(28)	(60)	(35)	(31)	(52)	(64)	(219)	(86)	(93)
N (university or >)	(165)	(74)	(79)	(53)	(127)	(148)	(115)	(216)	(222)	(261)	(138)	(221)

( ) Number of respondents.

TABLE 5.4 Association between Being in a Binational Couple and Interest in Politics on Different Scales, Controlling for City of Residence and for Socio-Demographic, Social Support, Network Embeddedness, and Psychological Variables (OLS)

	Local/National			Europe/World	
	(1)	*(2)*	*(3)*	*(4)*	*(5)*
Foreign in binational couple	−0.51 ⋆	−0.39 ⋆	−0.28 ⋆	0.59 ⋆	0.73 ⋆
National in binational couple	−0.23 ⋆	−0.22 ⋆	−0.26 ⋆	0.30 ⋆	0.21 ⋆
Age		0.06 ⋆	0.05 ⋆		0.04 ⋆
Years in relationship			0.01		
Gender (Female=1)			−0.43 ⋆		−0.48 ⋆
Education	0.25 ⋆	0.25 ⋆	0.23 ⋆	0.35 ⋆	0.32 ⋆
Income (PPS)			3.0E−03		6.0E−06 ⋆
Household size			−0.01		−0.04
Homeowner			0.02		−0.17 +
Unemployed			9.0E−03		0.06
Housework			−0.20		−0.21
Student			0.55		0.61 +
Other occupational status			−0.40		−0.21
Partner employed			8.0E−03		0.09
Psychological well-being (+=Less)			−0.07 ⋆		−0.06 ⋆
Perception of help available			0.01		−4.0E−03
Satisfaction with relationship			−9.0E−03		−0.03
Number of relatives and in-laws		0.05 ⋆	0.05 ⋆		0.01
Number of close friends		0.05 ⋆	0.04 +		0.03
Constant	3.22 ⋆	0.58	1.30	1.68 ⋆	0.46
R-Square %	8.6	10.7	13.0	11.1	15.3
N	2078	2078	2078	2078	2078

Controls for city of residence.
+: Significant at 0.10 level, two-tailed; ⋆: sig at 0.05 level, two-tailed.

origin and on their impact on assimilation. This chapter examines this topic with a focus on foreign partners in binational couples. Table 5.3 above corroborates what Portes and others have already shown for migrants in the United States: despite some variation across countries, foreign partners tend to express as much interest in national politics as in politics in their country of residence. In fact, those who express more interest in one also tend to show more interest in the

118 Civil and political engagement

other (correlation index = 0.44). In relative terms, however, the longer foreign partners have lived in the country of residence, the lesser their interest in politics in their country of nationality relative to their interest in politics in the country of residence (Table 5.5, column 1). The effect is certainly very small. On a scale from 0 to 3, individuals with ten years of residence just show about one-third of one unit more interest in politics in the country. This effect of years of residence, though small, must be brought together with other results that also highlight the role of social integration in explaining relative interest in local politics. Indeed, the bigger the foreign partners' social network, as measured by the number of relatives and in-laws in the country of residence and the better they feel psychologically, the less interested they are in politics in their country of nationality relative to politics in the country of residence (Table 5.5, column 2).

TABLE 5.5 Association between Years of Residence and Interest in Politics in the Country of Nationality relative to Interest in Politics in the Country of Residence, Controlling for City of Residence and for Socio-Demographic, Social Support, Network Embeddedness, and Psychological Variables (OLS) (Foreign Partners Only)

	(1)		(2)	
Years of residence	−0.04	⋆	−0.03	+
Age			−0.03	⋆
Years in relationship			0.02	
Gender (Female=1)			−0.13	
Education	−0.03		−0.03	
Income (PPS)			−3.0E−03	
Household size			−0.01	
Homeowner			0.02	
Unemployed			0.04	
Housework			0.23	
Student			−0.07	
Other occupational status			0.42	
Partner employed			0.22	
Psychological well-being (+=Less)			0.06	+
Perception of help available			0.01	
Satisfaction with relationship			−0.05	
Number of relatives and in-laws			−0.04	+
Number of close friends			−0.01	
Constant	0.84	⋆	2.16	⋆
R-Square %	13.6		17.6	
N	489		489	

Controls for city of residence.

Dependent variable: (Interest in National Politics − Interest in Politics in Country of Residence) (Range: 0–3).

+: Significant at 0.10 level, two-tailed; ⋆: sig at 0.05 level, two-tailed.

Political participation

Interest in politics is a pre-condition for political engagement, but the latter is best measured through information on levels of political participation. This study uses a well-known battery of indicators of political practices commonly observed in democracies: (1) contacting a politician and government officials, (2) work for a political party or action group, (3) work for another political association or action group, (4) the display of a badge or a sticker, (5) the signing of a petition, (6) participation in a public demonstration, and (7) the boycott of certain products. Whereas the first three indicators involve relatively direct contact with politicians and political organizations, the other four refer to occasional mobilization around issues. Political participation turns out to be relatively infrequent. On average, respondents in this study report having participated in about one type of political activity (Unweighted Country Average = 1.1).

The prevalence of non-institutional mobilization varies across practices, however (Table 5.6). For instance, the most frequent form of participation is signing a petition, an occasional and targeted activity that is not very time consuming and does not involve a major effort. It is practiced by between a third and a half of respondents, depending on level of education and type of couple. Meanwhile, less than one in twenty respondents claim to have volunteered to work for political parties and organizations. This testifies to people's political disaffection, as emphasized in the literature on the new populisms. Although Table 5.6 only provides unweighted average percentages across the four countries in the study, some political activities are more prevalent in some countries than in others. Taking part in a demonstration, for instance, is more central to the cultural repertoire of political action in Spain than in the other three countries. While one in three Spanish national respondents claim to have participated in a demonstration, less than one in ten national respondents have done so in the other three countries taken together.

From this study's standpoint, the most important finding is that nationals in binational couples participate slightly less in non-institutional forms of political mobilization than do nationals in national couples (esp. demonstrations and boycotts) and that foreign partners do so less than national partners in general. When one focuses on political participation in general, captured by an additive sum of all forms of participation (range = 0–7), statistical estimates confirm that partners in binational couples indeed participate less in non-institutional forms of mobilization than do partners in national couples (Table 5.7, column 1). The contrast, however, less than a third of a unit in the index of political mobilization, is small.

Less emotional attachment to place and shallower social embeddedness appear as the main explanation for the binational couples' lower levels of non-institutional political participation. The coefficient for the contrasts in levels of political mobilization between partners in binational couples and partners in national couples drop considerably when one controls for identification with the city of residence, for the number of relatives/in-laws and close friends people

120 Civil and political engagement

TABLE 5.6 Political Participation, by Type of Couple and Education (Unweighted Average of Country %)

	National Couple		Binational Couple (National)		Binational Couple (Foreign)	
Contact a Politician, Government or Local Government Official						
Less than university	10	(408)	10	(273)	6	(246)
University or more	15	(597)	14	(571)	12	(705)
Worked in a Political Party or Action Group						
Less than university	3	(409)	3	(273)	2	(247)
University or more	5	(596)	4	(570)	3	(707)
Worked in Another Organization or Association						
Less than university	14	(413)	10	(273)	9	(249)
University or more	18	(601)	16	(573)	14	(711)
Worn or Displayed a Campaign Badge/Sticker						
Less than university	10	(412)	7	(273)	5	(248)
University or more	11	(598)	9	(573)	7	(705)
Signed a Petition						
Less than university	48	(436)	40	(278)	28	(253)
University or more	50	(611)	47	(577)	34	(712)
Took Part in a Public Demonstration						
Less than university	18	(410)	11	(274)	12	(248)
University or more	16	(597)	12	(572)	14	(707)
Boycotted Certain Products						
Less than university	27	(429)	21	(275)	17	(254)
University or more	25	(612)	22	(571)	25	(714)

( ) Number of respondents.

have, for age, and for student status (Table 5.7, column 2). This is particularly the case for foreign partners. Low attachment to and a small circle of family and friends in the city in which one lives, which are more prevalent among partners in binational couples than among those in national couples, are associated with less frequent political mobilization. Partners in binational couples also tend to be younger and the proportion of students among them smaller. Since, except for students, younger people mobilize politically less than do older ones, compositional differences also explain the contrast between partners in binational couples and those in national ones.

The impact of other theoretically relevant variables on the contrast between the two types of couples is negligible (column 3). This is because their association with political mobilization is trivial and because the partners in binational and in national couples are quite similar along these variables. Wealthier individuals and people who identify more with their country of nationality tend to mobilize

TABLE 5.7 Association between Being in a Binational Couple and Political Participation, Controlling for City of Residence, Socio-Demographic Variables, Transnational Skills and Experience, Social Support Network Embeddedness, Identification, and Psychological Variables (OLS)

	(1)		(2)		(3)	
Foreign in binational couple	−0.27	★	−0.17	+	−0.18	★
National in binational couple	−0.17	★	−0.14	+	−0.18	★
Age					0.02	★
Years in relationship					0.02	★
Gender (Female=1)					0.0E−03	
Education	0.08	★	0.08	★	0.08	★
Income (PPS)					−6.0E−03	★
Household size					−0.03	
Homeowner					−0.12	
Unemployed			−0.11		−0.06	
Housework			−0.05		−0.04	
Student			0.87	★	0.82	★
Other occupational status			0.06		−3.0E−03	
Partner employed					−0.12	
Languages spoken					0.04	
Countries visited between 17 and meeting partner					0.02	★
Psychological well-being (+=Less)					−0.04	★
Perception of help available					3.0E−03	
Satisfaction with relationship					−0.04	★
Number of relatives and in-laws			0.04	★	0.04	★
Number of close friends			0.04	★	0.04	★
Identification with city			0.02	★	0.03	★
Identification with nation					−0.08	★
Identification with Europe					6.0E−03	
Constant	0.88	★	0.36	+	0.59	
R-Square %	3.9		5.5		10.3	
N	2078		2078		2078	

Controls for city of residence.
+: Significant at 0.10 level, two-tailed; ★: sig at 0.05 level, two-tailed.

politically less than do poorer individuals and people with less intense national feelings. The latter probably reflects that non-institutional forms of mobilization tend to be more prevalent among left-oriented people whereas national identification tends to be stronger among right-oriented people. Also, people who have been together with their partner for a longer time and who have travelled abroad more often in late adolescence and early adulthood tend to mobilize politically more than do those who have been together with their partner for a shorter time and people who have travelled less often. Finally, people whose psychological well-being is compromised and those who are happier in their relationship tend

122 Civil and political engagement

to mobilize politically less than do people who are fitter psychologically and who are less happy in their relationship.

The previous pages provide us with a detailed sketch of civil and political engagement in seven cities of four different European countries early in the second millennium. Adult Europeans, men and women alike, nationals and foreigners, emerge as well-integrated in their societies, joining clubs and associations, volunteering for diverse causes, and participating in political life. The statistical results consistently show partners in binational couples to be slightly less engaged than are partners in national ones, but the contrasts are small. When one evaluates this finding from the perspective of the literature on globalization and migration, this finding strengthens the position of those who claim that the transformations that the world is experiencing as a result of greater mobility across borders and greater transcultural communication do not undermine social integration and local and national democracies by detracting from civil and political participation.

Seen from this book's perspective, the finding that national and binational couples differ, but not greatly, in their level of civil and political engagement fulfills the first requirement of a European society: that individuals be well-integrated in their local setting, regardless of nationality and social condition. At the same time, the chapter has shown that partners in binational couples display significantly more interest in European and world political affairs than do partners in national couples. This finding shows that binational couples fulfill the second requirement for a cohesive European society. In this sense, they are distinct from individuals in national couples and can be said to represent an emergent social group whose horizon is no longer national but cosmopolitan. Finally, the chapter strengthens the view that binational couples, just like national couples, are segmented along socio-economic lines, as captured by differences in education. Less educated partners in national and binational couples alike not only display less civil and political engagement but also express less interest in European and world politics.

Notes

1   See Scharpf (1999), Moravcsik (2002), Schmitter (2003), Føllestall and Hix (2006).
2   Teney and Hanquinet (2012), Lie and Wheelock (2009), Crotty (1991), Lipset (1981), McVeigh and Smith (1999).
3   Delli Carpini and Keeter (1996), Campbell (2008), Klofstad (2007), Nie and Stehlik-Barry (1996), Gil de Zúñiga and Valenzuela (2011), Teney and Hanguiquet (2012), Brand (2010), Brand and Xie (2010).
4   Wilson (2000), Wilson and Musick (1997), Lim and Sander (2013), Lasby (2004).
5   Kasarda and Janowitz (1974), Fischer (1982), Sampson (1991), Kang and Kwak (2003), McCabe (2013).
6   Dooley and Catalano (1999), Burgard et al. (2007), Brand et al. (2008), Lim and Sander (2013).
7   This standardized index represents the factor scores for the factor solution corresponding tor four items, corresponding to interest in city, national, European, and world politics. The index has been re-scaled to a 0–100 range.

References

Bachmann, Ingrid, Kelly Kaufhold, Seth Lewis, and Homero Gil de Zúñiga. 2010. "News Platform Preference: Advancing the Effects of Age and Media Consumption on Political Participation." *International Journal of Internet Science* 5(1): 34–47.

Brady, Henry, Kay Lehman Schlozman, and Sidney Verba. 1999. "Prospecting for Participants: Rational Expectations and the Recruitment of Political Activists." *The American Political Science Review* 93(1): 153–168.

Brand, Jennie. 2010. "Civic Returns to Higher Education: A Note on Heterogeneous Effects." *Social Forces* 8(2): 417–433.

Brand, Jennie, Becca Levy, and William Gallo. 2008. "Effects of Layoffs and Plant Closings on Subsequent Depression among Older Workers." *Research on Aging* 30(6): 701–721.

Brand, Jennie, and Yu Xie. 2010. "Who Benefits Most from College? Evidence for Negative Selection in Heterogeneous Economic Returns to Higher Education." *American Sociological Review* 75(2): 273–302.

Burgard, Sarah, Jennie Brand, and James House. 2007. "Toward a Better Estimation of the Effect of Job Loss on Health." *Journal of Health and Social Behavior* 48(4): 369–384.

Burns, Nancy, Kay Lehman Schlozman, and Sidney Verba. 2001. *The Private Roots of Public Action: Gender, Equality, and Political Participation.* Cambridge, MA: Harvard University Press.

Campbell, David. 2008. *Why We Vote How Schools and Communities Shape Our Civic Life.* Princeton, NJ: Princeton University Press.

Clifford, Bob. 2005. *The Marketing of Rebellion: Insurgents, Media, and International Activism.* Cambridge, UK: Cambridge University Press.

Crotty, William. 1991. *Political Participation and American Democracy.* Westport, CT: Greenwood Pub Group.

Delli Carpini, Michael, and Scott Keeter. 1996. *What Americans Know about Politics and Why It Matters.* New Haven, CT: Yale University Press.

Dooley, David, and Ralph Catalano. 1999. "Unemployment, Disguised Unemployment, and Health: The US Case." *International Archives of Occupational and Environmental Health* 72: 16–19.

Enns, S., Todd Malinick, and Ralph Matthews. 2008. "It's Not Only Who You Know, It's also Where They Are: Using the Position Generator to Investigate the Structure of Access to Embedded Resources." In Nan Lin and B.H. Erickson (eds.), *Social Capital: An International Research Program.* New York: Oxford University Press, pp. 255–307.

Fischer, Claude. 1982. *To Dwell among Friends: Personal Networks and Places: Social Relations in the Urban Setting.* New York: Free Press.

Føllestall, Andreas, and Simon Hix. 2006. "Why There Is a Democratic Deficit in the EU: A Response to Majone and Moravcsik." *Journal of Common Market Studies* 44: 533–562.

Freeman, Richard. 1996. "Working for Nothing: The Supply of Volunteer Labor." *Working Paper* 5435. National Bureau of Economic Research.

Gil de Zúñiga, Homero, and Sebastián Valenzuela. 2011. "The Mediating Path to a Stronger Citizenship: Online and Offline Networks, Weak Ties, and Civic Engagement." *Communication Research* 38(3): 397–421.

Grillo, Michael, Miguel Teixeira, and David Wilson. 2010. "Residential Satisfaction and Civic Engagement: Understanding the Causes of Community Participation." *Social Indicators Research* 97: 451–466.

124 Civil and political engagement

Harlow, Robert, and Nancy Cantor. 1996. "Still Participating After All These Years: A Study of Life Task Participation in Later Life." *Journal of Personality and Social Psychology* 71(6): 1235–1249.

Helliwell, John F., and Robert Putnam. 2004. "The Social Context of Well-Being." *Philosophical Transactions of the Royal Society of London* 359: 1435–1446.

Itzigsohn, José, and Silvia Giorguli Saucedo. 2002. "Immigrant Incorporation and Sociocultural Transnationalism." *International Migration Review* 36(3): 766–798.

Kang, Naewon, and Nojin Kwak. 2003. "A Multilevel Approach to Civic Participation: Individual Length of Residence, Neighborhood Residential Stability, and Their Interactive Effects with Media Use." *Communications Research* 30(1): 80–106.

Kasarda, John, and Morris Janowitz. 1974. "Community Attachment in Mass Society." *American Sociological Review* 39(3): 328–339.

Klofstad, Casey. 2007. "Talk Leads to Recruitment: How Discussions about Politics and Current Events Increase Civic Participation." *Political Research Quarterly* 60(2): 180–191.

Lasby, David. 2004. *The Volunteer Spirit in Canada: Motivations and Barriers*. Toronto: Canadian Center for Philanthropy.

Lie, Mabel, Susan Baines, and Jane Wheelock. 2009. "Citizenship, Volunteering, and Active Aging." *Social Policy and Administration* 43(7): 702–718.

Lim, Chaeyoon, and Thomas Sander. 2013. "Does Misery Love Company? Civic Engagement in Economic Hard Times." *Social Science Research* 42: 14–30.

Lipset, Seymour Martin. 1981. *Political Man: The Social Bases of Politics*. Baltimore, MD: Johns Hopkins University Press.

McCabe, Brian. 2013. "Are Homeowners Better Citizens? Homeownership and Community Participation in the United States." *Social Forces* 91(3): 929–954.

McVeigh, Rory, and Christian Smith. 1999. "Who Protests in America? An Analysis of Three Political Alternatives—Inaction, Institutionalized Politics, or Protest." *Sociological Forum* 14: 685–702.

Mendelson, Sarah E., and John K. Glenn (eds.). 2002. *The Power and Limits of NGOs: A Critical Look at Building Democracy in Eastern Europe and Eurasia*. New York: Columbia University Press.

Moravcsik, Andrew. 2002. "In Defense of the 'Democratic Deficit': Reassessing the Legitimacy of the European Union." *Journal of Common Market Studies* 40: 603–624.

Musick, Marc, and John Wilson. 2008. *Volunteers: A Social Profile*. Bloomington: Indiana University Press.

Muxel, Anne. 2009. "EU Movers and Politics: Towards a Fully-Fledged European Citizenship?" In Ettore Recchi and Adrian Favell (eds.), *Pioneers of European Integration: Citizenship and Mobility in the EU*. Cheltenham, UK: Edward Elgar.

Nie, Norman, Jane Junn, and Kenneth Stehlik-Barry. 1996. *Education and Democratic Citizenship in America*. Chicago, IL: University of Chicago Press.

Portes, Alejandro, Cristina Escobar, and Renelinda Arana. 2009. "Divided or Convergent Loyalties? The Political Incorporation Process of Latin American Immigrants in the United States." *International Journal of Comparative Sociology* 50(2): 103–136.

Portes, Alejandro, Luis Guarnizo, and Patricia Landolt. 1999. "Introduction: Pitfalls and Promise of an Emergent Research Field." *Ethnic and Racial Studies* 22(2): 217–237.

Putnam, Robert. 1994. *Making Democracy Work*. Princeton, NJ: Princeton University Press.

Putnam, Robert. 2000. *Bowling Alone*. New York: Simon & Schuster.

Recchi, Ettore. 2015. *Mobile Europe: The Theory and Practice of Mobility in the EU*. Basingstoke, UK: Palgrave MacMillan.

Sampson, Robert. 1991. "Linking the Micro and Macrolevel Dimensions of Community Social Organization." *Social Forces* 70: 43–64.

Scharpf, Fritz. 1999. *Governing in Europe: Effective and Democratic?* Oxford, UK: Oxford University Press.

Schmitter, Philippe. 2003. "Democracy in Europe and Europe's Democratization." *Journal of Democracy* 14: 71–85.

Stark, David, Balazs Vedres, and Laszlo Bruszt. 2007. "Rooted Transnational Publics: Integrating Foreign Ties and Civil Activism." *Theory and Society* 35(3): 323–349.

Teney, Céline, and Laurie Hanquinet. 2012. "High Political Participation, High Social Capital? A Relational Analysis of Youth Social Capital and Political Participation." *Social Science Research* 41(5): 1213–1226.

Wilson, John. 2000. "Volunteering." *Annual Review of Sociology* 26(1): 215–240.

Wilson, John, and Marc Musick. 1997. "Who Cares? Toward an Integrated Theory of Volunteer Work." *American Sociological Review* 62(5): 694–671.

6

TASTE AND CULTURAL PRACTICES

Taste and consumption have been at the center of sociology since the discipline's early days.[1] In post-industrial society, they complement and arguably supersede work as the most important individual sources of identity (Bauman, 1991; Warde, 2017). Not only are we what we consume but we consume in order to become who we want to be and in order to present ourselves to others. Also, consumption contributes to people's sense of group affiliation, by making them aware of others who engage in similar consumption practices and by facilitating social relations with people with similar taste and lifestyles. Based on these premises and on the assumption that nationality and education are somewhat coterminous with distinctive consumption cultures, this chapter examines contrasts in taste and consumer practices between partners in binational and national couples and between less and more educated partners in binational couples. In addition to this, it explores whether partners in a couple influence each other's taste and consumption practices. Finally, the chapter examines the relevance of personality, in the form of openness to variety and of exposure to the foreign partner's taste and cultural practices, for the explanation of contrasts between partners in binational and national couples. I show that openness and exposure contribute to explain why the former display a more developed international taste and more frequently engage in international practices than do the latter.

In the literature on lifestyles, taste, and cultural consumption, exposure and attitudinal openness emerge as major structural and individual determinants of taste.[2] Exposure makes a taste for and consumption of certain products conceivable. Liking and consuming a product require that one be familiar with the product in question. It follows that the more cultural objects and forms people know, the broader their taste *palette* and the more varied their consumption practices are likely to be. Lizardo has demonstrated that more educated people are omnivorous because they can recognize and name many genres and subgenres

(Lizardo, 2014; Savage and Gayo, 2011). At the same time, says Bourdieu, repeated exposure to a particular range of cultural objects and practices since early childhood shapes a person' modular aesthetic disposition. Early exposure to certain forms of consumption, through its impact on the aesthetic disposition, influences what people like and consume as adults. In developing this broad theoretical point further, Lizardo and Skiles argue that children of the relatively well-off educated classes from early on develop the capacity to abstract form from function when apprehending cultural objects, which then broadens "the potential number of objects that could be found to have aesthetic appeal" (Lizardo and Skiles, 2012, pp. 268–269).

Lizardo's and Skiles's reflection above takes us to a second relevant concept in the literature on taste and cultural practices, which is openness. In psychology, openness to experience is a basic personality trait. It covers "tolerance of ambiguity, low dogmatism, need for variety, esthetic sensitivity, absorption, unconventionality, intellectual curiosity, and intuition" (McCrae and Costa, 1997; Roose et al., 2012; Warde et al., 2007). Openness is one of the many forms that a person's aesthetic disposition, acquired through early and repeated exposure to particular cultural objects and practices, can take. What makes a person more or less open, however, depends on a wider range of factors, which justifies treating it as a partly exogenous variable influencing taste and cultural practices.

Work by Saito is particularly relevant to the comparison of taste and cultural practices among individuals in national and binational couples (Saito, 2011). He draws on studies of globalization and on Bruno Latour's actor-network theory in order to emphasize the role of networks and relationships in facilitating both exposure and openness to cultural objects that are typical in different parts of the world (Latour, 2005). He defines cosmopolitanism as more than "an intellectual and aesthetic stance." It is broader than this: a general orientation (i.e. disposition) to foreign others and cultures, which can be broken down into three elements: cultural omnivorousness (openness to foreign non-humans), ethnic tolerance (openness to foreign humans), and cosmopolitics. Saito then highlights that interaction with other individuals provides information and incentives to like and consume particular objects. Meanwhile, shared taste and consumption practices facilitate interaction and the development of social bonds between people, which, once established, further shape a person's taste and consumption practices. The stronger the bond between two individuals, the greater the likelihood that they each will acquire the other's taste and engage in the other's cultural practices. Regarding the role of shared taste in propitiating interaction and the development of social bonds, Saito refers to Erickson and Lizardo (Erickson, 1996; Lizardo, 2006). He remarks that popular cultural objects, such as sports, "provide focal points of interaction for people from different classes and cultural origins ... through these weak ties, nonredundant information about cultural objects belonging to different classes flows." This contributes to people becoming more omnivorous and acquiring a taste for consumption goods from different cultures than one's own.

128 Taste and cultural practices

The theoretical discussion above has empirical implications for the comparison between partners in national couples and partners in binational ones. It leads to the expectation of a correlation between being in a binational couple and having a more varied, more international, taste. One would expect that partners in binational couples are more open to consuming foreign cultural products than are partners in national couples. They are also more likely to be exposed to foreign cultural products. A binational couple is a strong tie. Following Saito, I expect that partners to these couples will become similar in their cultural tastes with the passing of time and thus become more international in their consumer practices. Beyond Saito, but still drawing on the fact that a binational couple is a strong tie, I also expect that liking what the partner likes will be more likely, the stronger or more central the partner's taste for a particular product is and the more the reproduction of the relationship between the partners involves sharing this particular taste. For instance, if my partner earns a living by playing French Hip-Hop music as a DJ, I will not only be exposed to French hip-hop in a more informed way, which will make the music more interesting than if I just listen to it on the radio; in addition to this, I will have a greater incentive to like it in order to maintain the quality of our relationship. This adoption of my partner's taste for French Hip-Hop may not be as likely if my partner is a business consultant who just happens to like this and many other styles.

When one moves from the level of inter-personal relationships to the inter-group level, a bi-directional causal relationship between the spread of an international taste and the formation of binational couples may in the long turn contribute to greater mutual understanding between Europeans of different nationalities and propitiate a greater collective European awareness and solidarity between Europeans.

In what follows, I examine different dimensions of taste and consumer practices: music, film, books, and cuisine. I show that individuals in binational couples like Jazz and Contemporary Classic music and Non-English film more, that they display a greater propensity to read books in foreign languages, and that they like a broader range of world cuisines than do individuals in national couples. At the analytical level, I provide empirical evidence that supports the claim that both attitudinal openness and exposure play a role in the development of international taste and that being a partner in a binational couple contributes to greater attitudinal openness and exposure to foreign cultural products. Finally, the empirical analysis below provides insights on the role of other factors, such as country of residence, gender, education, and transnational practices, in shaping both cosmopolitan taste and consumer practices. In particular, it highlights the cultural divide between less educated and more educated binational couples.

Musical taste

Respondents to the *Eumarr* survey reported whether they like jazz, classic music, contemporary classic music, pop, rock, folk/ethnic/roots music, and music by singer-songwriters.[3] Close similarity in the distribution of answers across cities and across major socio-demographic categories suggests that participants understood the meaning of the various musical genres (see Table 6.1). Pop and rock are the most popular music genres in all countries. Contemporary classic and folk/ethnic/roots are the least popular ones. Whereas more than half the respondents like the former, about a third or less like the latter (based on unweighted average of country percentages). Also, as the literature shows, highly educated respondents like classic music and jazz more than do less educated ones. Finally, there are no obvious contrasts between partners in binational couples and those in national couples.

An underlying assumption in the literature is that music is central or, at least, very important for individuals. This assumption needs to be empirically tested. The qualitative interviews that I conducted as part of the *Euromarr* project suggest that, except for musicians and professionals in the music industry, people in their thirties and forties do not have more than a fleeting interest in music and fall into the category that Savage labels as "consumers" (Savage et al., 2005). This applies even to those who checked many styles while filling-out the *Eumarr*

TABLE 6.1 Musical Taste, by Type of Couple and Education (Unweighted Average of Country %)

	National Couples		Binational Couples			
			National		Foreign	
Jazz						
Less than university	37	(460)	45	(283)	36	(269)
University or more	44	(625)	48	(592)	52	(720)
Classical						
Less than university	43	(460)	47	(283)	43	(269)
University or more	55	(625)	56	(592)	59	(720)
Contemporary Classic						
Less than university	28	(460)	31	(283)	25	(269)
University or more	26	(625)	26	(592)	28	(720)
Pop						
Less than university	67	(460)	62	(283)	56	(269)
University or more	62	(625)	58	(592)	53	(720)
Rock						
Less than university	63	(460)	53	(283)	47	(269)
University or more	54	(625)	52	(592)	50	(720)
Folk						
Less than university	28	(460)	35	(283)	22	(269)
University or more	27	(625)	32	(592)	31	(720)
Singer-Songwriters						
Less than university	46	(460)	45	(283)	36	(269)
University or more	44	(625)	48	(592)	40	(720)

( ) Number of respondents.

130 Taste and cultural practices

questionnaire. The respondents' typical reaction when I asked them about their music likes and dislikes was to say that they like to have music in the background and that's it. Others were more apologetic and said that they are too busy, "children and all that," to pay attention to music. In fact, most of the times it felt awkward to start asking respondents about their musical tastes since nothing in the home environment (e.g. music in the background, CD's in the living room, music equipment) suggested that music is an important part of their lives. This relative indifference to music is consistent with the conclusion reached in other studies that omnivorousness measured as the number of music genres checked in a questionnaire mainly measures the respondents' musical vocabulary.

I further explored the relationship between being in a binational couple and musical taste through multiple regression. Partners in binational couples display a slightly greater preference for jazz and contemporary classic music (Table 6.2, columns 1 and 5). This contrast varies between 5% and 9% points, depending on the genre and whether one focuses on the national or the foreign partner in these couples. Both jazz and contemporary classic music, especially the latter, are genres only liked by a minority in the population. They can be difficult for those who listen to it occasionally or who are less used to sounds that, very often, break free from the laws of traditional Western melody and harmony (e.g. free jazz or serialism, for instance). The contrast between partners in binational and national couples perhaps reflects differences in cultural capital and associated dispositions, such as greater or lesser openness to non-hegemonic and complex forms of artistic expression (Bourdieu, 1984). The even-numbered columns in Table 6.2 confirm this interpretation. I examined the impact of being in a binational couple, controlling for gender, age, education, parents' education, and knowledge of foreign languages. Age stands for differences between generations and over the life cycle (Savage and Gayo, 2011). Other controls, like education, parents' education and knowledge of foreign languages relate to education and educational capital. For Lizardo and Skiles education and educational capital are "the primary drivers of differences in tastes and culture consumption in all contemporary national contexts" (Lizardo and Skiles, 2012). Meanwhile, Prieur and Savage empirically demonstrate that in Britain and Denmark cultural capital also differentiates individuals with an international versus local cultural orientation (Prieur and Savage, 2011; see also Saito, 2011).

The very small R-square coefficients in Table 6.2 mean that there is a great deal of variation in people's taste for different musical genres within theoretically relevant socio-demographic categories of the population (see coefficients in even-numbered columns). This is consistent with the view that while adults very often like music, what music they listen to and what genre they like is not central to their identity. Still, liking jazz and classic music is more prevalent among older people than among younger people in the 30–46 age group. Also, women like jazz and rock music less and like classic and pop music more than do men. Finally, cultural capital enters in the explanation of whether people like music genres in the list, other than pop and rock. Depending on the genre, being highly educated, having parents that are highly educated, or speaking

TABLE 6.2 Association between Being in a Binational Couple and Taste for Different Music Genres, Controlling for City of Residence, Socio-Economic Variables, and the Number of Spoken Languages (OLS)

	Jazz (1)	Jazz (2)	Folk (3)	Folk (4)	Contemp. Classic (5)	Contemp. Classic (6)	Classic (7)	Classic (8)	Pop (9)	Pop (10)	Rock (11)	Rock (12)	Singer-Songwriters (13)	Singer-Songwriters (14)
Foreign in a binational couple	0.09 ★	0.08 ★	0.03	0.02	0.07 ★	0.06 ★	0.04	0.02	−0.08 ★	−0.09 ★	−0.06 ★	−0.06 ★	−0.03	−0.04
National in a binational couple	0.06 ★	0.04	0.08 ★	0.07 ★	0.05 +	0.04	0.03	0.02	−0.03	−0.03	−0.04	−0.05	+0.02	0.01
Gender (1=Woman)		−0.06 ★		9.0E−03		−9.0E−03		0.05 ★		0.04 ★		−0.06 ★		0.03
Age		−2.0E−03		5.0E−03 ★		6.0E−03		0.01 ★		−1.0E−03		−1.0E−03		2.0E−03
Education	0.03 ★	0.01	2.0E−03	−3.0E−03	0.00	−5.0E−03	0.04 ★	0.03 ★	−0.01	−3.0E−03	−4.0E−03	−5.0E−03	−1.0E−03	−1.0E.03
Parents' education		0.02 ★		8.0E−03		6.0E−03		0.03 ★		−9.0E−03		−7.0E−03		9.0E.03
Languages known		0.04 ★		0.02 +		0.02 ★		0.04 ★		0.01		0.02		0.03 ★
Constant	0.24	0.21	+ 0.30	0.04	0.33	0.05	0.32 ★	−0.24 +	0.72 ★	0.73 ★	0.69	0.75 ★	0.46 ★	0.29 ★
R-Square (%)	1.9	3.2	1.9	2.3	1.6	2.1	3.8	5.5	1.1	1.4	1.8	2.3	1.2	1.6
N	2300	2300	2300	2300	2300	2300	2300	2300	2300	2300	2300	2300	2300	2300

Controls for city of residence.
+: Significant at 0.10 level, two-tailed; ★: Significant at 0.05 level, two-tailed.

132 Taste and cultural practices

foreign languages is associated with a greater prevalence of people who like those genres. Since partners in binational couples have more cultural capital than do those in national couples, one can speculate that cognitive factors, in the form of greater openness to non-hegemonic forms of artistic expression and to complexity, which the literature associates to cultural capital, contribute to explain why partners in binational couples like jazz and contemporary classic music more.

Film taste

The *Eumarr* survey also inquired about people's taste in film. Because of our focus on international taste and consumer practices, the questionnaire differentiated between the film's geographical origins instead of differentiating between genres, as one usually finds in the literature on musical taste. This is because geographic origin tends to leave a specific imprint in film that is more infrequent in music, except for the music style that we labeled folk/ethnic/roots. The "remake," that is, the localization of a given film achieved by first buying the rights to the film and then re-filming it, usually with local actors, with different pace and production values, sometimes through changes in both setting and script (e.g. Fukua's *Magnificent Seven* and Kurosawa's *The Seven Samurai*), is thus typical in film but not in music (e.g. one does not imagine anybody "remaking" Radiohead's *OK Computer* to suit a French audience).[4]

The survey questionnaire differentiates between (1) American; (2) Host Country; (3) Non-English European; and (4) Non-English, Non-European film. As expected, people prefer American film to films from other world regions (with the exception of highly educated Zurich respondents who like non-English European films better) (see Table 6.3). Then, Spanish and Belgian respondents like national film more than do Dutch and Swiss respondents. This may reflect the relative strength of a country's film industry. Spain and Belgium, especially the former, are bigger film producers and co-producers than are the Netherlands and Switzerland and have comparatively prestigious film traditions. Finally, Table 6.3 reveals that highly educated people tend to like non-English films more than do less educated people. Although the availability of films in original version (more below) and greater openness perhaps play a part in the explanation of this relationship, the empirical observation that liking American films is negatively correlated with liking non-English films ($r = -0.04$ for non-English European films; -0.12 for non-English non-European films) suggests that other factors, such as strategies of distinction or anti-Americanism, also play a role. This was obvious, for instance, in one of my qualitative interviews, where the respondent made a point of stating that

> the prototypical American film has never appealed to me, neither action movies nor American comedy, not at all. I do not dig much American things although I'd love to visit the United States; it must be a great country to discover, but I like things European more.
>
> *(Interview # 1)*

TABLE 6.3 Film Taste, by City of Residence, Type of Couple, and Education (%)

	Spanish Cities			Belgian Cities			Dutch Cities			Swiss City		
	National Couples	Binational Couples		National Couples	Binational Couples		National Couples	Binational Couples		National Couples	Binational Couples	
		National	Foreign		National	Foreign		National	Foreign		National	Foreign
American												
Less than university	91	87	89	75	94	95	88	82	88	62	72	67
University or more	91	88	82	79	75	82	81	83	82	60	63	59
Own Country												
Less than university	78	80	66	75	70	82	53	57	33	56	53	39
University or more	79	75	70	78	79	74	56	55	46	54	45	38
Non-Anglo, European												
Less than university	36	56	36	34	57	59	38	50	28	72	78	54
University or more	61	73	64	67	80	74	58	73	66	79	80	69
Non-Anglo, Non-European												
Less than university	22	35	27	19	46	41	21	43	21	50	52	39
University or more	32	53	49	50	62	66	31	49	44	65	69	60
N (< than Uni)	(157)	(71)	(62)	(32)	(67)	(39)	(35)	(55)	(67)	(236)	(90)	(101)
N (Uni. Or >)	(166)	(77)	(80)	(58)	(142)	(174)	(116)	(224)	(227)	(285)	(149)	(239)

( ) Number of respondents.

134 Taste and cultural practices

National partners in binational couples like non-English films more than do partners in national ones, except in Zurich. Foreign partners, on the other hand, vary in the extent to which they like non-English films. In some countries they like them as much as nationals and in other countries they like them less. Probably, the different national composition of the foreign population in each of the seven cities contributes to explain this empirical finding. Foreign partners in binational couples coincide, however, in liking host country films less than do nationals from those countries.

Multiple regression analysis helps to better assess the association between being in a binational couple and taste in film, as well as possible interactions between types of respondents and the country in which they live (see Table 6.4). The statistical results show that taste for film is more defined than is taste for music, as reflected in slightly higher R-square coefficients than those obtained in the analysis of musical taste. Still, low R-square coefficients suggest that just like listening to music, watching movies is more a distraction than a meaningful identity-giving activity. It also confirms that partners in binational couples generally like films from the country of residence less than do nationals. Furthermore, while nationals in binational couples like non-English foreign films more than do nationals in national couples, foreign partners in these couples do not differentiate themselves from nationals in national couples so clearly (see columns 1, 3, 5, and 7). The fact that the contrast in film taste between nationals in binational couples and nationals in national couples is similar to that of highly educated individuals with respect to less educated ones and to that of polyglots relative to individuals who speak one or two languages only (columns 2, 4, 6, and 8) suggests that greater openness underlies all these contrasts.

Another potentially relevant source of differentiation between individuals in national and binational couples is the appreciation of film in original version. European countries differ from one another in their propensity to subtitling or dubbing foreign films. Whereas Anglo-Saxon, Benelux, and Scandinavian countries rarely dub film, there are very strong dubbing traditions in the German-speaking countries and in Spain and Italy. In these countries, professionals in the art of dubbing enjoy prestige and constitute a powerful lobby against the trend toward subtitling. In a self-reinforcing process, the population displays different degrees of openness to watching films in the original language. This is reflected in the survey data collected for *Eumarr*. Whereas more than 80% of Dutch and Belgian partners in national couples said that they like to watch films in original version, nationals in the Spanish cities and in Zurich express a greater preference for the dubbed version. In Spain, although most films and series can be watched on T.V. in original version by the click of a button on the remote, about two-thirds of the national respondents prefer the dubbed version (see Table 6.5). In Zurich, part of German-speaking Europe, where dubbing is also prevalent, the percentage of respondents who like to watch films in original version is significantly higher than in Spain but still lies below the numbers for Belgium and the Netherlands.

As one would expect, individuals with university education like to watch films in original version more than do individuals with less than university education. The

TABLE 6.4 Association between Being in a Binational Couple and Taste for Films from Different World Regions, Controlling for City of Residence and for Socio-Demographic Variables and the Number of Spoken Languages (OLS)

	American		American		Country of Residence		Country of Residence		Non-National, non-Anglo European		Non-National, non-Anglo European		Non-National, Non-Anglo, Non-European		Non-National, Non-Anglo, Non-European	
	(1)		(2)		(3)		(4)		(5)		(6)		(7)		(8)	
Foreign in binational couple	2.0E−03		0.02		−0.14	★	−0.14	★	−0.04	+	−0.06	★	0.06	★	0.03	
National in Binational couple	−6.0E−03		−7.7E−05		−0.04	+	−0.04	+	0.09	★	0.07	★	0.13	★	0.12	★
Gender (1=Woman)			−0.04	★			0.04	+			0.00				0.02	
Age			−5.0E−03	★			2.0E−03				5.0E−03	★			−3.0E−03	
Education	−0.02	★	−0.02	★	0.01	+	0.01	+	0.06	★	0.04	★	0.05	★	0.03	★
Parents' education			−0.01	★			−2.0E−03				0.02	★			0.02	★
Languages known			−0.03	★			7.0E−03				0.06	★			0.07	★
Constant	0.84	★	1.18	★	0.48	★	0.39		0.36	★	−0.02		0.16	★	−0.17	
R-Square (%)	5.4		6.5		7.9		8.0		11.2		13.3		8.7		10.7	
N	2300		2300		2300		2300		2300		2300		2300		2300	

Controls for city of residence.

+: Significant at 0.10 level, two-tailed; ★: Significant at 0.05 level, two-tailed.

136 Taste and cultural practices

TABLE 6.5 Preference for Films in Original Version, by City of Residence, Type of Couple, and Education (%)

	National Couple		Binational Couple (National)		Binational Couple (Foreign)	
Spanish Cities						
Less than university	17	(155)	30	(69)	53	(60)
More than university	37	(164)	69	(74)	74	(80)
Belgian Cities						
Less than university	86	(29)	79	(67)	64	(39)
More than university	82	(57)	92	(141)	83	(173)
Dutch Cities						
Less than university	97	(34)	92	(53)	88	(64)
More than university	94	(116)	99	(222)	87	(224)
Swiss City						
Less than university	53	(215)	58	(85)	50	(91)
More than university	80	(259)	88	(138)	73	(217)

( ) Number of respondents.

effect of education, however, is greater in countries with less tradition in showing films in original version. The relationship between being in a national or binational couple and liking film in original version varies also across countries. In Spain, it is clear than the proportion of those who like them this way is higher among partners in binational couples. In Zurich, the proportion is higher among nationals in binational couples than among nationals in national couples but foreign partners in binational couples do not differ from nationals in national couples. Finally, in Belgium and the Netherlands, where films are traditionally shown in original version, the proportion of foreign partners in binational couples who like them this way is lower than the proportion observed among nationals. Table 6.5 also shows that the proportion of foreign partners who like films in the original language is higher in countries where the proportion of nationals who like them is higher and is lower in countries where the proportion of nationals who like them is lower. In sum, being in a binational couple is associated with a greater propensity to liking films in original version but only among nationals and only in countries where the national population generally prefers the dubbed version. Meanwhile, foreign partners in binational couples assimilate to the traditional way of watching films in the country where they live. The more exposed they are to films in original version, as in Belgium or the Netherlands, the higher the proportion of those who prefer them to the dubbed version.

Since liking films in original version varies significantly across countries, which then impacts on how partners in national and binational couples differ from one another, I further explore the association between the type of couple to which individuals belong and preference for films in original version, separately for each country. Table 6.6 confirms that nationals in binational couples like film in original version more than do nationals in national couples only in the

TABLE 6.6 Association between Being in a Binational Couple and Taste for Films in Original Version, Controlling for City of Residence and for Socio-Demographic Variables and the Number of Spoken Languages (OLS)

	Spanish Cities (1)		Spanish Cities (2)		Belgian Cities (3)		Belgian Cities (4)		Dutch Cities (5)		Dutch Cities (6)		Swiss City (7)		Swiss City (8)	
Foreign in binational couple	0.42	★	0.34	★	−0.07		−0.08		−0.08	★	−0.08	★	−0.09	★	−0.08	★
National in binational couple	0.28	★	0.23	★	0.03		6.0E−03		0.02		0.02		0.09	★	0.09	★
Gender (1=Woman)			−0.02				−0.04				0.01				−8.0E−03	
Age			2.0E−03				1.0E−03				−5.0E−03				5.0E−03	
Education	0.07	★	0.06	★	0.02		0.01		8.0E−03		7.0E−03		0.11	★	0.07	★
Parents' education			6.0E−03				0.02	+			−4.0E−03				0.04	★
Languages known			0.07	★			0.06	★			−4.0E−03				0.10	★
Constant	−0.17	+	−0.40	+	0.77	★	0.57	★	0.90	★	1.10	★	−0.07		−0.57	★
R-Square (%)	17.9		20.2		1.8		11.6		3.0		4.0		9.3		14.6	
N	505		505		417		417		618		618		760		760	

Controls for city of residence.

+: Significant at 0.10 level, two-tailed; ★: Significant at 0.05 level, two-tailed.

138 Taste and cultural practices

Spanish cities and in Zurich and that foreign partners in binational couples like film in original version more than do nationals only in the Spanish cities. In the Netherlands, in fact, the proportion of foreign partners who prefer to see films in original version is lower than that of nationals (column 5).

Table 6.6 also supports the expectation that openness influences whether people prefer film in original version or prefer the dubbed version instead. Except for the Netherlands, where there is an overwhelming preference for films in original version among the population, the proportion of individuals who do so increases as the number of languages they know increases (columns 2, 4, 8). While knowing foreign languages makes it easier to follow films in original version (even if subtitled), it is also a cause and indicator of openness to other cultures (Díez Medrano, 2006). In fact, I could show that there is no correlation between knowing English only and preference for films in original version. In sum, one cannot generalize as to contrasts in taste for film in original version between partners in national and partners in binational couples. Preference for a foreign film's original or dubbed version is rooted in national traditions, in exposure, and in how open people are.

Reading books in foreign languages

A more demanding way to get exposure to foreign cultures is to read foreign books in their original language. Here, as opposed to when watching subtitled films in the original language, one really needs to know foreign languages. In the cities included in *Eumarr*, people do not read foreign literature as frequently as they engage in other cultural activities. Only in the Netherlands did about one half of the population read at least one book in a foreign language in the year preceding the study (see Table 6.7). As one would expect, this habit is also more prevalent among the more educated than among the less educated. From this book's perspective, however, the most relevant finding is that, regardless of their level of education, partners in binational couples are more likely to have read a book written in a foreign language in the year before the survey than are partners in national couples. Spain is the only country where foreign partners in binational couples display a clearly higher propensity to read books in foreign languages than do national partners in binational couples. This probably reflects that Spaniards are less fluent in foreign languages than are most other Europeans.

Table 6.8 shows that the probability of having read a book in a foreign language is on average 16% points higher among foreign partners in binational couples than among nationals in national couples. Meanwhile, the contrast between nationals in binational couples and nationals in national ones amounts to 10% points. The contrast between partners in binational couples and partners in national ones can be partly explained by the fact that knowledge of foreign languages is more widespread among the former (i.e. see decline in the regression coefficients for the relevant variables between columns 1 and 2 in Table 6.8).

Taste and cultural practices **139**

TABLE 6.7 Read a Book in a Foreign Language the Previous Year, by City of Residence, Type of Couple and Education (%)

	National Couple		Binational Couple (National)		Binational Couple (Foreign)	
Spanish Cities						
Less than university	25	(133)	42	(57)	84	(43)
More than university	45	(162)	61	(70)	88	(76)
Belgian Cities						
Less than university	24	(25)	41	(53)	29	(31)
More than university	55	(49)	58	(132)	62	(164)
Dutch Cities						
Less than university	37	(27)	57	(47)	76	(54)
More than university	69	(109)	78	(216)	76	(212)
Swiss City						
Less than university	30	(205)	42	(76)	58	(88)
More than university	62	(250)	72	(130)	69	(149)

( ) Number of respondents.

TABLE 6.8 Association between Being in a Binational Couple and Reading Books in Foreign Languages, Controlling for City of Residence and for Socio-Demographic Variables, and the Number of Spoken Languages (OLS)

	(1)		(2)	
Foreign in binational couple	0.20	★	0.16	★
National in binational couple	0.14	★	0.10	★
Gender (1 = Woman)			−0.05	★
Age			−1.0E−03	
Education	0.08	★	0.05	★
Parents' education			0.00	
Languages known			0.15	★
Constant	−0.09	+	−0.31	★
R-Square (%)	11.8		18.3	
N	2300		2300	

Controls for city of residence.
+: Significant at 0.10 level, two-tailed; ★: Significant at 0.05 level, two-tailed.

Since the contrast between partners in binational couples and partners in national ones remains even after one takes into account differences between the two groups in the number of languages they know, I would argue, however, that it also reflects both greater openness to other cultures and greater access to foreign books through one's foreign partner (column 2).

140 Taste and cultural practices

Taste for foreign cuisine

International migration and a growing interest in the health impact of nutrition has fundamentally transformed people's eating habits. Not long ago, and with the exception of isolated Chinese, Turkish, Greek, or Italian restaurants, depending of where one lived in Europe, most restaurants only specialized in regional or national dishes. Similarly, supermarkets only offered local products. As a child growing up in Spain, I only discovered kiwi fruit in the late 1970s. To get packaged corn on the cob or even cornflakes in the late 1960s my mother had to travel far to a Woolworth supermarket that had opened in Madrid, probably to serve the U.S. expatriate community living in the city (the store sat about 100 meters away from the U.S. cultural center) and thus spare them even longer trips to the supermarket at U.S. Torrejón military base located well outside the city. Both my discovery of kiwi fruit and my mother's interest in buying corn on the cob and cornflakes resulted from transnational contact or experience: an invitation to visit a friend in Belgium in the first case, and my parents' previous two-year residence in the United States in the second case. Experiences like these were infrequent in the 1960s and 1970s, especially in a backward and relatively closed country like Spain. In the globalization age, they have multiplied exponentially with the elimination of barriers to foreign trade and with increasing international mobility and exchange. In fact, in the European Union one no longer needs to travel or do deep searching in order to buy or eat food from a huge variety of world regions. Price is not a barrier either. Very often foreign food and restaurants are cheaper than local ones. One would thus think that what matters most is the motivation and willingness to try and the disposition to like new and different flavors. As I show below, however, strong ties, such as living with a foreign partner, can still influence eating preferences.

I focus both on the number of cuisine's types people like and on the extent to which they like Asian cuisine, measured as a factor that takes into account taste for different kinds of Asian cuisine: Japanese, Chinese, Thai, Vietnamese, Korean, and Indian food. The *Eumarr* survey to a large extent confirms the thesis that in the globalization age people are exposed and like a whole range of cuisines. The populations of the four countries in the *Eumarr* study like an average of nine different national cuisines, an admittedly high number (see Table 6.9). Also, more educated individuals like a more varied array of cuisines than do less educated ones and they tend to like Asian food more. Finally, and controlling for country and education, partners in binational couples have more omnivorous taste and like Asian food more than do partners in national couples.

Regression analysis confirms the findings above (Table 6.10). Partners in binational couples are more omnivorous than are partners in national ones and this is so even after one controls for socio-demographic and transnational experience and skills (columns 1 and 4). Furthermore, those who know foreign languages and who have travelled to many countries since they were children are also more omnivorous than those who do not know foreign languages and have travelled

TABLE 6.9 Number of National Cuisines Liked and Taste for Asian Food, by Type of Couple and Education (Unweighted Average of Country Means)

		National Couple		Binational Couple (National)		Binational Couple (Foreign)	
Number of national cuisines liked	Less than university	7.41	(466)	8.93	(288)	8.33	(271)
	More than university	9.13	(638)	10.42	(606)	10.19	(733)
Likes Asian food	Less than university	3.41	(458)	4.32	(282)	3.77	(268)
	More than university	4.56	(626)	5.19	(592)	4.89	(720)

( ) Number of respondents.

TABLE 6.10 Association between Being in a Binational Couple and both the Number of National Cuisines Liked and Taste for Asian Food, Controlling for City of Residence and for Socio-Demographic and Transnational Experience and Skills Variables (OLS)

	Number of National Cuisines Liked			Likes Asian Food		
	(1)	(2)	(3)	(4)	(5)	(6)
Foreign in binational couple	0.88 ★	0.74 ★	0.91 ★	0.33 ★	0.24	0.34 ★
National in binational couple	0.98 ★	0.72 ★	0.52 ★	0.62 ★	0.51 ★	0.40 ★
Gender (1 = Woman)		−1.00 ★	−0.84 ★		−0.25 ★	−0.16
Age		−0.02	−0.03		7.0E−03	1.0E−03
Education	0.50 ★	0.30 ★	0.23 ★	0.29 ★	0.19 ★	0.14 ★
Parents' education		0.18 ★	0.04		0.12 ★	0.04
Languages known		0.55 ★	0.36 ★		0.26 ★	0.14 ★
Countries visited before 17			0.14 ★			0.08 ★
Countries visited between 17 and before meeting Partner			0.16 ★			0.10 ★
Constant	7.24 ★	7.30 ★	7.26 ★	3.00 ★	2.12 ★	2.10 ★
R-Square (%)	10.5	12.6	16.2	14.3	15.4	18.7
N		2300			2300	

Controls for city of residence.
+: Significant at 0.10 level, two-tailed; ★: Significant at 0.05 level, two-tailed.

142 Taste and cultural practices

abroad less often during their lifetime. In fact, knowing foreign languages and transnational travel experience explain to a great extent why nationals in binational couples are more omnivorous than are nationals in national couples and why they like Asian food more (i.e. the corresponding regression coefficient becomes smaller as one moves from column 2 to column 3 and from column 5 to column 6). This finding suggests that partners in binational couples are more omnivorous than are those in national ones because they have been exposed and have become more open to other cultures since childhood. I decided to explore the issue further by focusing on a controlled comparison between nationals in national and binational couples and through close inspection of the type of cuisine individuals like.

Anthropology and psychology argue that eating is central to one's individual and collective identity (Douglas, 1966, 1979; Fischler, 1988). Scholars have remarked that one of the most enduring features in immigrant populations' gradual assimilation to a host society is what they eat and how they prepare it (Billig, 1995; Calvo, 1982). Furthermore, sociological and anthropological studies have highlighted the centrality of food in how couples negotiate their lives together (Cross and Gilly, 2014; Darmon and Warde, 2016). Studies of intercultural couples also emphasize individuals' openness to adapting to their partners' culinary preferences. These studies, however, generally focus on highly educated bicultural couples and on the foreign partner in the couple. The analysis that follows contributes a quantitative perspective to this literature at the same time as it explores the impact of being in a binational couple for native partners, controlling for education.

Data on the foreign partners' food taste provide a first indication that individuals tend to adapt to their partners' food taste. As foreigners in their partner's country of residence, these individuals are doubly exposed to their partner's cuisine, both at home and outside the home. The *Eumarr* survey questionnaire collected information on whether respondents like Spanish, Swiss, and Dutch cuisine (it did not ask about Belgian cuisine—although it can be as good as the others or more!) (see Table 6.11). In all cases, one sees that foreign partners in binational couples like the host country's cuisine more or less the same as nationals and considerably more than do respondents in the four countries taken together, regardless of level of education. Taste for Dutch cuisine in the Netherlands is particularly interesting, for there are large contrasts between less educated and more educated respondents in national couples. This may perhaps reflect starker contrasts between popular and high-end cuisine in the Netherlands than in Spain or Switzerland, where popular dishes are highly appreciated (e.g. Paella, Raclette).

An exclusive focus on the national partners in national and binational couples provides even stronger confirmation of how partners impact on a person's culinary taste, for one can disentangle the effects from the country of residence and the nationality of the partner (Table 6.12). For seven different cuisines, I checked whether having a partner with the same nationality as the cuisine that one is

TABLE 6.11 Taste for Host Country's Cuisine, by Type of Couple, Education, and Country (%)

	Likes Spanish Cuisine in Spain		Likes Dutch Cuisine in the Netherlands		Likes Swiss Cuisine in Switzerland	
National in National Couple						
Less than university	95	(159)	10	(38)	89	(236)
More than university	92	(171)	32	(121)	82	(285)
National in Binational Couple						
Less than university	97	(71)	32	(56)	88	(90)
More than university	91	(79)	38	(230)	84	(149)
Foreign in Binational Couple						
Less than university	90	(63)	28	(67)	75	(101)
More than university	91	(85)	45	(232)	76	(239)
Total						
Less than university	95	(293)	26	(161)	85	(427)
More than university	92	(335)	40	(583)	80	(673)

( ) Number of respondents.

TABLE 6.12 Association between Being in a Binational Couple and Liking Different Cuisines, Controlling for Socio-Demographic Variables, and for Having a Partner of a Particular Nationality or from a particular European Region (Respondents who have the Country of Nationality Only) (OLS)

	Likes French (1)	Likes German (2)	Likes Greek (3)	Likes Italian (4)	Likes Polish (5)	Likes Scandinavian[1] (6)	Likes Hungarian (7)
In a binational partnership with person with same nationality/ region as cuisine	0.23 ★	0.41 ★	0.43 ★	0.07 +	0.92 ★	0.57 ★	0.75 ★
In a binational partnership with person with same nationality/ region as cuisine						0.57 ★	
In a binational partnership	−0.03	−0.06 ★	0.06 ★	−0.01	9.0E−03	9.0E−03	−0.02
R–Square (%)	10.6	16.0	5.8	2.3	17.7	4.5 4.1	7.6
N				1531			

Controls for city of residence.
+: Significant at 0.10 level, two-tailed; ★: Significant at 0.05 level, two-tailed.
1: Finland in row 1 and Sweden in row 2.

144 Taste and cultural practices

examining increases the probability that a national will like that particular cuisine. All models, except for one, confirm that this is the case (first row of columns 1 to 7). The one that does not work as predicted involves Italian cuisine. This, of course, is not surprising: Italian cuisine, especially its most popular dishes (i.e. pizza, pasta), has been completely denationalized and is liked by virtually everybody in Europe, regardless of nationality. Nine out of ten respondents in the *Eumarr* study said they like Italian cuisine.

Another way of looking at the effect of the foreign partner's nationality on whether one likes a particular cuisine is to focus only on the subsample of national respondents whose partner belongs to any of the nationalities whose cuisine was part of the list provided in the questionnaire (i.e. French, German, Greek, Scandinavian, Hungarian, and Polish). For respondents who had selected their foreign partner's national cuisine, I subtracted one from the total count of national cuisines they had checked. Then, I re-estimated the regression model to see whether these respondents are more omnivorous than respondents in national couples. I found that once one subtracts the foreign partner's cuisine from the count of cuisines that one likes, the relationship between being in a binational couple and omnivorous taste becomes much smaller and is no longer statistically significant ($N = 1887$).

Partners in binational couples thus come to like their partner's national cuisines. This is a significant finding for it shows that the impact that exposure to cultural objects through one's strong ties has on taste depends on the cultural object being considered. Of course, one cannot rule out the opposite causal process to be at work: one enters a relationship with a foreign national because one likes his or her national cuisine. Admittedly, one can imagine this happening or, what is more realistic, that liking the foreign partner's national cuisine works as a focal point on which the relationship is built. In general, however, exposure through marriage or cohabitation probably precedes liking a partner's national cuisine.

Does taste differentiate nationals in national and binational couples?

This chapter has examined taste in music, film, literature, and cuisine. Except for music, the focus has primarily been on international cultural taste and not on differences between genres as is typical in the literature. This is because cosmopolitanism is the dimension that I expect will differentiate individuals who are in national couples from those who are in binational couples. Despite the wide accessibility to cultural goods from foreign countries that results from European integration and globalization trends, cosmopolitan strong ties (i.e. being part of a binational couple) more directly expose partners to foreign cultural products than do national strong ties, and provide a stronger incentive or motivation to like them, especially when they originate in the partner's country of origin.

The statistical analysis above suggests that nationals in national and binational couples are not all that different in their tastes. This is probably because of the aforementioned global and European integration trends, which give everybody access to products of mass consumption produced anywhere in the world; because European cultural habits have become quite homogeneous; and because although people like and dislike many things in the world of material and cultural consumption, they generally do not care so much about any of them in particular (Schwimm, 2006).[5] Another factor that explains the similarity between national and binational couples is that nationally specific cultures have a quite strong impact on partners in national and binational couples, simultaneously inducing heterogeneity between individuals in binational couples across different countries.

There are some relevant contrasts, however, between the group of individuals in national couples and the group of individuals in binational couples: the latter have a more developed international taste in the areas that I have explored. The main contrasts concern Jazz, Contemporary Classic, non-English films, books in foreign languages, and cuisine from different parts of the world. One question one may want to answer is how distinct the cultural and consumer taste of partners in binational couples is from that of partners in national couples, once one takes all these contrasts together. Another interesting question is whether and how the taste of nationals in binational couples differentiates itself from the taste of foreign partners in these couples. Then, since many of these variables are correlated, one would want to know whether all of them differentiate partners in binational couples from partners in national ones, once one holds the others constant. A multinomial regression model (Table 6.13) allows to answer these questions and discover which among the different areas of cultural and consumer taste distinguish people in national and binational couples most. The statistical results confirm that the cultural and consumer taste expressed by partners in binational couples does not differ very much from that of partners in national couples (Cox-Snell Pseudo-R-Square = 18.5). In a guessing game, where people would ask us to say whether an individual with a particular taste in music, film, foreign books, and cuisine is a national partner in a national couple, a national partner in a binational couple, or a foreign partner in a binational couple, our guess would be wrong most of the times.

At the same time, all the dimensions of taste that emerged as relevant for the distinction between partners in binational couples and partners in national ones, are still relevant once we control for the others (columns 1 to 3). Of all these dimensions, the one that differentiates them most is reading books in foreign languages, which as I show above, is due in part, but only in part, to the fact that partners in binational couples are competent in more languages on average than are partners in national couples. The analysis also shows that national and foreign partners in binational couples are not quite identical in their cultural and consumer taste. Foreign partners, for instance, like film from the country of residence and from non-European non-English speaking countries significantly less than do national partners in these couples. On the other hand, their food taste is more omnivorous than their national partners' food taste (column 3: −0.05).

146 Taste and cultural practices

TABLE 6.13 Association between Taste in Music, Taste in Film, Reading Habits, and Taste for Cuisine and Being in a Binational Couple instead of a National Couple (Multinomial Logit Model—Logit Coefficients).

	National in Binational Couple vs. National in National Couple (Controlling for city and Education) (1)		Foreign in Binational Couple vs. National in National Couple (Controlling for City and Education) (2)		National in Binational Couple vs. Foreign in Binational Couple (Controlling for City and Education) (3)	
Likes Jazz	0.09		0.22	+	−0.14	
Likes contemporary classic	0.14		0.26	★	−0.11	
Country of residence films	−0.28	★	−0.66	★	0.37	★
Non-English, Non-European Films	0.50	★	0.20	+	0.29	★
Read a foreign book in past 12 months	0.53	★	0.80	★	−0.27	★
Omnivorous (Cuisine)	0.01		0.06	★	−0.05	★
Asian food	0.04		−0.07	★	0.11	★
Constant	7.04	★	5.12	★	1.92	★
Cox-Snell Pseudo R-Square (%)	18.5					
N			2300			

Controls for city of residence and education.
+: Significant at 0.10 level, two-tailed; ★ = Significant at .05 level, two-tailed test.

Time and cultural and consumer taste

The migration literature has shown great interest in the migrants' assimilation to the host culture. Its focus, however, has mainly been on language and values. The *Eumarr* data allow for a unique examination of the consumer dimension. One would expect that some of the contrasts between national and foreign partners in binational couples diminish over time, as the foreign partner develops an appreciation for things local. I have already shown that foreign partners like the local food as much as nationals. I have also shown that foreign partners like films from the country of residence less than do nationals and that they prefer film in original version more when they live in countries where films are traditionally shown this way than when they live in countries were films are traditionally dubbed. The *Eumarr* survey also asked respondents whether they like local versions of the different music genres examined above. For some genres, like pop, rock, folk, and singing song-writers, the local distinction makes more sense than for others, like jazz, classic, or contemporary classic. Of those four, pop and rock are the most relevant because they are popular genres and respondents may be

Taste and cultural practices **147**

able to provide more reliable answers. One can thus analyze whether foreign partners in binational couples like local music, local film, and local cuisine more the longer they have lived in the country or with their national partner. In addition to this, one can analyze whether foreign partners gradually assimilate to the preferred way of watching films in the country where they live. Table 6.14 displays the statistical coefficients for models that explore the role of time in the country and the duration of the relationship on these variables, controlling for city of residence, socio-demographic variables, and language skills. The longer foreign partners have lived in the country of residence the more they like local pop music. Also, when in the Netherlands or Belgium, with long traditions of showing film in original version, the longer foreign partners have been married or in cohabitation, the more they like to watch films this way. When in Spain or Switzerland, countries where films are usually dubbed, the longer foreign partners have been married or in cohabitation, the less they like films in original version. This is a quite elegant and convincing finding; the assimilation hypothesis predicts that taste in Belgium and the Netherlands on the one hand and in Spain and Switzerland on the other will evolve in opposite directions, which is exactly what happens. Other findings discussed above are more puzzling and raise more

TABLE 6.14 Associations between Years of Residence and Duration of Relationship on Taste for Music, Film, and Cuisine among Foreign Partners in Binational Couples, Controlling for City of Residence, Gender, Age, Education, Parents' Education, and the Number of Spoken Languages (OLS Regression Coefficients)

	Independent Variable: Years of Residence (1)		Independent Variable: Duration of Relationship (2)	
Likes pop from the Country of residence	0.01	★	−1.0E−03	
Likes rock from the Country of residence	4.0E−03		1.0E−03	
Likes folk from the Country of residence	2.0E−03		1.0E−03	
Likes singer-songwriters from Country of residence	−4.0E−03		−0.01	
Likes Film from Country of residence	1.0E−04		−0.01	+
Likes Cuisine from Country of residence	1.0E−03		−1.0E−03	
Likes film in original version (Belgian and Dutch Cities)	3.0E−03		6.0E−03	+
Likes film in original version (Spanish Cities and Zurich)	−4.0E−03		−0.02	★
N (Belgium/Netherlands + Spain/Switzerland)	(364 + 250)			

Note: Sixteen independent multiple regression models (8 rows ★ 2 columns). Cells represent the regression coefficient for the association between an independent variable (years of residence or duration of relationship) and the row dependent variable, in each case after controlling for city of residence, gender, age, education, parents' education, and the number of languages spoken.
+: Significant at 0.10 level, two-tailed; ★= Significant at .05 level, two-tailed test.

148 Taste and cultural practices

questions than provide answers. While some hint at assimilation as a function of time, others, like the one referring to films produced in the country of residence, are difficult to interpret.

In sum, this chapter shows that partners in binational couples display distinct cultural and consumer taste and practices when compared with partners in national couples. This taste can be described as more international. It also shows that since education structures taste and consumption, less educated partners in binational couples are slightly less international than are more educated ones. The chapter has explored the bridging role of being in a binational couple, that is, how being in a binational couple instead of a national couple makes it more likely that partners will get exposure to foreign consumer products and come to like them. I have shown that foreign partners like food from particular countries more when they live or are married with someone from that country. Reciprocally, national partners in binational couples like particular cuisines more when they live or are married from the same country as the cuisine under examination.

I have also found evidence for the effect of exposure on film viewing preferences. When foreign partners in binational couples live in countries where film is usually shown in the original language, they express greater preference for this form of viewing than when they live in countries where films are usually dubbed. Finally, this chapter has also addressed the theoretically relevant issue of the role of openness as a personality trait in shaping taste and cultural practices. Systematic associations between fluency in foreign languages, an indicator of openness, and the different indicators of taste, as well as the fact that fluency in foreign languages usually contributes to the explanation of the observed contrasts between partners in binational and partners in national couples, is consistent with openness playing some role in explaining both taste and the contrasts.

Notes

1 Foundational sociological works on taste and consumption: Weber (2013 [1922]), Veblen (1994 [1899]), Bourdieu (1984).
2 The list of publications in this area is very long. Some important contributions aside from Bourdieu's are DiMaggio and Useem (1978), Peterson (1992), Bryson (1997).
3 The questionnaire also included the category Adult Contemporary. Data inspection suggests, however, that respondents in Switzerland understood the category very differently from those in other countries. In Switzerland (Zurich) the percentage of respondents who reported liking this genre is much lower. This is the only country where the questionnaire did not translate the term from English into an equivalent national expression. As a result, many respondents may not have understood what it meant It is also unclear what respondents in the other countries understood from the term since the Spanish questionnaire was the only one that included selected representatives of that music (Julio Iglesias, Nana Mouskouri, Tom Jones).
4 Of course, singers and musical groups have always made versions of songs first released in other countries and languages, but the explicit and underlying reasons for this were generally not to indigenize the original ones.
5 Schwimm suggests that homogenization under globalization is more likely in areas that are not formally institutionalized (i.e. consumption), than in those that are (e.g. norms, beliefs).

References

Bauman, Zygmunt. 1991. *Modernity and Ambivalence*. Cambridge, UK: Polity Press.

Billig, Michael. 1995. *Banal Nationalism*. London, UK: Sage.

Bourdieu, Pierre. 1984. *Distinction: A Social Critique of the Judgement of Taste*. Cambridge, MA: Harvard University Press.

Bryson, Bethany. 1997. "What about the Univores? Musical Dislikes and Group-Based Identity Construction among Americans with Low Levels of Education." *Poetics* 25(2–3): 141–156.

Calvo, Manuel. 1982. "Migration et Alimentation." *Social Science Information* 21(3): 383–446.

Cross, Samantha, and Mary C. Gilly. 2014. "Consumption Compromises: Negotiation and Unification within Contemporary Families." *Journal of Business Research* 67(4): 449–456.

Darmon, Isabelle, and Alan Warde. 2016. "Senses and Sensibilities." *Food, Culture & Society* 19(4): 705–722.

DiMaggio, Paul, and Michael Useem. 1978. "Social Class and Arts Consumption: The Origins and Consequences of Class Differences in Exposure to the Arts in America." *Theory and Society* 5(2): 141–161.

Douglas, Mary. 1966. *Purity and Danger*. London, UK: Routledge and Kegan Paul.

Douglas, Mary. 1979. "Les structures du culinaire." *Communications* 31: 145–170.

Erickson, Bonnie H. 1996. "Culture, Class, and Connections." *American Journal of Sociology* 102(1): 217–251.

Fischler, Claude. 1988. "Food, Self and Identity." *Social Science Information* 27(2): 275–292.

Latour, Bruno, 2005. *Reassembling the Social: An Introduction to Actor-Network Theory*. Oxford, UK: Oxford University Press.

Lizardo, Omar. 2006. "How Cultural Tastes Shape Personal Networks." *American Sociological Review* 71(5): 778–807.

Lizardo, Omar. 2014. "Omnivorousness as the Bridging of Cultural Holes: A Measurement Strategy." *Theory and Society* 43(3–4): 395–419.

Lizardo, Omar, and Sara Skiles. 2012. "Reconceptualizing and Theorizing Omnivorousness: Genetic and Relational Mechanisms." *Sociological Theory* 30(4): 263–282.

McCrae, Robert R., and Paul T. Costa. 1997. "Conceptions and Correlates of Openness to Experience." In Robert Hogan, John A. Johnson, and Stephen R. Griggs (eds.), *Handbook of Personality Psychology*. San Diego, CA: Academic Press, pp. 825–847.

Peterson, Richard A. 1992. "Understanding Audience Segmentation: From Elite and Mass to Omnivore and Univore." *Poetics* 21(4): 243–258.

Prieur Annick, and Mike Savage. 2011. "Updating Cultural Capital Theory: A Discussion Based on Studies in Denmark and in Britain." *Poetics* 39(6): 566–580.

Roose, Henk, Koen van Eijck, and John Lievens. 2012. "Culture of Distinction or Culture of Openness? Using a Social Space Approach to Analyze the Social Structuring of Lifestyles." *Poetics* 40(6): 491–513.

Saito, Hiro. 2011. "An Actor-Network Theory of Cosmopolitanism." *Sociological Theory* 29(2): 124–149.

Savage, Mike, Gaynor Bagnall, and Brian Longurst. 2005. *Globalization and Belonging*. London, UK: Sage.

Savage, Mike, and Modesto Gayo. 2011. "Unravelling the Omnivore: A Field Analysis of Contemporary Musical Taste in the United Kingdom." *Poetics* 39(5): 337–357.

Schwimm, Thomas. 2006. "Konvergenz, Divergenz, or Hybridisierung." *Kölner Zeitschrift für Soziologie und Sozialpsychologie* 58(2): 201–232.

150 Taste and cultural practices

Veblen, Thorsten. 1994 [1899]. *The Theory of the Leisure Class.* New York: Dover Publications.

Warde, Alan. 2017. *Consumption: A Sociological Analysis.* London, UK: Palgrave MacMillan.

Warde, Alan, David Wright, and Modesto Gayo-Cal. 2007. "Understanding Cultural Omnivorousness: Or, the Myth of the Cultural Omnivore." *Cultural Sociology* 1(2): 143–164.

Weber, Max. 2013 [1922]. *Economy and Society.* Berkeley: University of California Press.

7

IDENTITIES

From marriage to Europe? Most likely, this is not the thought that inspired Monnet's grand design for European integration. And yet, sociologists interested in European integration have started to examine its impact on European identification (e.g. Mau, 2010; Kuhn, 2015; Pötzschke and Braun, 2019). This chapter shows that binational marriage and cohabitation between Europeans makes people more aware of being European. Considered together with other features that distinguish partners in these couples as cosmopolitan, this finding strengthens the case for viewing binational couples as a significant source of social transformation in Europe. Europeanness, however, is just one dimension of a complex set of geographical and geopolitical identifications that differentiate binational from national couples and that this chapter explores. These include identification with the country of nationality, identification with the country and with the city of residence, emotional attachment to the European Union, and horizontal solidarity with other Europeans. The combined study of these identifications, attachments, and solidarities, helps evaluate the limits of binational marriage's transformative potential and at the same time provides insights into the transformation potential of other forms of social transnationalism.

European identification

The reciprocal relationship between nation and state has intrigued scholars for more than 100 years. Irrespective of how one defines the 'nation' or 'demos,' the dominant assumption is that a shared feeling of belonging to a community is a pre-condition for political stability and for a state's legitimacy. Interest in European identification dates back to the 1970s when "Euro-sclerosis" became a popular term used to describe the European Community. Low participation in the first democratic election to the European Parliament, in particular, moved

152 Identities

policy-makers and advisors in Brussels to discuss strategies to instill a feeling of attachment to Europe in the population (Calligaro, 2013). Meanwhile, scholars began to reflect on support for European integration and on European identification.[1] Political discussion and research on European identification intensified again in the 1980s, as the European Community prepared itself for the great leap forward toward a more political European Union; and it has resurfaced time and again since then, whenever the European Union has faced crises of legitimacy (e.g. the French and Dutch 2005 referenda on a European Constitution) or solidarity (e.g. during the 2008-financial and economic crisis) (Etzioni, 2013; Smith, 1992).

The available evidence suggests that neither the European Union's symbolic and policy measures undertaken to produce a European *demos*—e.g. the European flag, the European anthem, the concept of European citizenship—nor the creation of both a single market and a single currency have succeeded in turning nationals into Europeans.[2] Although the post-financial crisis years have witnessed an unambiguous linear increase in the proportion of EU citizens who see themselves as both 'national and European,' almost 40% among them still identify as 'only national.' Sixty percent of 'Europeans' in a pluri-national Europe compares very poorly with the 90% of 'nationals' found in pluri-national European states like Switzerland or Spain. It is also unclear whether reported identification as European entails a focused sense of Europeanness. Self-reports may just capture diffuse "cosmopolitan" feelings or even favorable attitudes to the European Union. Finally, when one interprets answers to survey questions of identification, it is worth distinguishing between emotionally charged identifications and assertions concerning the objective validity of adscription to a particular category. In contrast with national or sub-national identifications, European identification does not come up at all in daily conversations and interaction, whereas identification with the national or sub-national units does. Qualitative research concerning the meaning that respondents attach to questions on identity has also established that what individuals generally mean when they say that they identify as Europeans is that they recognize themselves as members of that category, as when they state "My passport says that I'm European; therefore, yes, I identify myself as European" or "I was born and live in Europe; thus, I am European" (Díez Medrano, 2010).

Although European integration and the European Union's cultural policies have not yet succeeded in creating a European *demos*, this does not mean that there is no variation in the population or that individual identifications are fixed. In recent years, sociologists who are interested in the study of European identification have shifted their explanatory focus from the aggregate impact of EU institutions and policies to the impact of micro-sociological processes related to geographical mobility and transnational skills (Fligstein, 2008; Kuhn, 2015; Recchi, 2014). Binational marriage is an offshoot of geographical mobility and there is a growing literature interested in its effects on identification (Chen and Takeuchi, 2011; Dribe and Lundh, 2008; Waters and Jiménez, 2005). There are indeed good reasons to expect an association between the two. Marriage and cohabitation are arguably the most emotionally intense and interaction-rich forms of sociation. Identity must thus enter into play in the choice of partner and at the same time be influenced by this choice. The strong salience of national identification (if only because state institutions invest so much in its development and reproduction; see Hobsbawm, 1990; Weber, 1976), logically implies that it should be the object of subjective and inter-subjective negotiation, both before and during a partnership with a person of different nationality. The following quote from a Spanish woman married to a German man illustrates both the salience of the "national" and the negotiation process that goes on in binational couples:

> Being married to a German makes you see things differently. A clear example is recycling; or the issue with water: not letting the water in the kitchen run. These are examples of things that I had not understood so well and where he has helped me to become better and to change my perspective. On other issues, however, no matter what, I will never change. I imagine that it is the same in all couples. At the end of the day, you live with it, you try to deal with it as well as you can, but you do not change: 'because I like it better the way <u>we</u> do it, how <u>we</u> see it, and not the way <u>they</u> see it; or, as in our case, the way <u>he</u> sees it.'
>
> *(Interview # 1)*

Thus far, the literature has treated binational partnerships mainly from the perspective of the acculturation of foreign partners to host societies and from the perspective of the identity of the children resulting from these partnerships (Varro, 1995). Marriage to a local is viewed as a step in the migrant's acculturation process, further validated by the adoption of a hyphenated identification or by the substitution of the host country's national identification for the home country's [Acculturation Thesis] (Chen and Takeuchi, 2011; Dribe and Lundh, 2008; Waters and Jiménez, 2005). The European context adds an element of complexity to the study of identification among partners in binational couples because European integration and European citizenship have led to the emergence of European identification as a plausible alternative to hyphenation or substitution.

Since identifications are situational, one can propose that the most basic reason why partners in binational couples would identify as Europeans is that being in a binational couple increases their awareness of being European [Awareness Thesis] (see Rother and Nebe, 2009). In addition to this, partners in binational couples may identify as Europeans due to status considerations. Citizens from poorer European countries often see Europe as enjoying higher status than does their own national community. It is thus conceivable that marriage to or cohabitation with a person from another European country instill a feeling of entitlement to European status among individuals from such countries.[3] Status also plays a role

154 Identities

when foreign partners in binational couples embrace a European identification in order to disactivate negative societal reactions in the host country. Identification as European may express the foreign partner's effort to re-establish status balance when she or he is treated dismissively by the partners' close relatives and friends, an attempt to diffuse conflict with unwelcoming close relatives and friends through asserting that one shares a European identity with both them and the partner [Status Thesis].

This chapter examines whether partners in binational couples display a greater propensity to identify as Europeans. The causal mechanisms outlined above in the discussion of the relationship between being in a binational couple and identification—acculturation, awareness, status—also lend themselves to specific empirical expectations that this chapter will contrast with the survey data collected in Belgian, Dutch, Spanish, and Swiss cities. If *acculturation* is the only mechanism, national partners in binational couples should not differ from foreign partners in binational couples in how strongly they identify as Europeans. If *awareness* plays a role, one would expect European identification to be stronger in Belgian, Spanish, and Dutch cities than in Zurich since Switzerland is part of the Schengen space but is not a member of the European Union. One would also expect that partners in binational couples identify as Europeans more than do partners in national couples. Finally, if *status* plays a role, one would expect greater levels of European identification and a greater contrast between members of binational couples and members of national couples in countries where Europe is a salient and positively valued category than in countries where Europe is a less salient and less positively valued category. The literature shows that frames about Europe and European integration are uniquely positive in Spain, so it is in the Spanish cities where one should find a stronger European identification and the biggest contrast between partners in national couples and partners in binational couples. A status perspective also leads to the expectation that foreign partners from poorer countries will express higher levels of European identification than do foreign partners from richer ones (Díez Medrano, 2003).

Measuring identification is not an easy task, mainly because it is an ambiguous concept (e.g. it captures both social classifications—who am I from society's standpoint—and subjective agreement with these classifications—who am I from my own standpoint). Another problem that researchers confront when measuring identifications is that these are situational. They become more salient and more intense in some contexts than others. These complexities imply that answers to questions of identification are extremely sensitive to wording (Citrin and Sides, 2004). This study measures geo-political identification through a battery of statements with which respondents had to express their level of agreement or disagreement on a 1 to 10 scale. The standard wording of these statements is "I feel [identification]"and they apply to the city, the region, the home country, the country of residence, Europe, and the world at large, in this order. On face value, the sentences measure subjective identifications, but one cannot rule out that some respondents read it as "I am [identification]" and thus answer primarily in terms of social categories. Therefore, one cannot distinguish respondents who evaluate the truth of the statement as far as their objective membership in a political/administrative unit and other respondents who provide information about the strength of their feelings of identification. A second problem one must deal with is that many respondents use the value for their earlier answers as anchors for their subsequent answers (see Bollen and Díez Medrano, 1998). Last but not least, there is also a problem of validity, for it is conceivable that when asked about their feelings as European, many respondents treat the concept "European" as short for any form of transnational or supranational form of identification.

In general, respondents in both national and binational marriages agree strongly with the statement "I feel European." The average value lies between 7 and 8 among both types of respondents, and in all four countries' cities, which suggests that 30- to 46-year-old married individuals in these cities generally recognize themselves as European. A comparison between binational and national couples also reveals that partners in the former display higher average values than do those in the latter. The average contrast between the two types of couples and across levels of education is less than 1% point in all countries. This difference represents one-tenth of the identification scale's full range from 1 to 10 but 20% of the typical empirical range (i.e. the inter-quartile range) for national respondents. Meanwhile, cross-city comparisons show that the average values for European identification are consistently lower in Zurich than in the Spanish, Belgian, and Dutch cities. This finding, which is replicated in the more complex statistical models below, is consistent with the *awareness* hypothesis outlined above, for Europe is less politically and socially salient and valued in Switzerland than in European Union countries (Table 7.1).

TABLE 7.1 Average European Identification, by Type of Couple, Education, and Country

		Spanish Cities	Belgian Cities	Dutch Cities	Swiss City
	National	7.41	6.54	5.28	6.70
		(145)	(28)	(32)	(209)
No university education	Binational	7.96	7.72	7.06	6.91
	(national partner)	(68)	(58)	(53)	(86)
	Binational	8.77	7.32	7.48	7.29
	(foreign partner)	(57)	(34)	(64)	(90)
	National	7.48	6.92	7.13	7.05
		(166)	(52)	(115)	(258)
University education	Binational	7.97	7.84	8.05	7.40
	(national partner)	(73)	(128)	(220)	(139)
	Binational	8.86	8.37	8.36	8.02
	(foreign partner)	(78)	(146)	(222)	(220)

( ) Number of respondents.

156 Identities

An empirical association between being in a binational couple and European identification does not necessarily mean that there is a causal nexus between the two. Other individual characteristics that are associated with whom respondents marry and with their degree of European identification can underlie this association. The biographies of many of those who get together with or marry a European are already quite transnational, which in turn has made their outlook more cosmopolitan. At the same time, people's degree of European identification can itself explain the choice of partner, with more "European" or cosmopolitan respondents more likely to enter a relationship with a European from another country if the opportunity arises. Here is, for instance, how a British woman married to a Spaniard reflects on her decision to marry him:

> There is a before and after my Canada trip [end of high school] in how I saw the world, really. I somewhat thought or imagined that I would not be with somebody English, but with someone from somewhere else, with a different perspective. So, I always somehow imagined that there would be more than one language at home, which is odd. I have not tried that hard to make it this way, but that's what has happened. But I don't know, maybe you just are attracted to these persons because of the way you see things.
>
> *(Interview # 5)*

The following paragraphs examine the association between being in a binational couple and identification as European so as to provide a plausible interpretation of the causal processes at work. Through multiple regression analysis, I estimate the contrasts in European identification between partners in binational and national couples, while I sequentially control for theoretically relevant antecedent, correlated, or intervening variables. These variables measure the individuals' socio-economic background, their current socio-economic status, and their transnational background, skills, and experiences. This analysis confirms that European identification is highest among foreign partners in binational couples and lowest among national partners in national couples. In fact, the contrasts hold even after controlling for all the sets of variables listed above (see Table 7.2). The average level of European identification among foreign partners lies around 1.7 points above that for national partners in national couples and the average level of European identification among national partners in binational couples lies around 0.7 points above that for national partners in national couples (columns 1 to 6). I found no statistically significant contrasts between average European identification among foreign partners from poorer countries and European identification among foreign partners from richer countries, which is inconsistent with the *status* hypothesis.

The findings above are more congruent with the *awareness* hypothesis, with the possibility that being in a binational couple makes individuals more conscious of the fact that they are European, at least in a geographical sense. This interpretation is all the more plausible since national partners in binational couples appear to identify more as European, the longer they have been together with their partner

TABLE 7.2 Association between being in a Binational Couple and European Identification, Controlling for City of Residence and for Socio-demographic and Transnational Background and Experience Variables (OLS)

	(1)		(2)		(3)		(4)		(5)		(6)		(7)	
-Foreign in a binational couple	1.66	★	1.72	★	1.69	★	1.71	★	1.72	★	1.69	★	1.49	★
-National in binational couple	0.75	★	0.74	★	0.75	★	0.76	★	0.69	★	0.64	★	0.05	
-Age			0.04	★	0.05	★	0.05	★	0.05	★	0.05	★	0.04	★
-Gender			0.10		0.12		0.14		0.08		0.10		0.10	
-Binational parents			0.03		0.06		0.06		0.02		0.04		0.04	
-Average parental education			0.08	★	5.0E-03		-4.4E-05		-0.01		-0.03		-0.04	
-Number of countries visited before 17			0.04	★	0.03	+	0.03	+	0.02		0.02		0.01	
-Education	0.25	★			0.26	★	0.22	★	0.18	★	0.11	★	0.10	+
-Unemployed							0.04		0.01		0.05		0.05	
-Housework							0.18		0.16		0.11		0.08	
-Student							0.17		0.15		0.08		0.12	
-Other							0.52		0.41		0.35		0.32	
-High status occupation (managers, professionals, technical professions)							0.32	+	0.29		0.28		0.25	
-Low status service occupations							-0.06		-0.08		-0.09		-0.09	
-Income (PPS)							0.00		-1.2E-05		0.00		-1.0E-03	
-Number of languages known before meeting partner									0.36	★	0.34	★	0.32	★
-Duration of the relationship											-1.0E-03		-0.01	

(*Continued*)

	(1)		(2)		(3)	(4)	(5)	(6)		(7)	
-Number of countries visited between 17 and living with partner											0.03	⋆
-Partner's education									0.17	⋆	0.17	⋆
-Number of countries visited since with partner											2.0E-03	
-Duration of the relationship⋆ foreign in binational couple											0.01	
-Duration of the relationship ⋆ National in binational couple											0.06	+
-Constant	1.61	⋆	1.15	+	−0.53	−0.49	−1.07	−1.69	⋆	−1.24	
R-square %	14.6		13.9		15.2	15.5	16.7	17.3		17.8	
N							2115				

Controls for city of residence and for identification with city of residence, identification with region, and identification with the country of nationality. +. Statistically significant at 0.10 level, two-tailed; ⋆. Statistically significant at 0.05 level, two-tailed.

(see positive coefficient for interaction term between duration of relationship and being a national in a binational couple at bottom row of column 7: b = 0.06+).[4]

Education and the number of languages individuals spoke before meeting their partner are also related to European identification. More educated people and polyglots report a higher level of European identification than do less educated people and monolinguals. Although the associations between these two variables and European identification are among the most consistent ones in the literature, few studies have tested for the mechanisms that mediate them. The few that have, however, suggest that cognitive processes, such as greater familiarity with and openness to other cultures and, in the case of Europe, greater awareness of being part of Europe, are the main mechanisms at work, as Inglehart already anticipated five decades ago (Inglehart, 1970; see also, Díez Medrano, 2018; Verhaegen et al., 2013). Knowing more languages before meeting one's partner in fact explains part of the education effect and also part of the contrast between nationals in binational couples and nationals in national couples. When one controls for the number of languages known before meeting one's partner (column 5), the coefficient for nationals in binational couples becomes about 9% smaller (from 0.76 to 0.69). This is most likely because knowing several languages facilitates communication with foreigners, which increases the probability of entering a binational couple. The reduction in the size of this coefficient may also capture some antecedent impact of European identification on the probability of entering a binational couple.

The partner's level of education is another variable that both explains European identification and at the same time helps account for the relationship between type of couple and identification as European. Holding the respondents' level of education constant, the more educated the respondents' partners are, the stronger the respondents' European identification (column 6: b = 0.17*). This finding reflects the mutual impact that partners in a couple exert on each other's sense of who they are. Indeed, since more educated individuals feel more European and are likely to communicate it to their partners, one would expect that the more educated one's partner is, the more likely it is that he or she will become more aware of being European. One of our respondents, a British woman living near Barcelona, speaks to this issue, as she discusses the influence she has had on her husband:

> He is from X, both his parents are from here, and he has not had the travel experience I have had. But now he's working a lot abroad and getting this experience. Seeing all the experiences I've had makes him very jealous, because he wished he had had the same opportunities. He just didn't have them. And I think that he has the vision now of wanting, you know, a multicultural life and international view. I think that this is something I possibly instilled in him. He wants to break away a bit from this fairly traditional model that there is here.
>
> *(Interview # 5)*

160 Identities

The combined effect of educational homogamy and higher average levels of education among partners in binational couples than among partners in national ones partly explains why the former identify more strongly as Europeans. Thus, when one controls for the partner's level of education, the coefficients for the contrast declines from 0.69 to 0.64 for nationals in binational couples and from 1.73 to 1.70 for foreign partners in binational couples (columns 5 and 6).

The statistical results displayed in Table 7.2 reveal that opportunities and challenges that the European market entails for people with different occupational skills and travel to foreign countries also explain how strongly people identify as Europeans. Column four shows that after controlling for education and income, people in managerial, professional, and technical occupations express a stronger European identification than do other respondents. Meanwhile, column seven shows that the higher the number of states that respondents visited between the seventeenth birthday and the year in which they met their current partner, the stronger their European identification (column 7). The observation of an effect of transnational travel is consistent with previous research on European identification. The fact that travel during adolescence or later matters more than travel frequency in early childhood is consistent with the central roles that adolescence and early adulthood play in the development of people's more deeply anchored values and identifications (Inglehart, 1977). We still remain in the dark, however, as to the mechanisms that mediate the relationship between travel and European identification. The dominant hypothesis, grounded in Deutsch's communication perspective, is that interaction with others and friendships abroad are the relevant ones (Fligstein, 2008; Kuhn, 2015; Recchi, 2014). No study has tested it, however, and one cannot rule out that cognitive processes unrelated to inter-personal interaction play as important or a more important role. The fact that travel frequency is associated with European identification even after controlling for the number of languages respondents spoke before meeting their current partner supports this view. Ties abroad, greater openness, familiarity with other European countries, awareness of being European based on the situational experience of being abroad, thus probably underlie the association between the number of countries people visited between the seventeenth birthday and the time when they met their partner and European identification.

Binational couples thus contribute to the emergence of a community of Europeans, mainly because the partners to these couples become more conscious of being part of a geographic, political, social, or cultural European space. This finding highlights the situational character of identifications. Relative to the amount of empirical variability in the indicator used to measure European identification the effect is not negligible. Of all the variables that I include in the statistical models above, only the number of languages that people speak, the partner's level of education, and travel between the seventeenth birthday and meeting the current partner have as big an effect on European identification among nationals. Being in a binational couple activates a pre-existing category of identification; it increases the partners' awareness that they are European. The trigger of this greater awareness is the other partner's European nationality itself.

I checked for the robustness of the findings above with another item on European identification included in the *Eumarr's* survey questionnaire. The item asked respondents how they would like to be seen primarily if they were in the United States or Japan. Non-European settings were chosen with the situational character of identifications in mind, in order to create a favorable scenario for the mobilization of a European identification. The choice options included the city of residence, the region of residence, the country of residence, the country of birth, Europe, or other location specified by respondents. The percentages in Table 7.3 show that less than one in four respondents (less than one in five if one focuses on nationals only) choose Europe as a category. They also show that the probability of choosing Europe as the category of identification is greater among respondents in binational couples than among those in national couples.

Multiple regression models that control for potential confounding factors confirm the finding above. In particular, they show that, holding other factors constant, the probability of choosing European over other identifications is 20% points higher among foreign partners in binational couples than among national partners in national couples and about 6% points higher among national partners in binational couples than among national partners in national couples (see Table 7.4). Also, just as in Table 7.2, the duration of the relationship (for nationals in binational couples), knowledge of foreign languages, the partner's level of education, and travel emerge as relevant factors in the explanation of European identification and in accounting for the contrasts between partners in binational and partners in national couples (columns 5, 6, and 8).

TABLE 7.3 Choice of European over Other Identifications, by Type of Couple, Education, and Country (%)

		Spanish Cities	Belgian Cities	Dutch Cities	Swiss City
	National	12	7	9	10
		(152)	(29)	(32)	(221)
No university education	Binational	17	15	20	18
	(national partner)	(70)	(61)	(54)	(89)
	Binational	44	23	25	32
	(foreign partner)	(59)	(35)	(64)	(94)
	National	21	8	15	14
		(166)	(52)	(115)	(264)
University education	Binational	24	16	25	16
	(national partner)	(75)	(127)	(217)	(140)
	Binational	41	35	38	34
	(foreign partner)	(78)	(146)	(224)	(224)

( ) Number of respondents.

TABLE 7.4 Association between being in a Binational Couple and Choice of European Identification, Controlling for City of Residence and for Socio-demographic and Transnational Background and Experience Variables (OLS)

	(1)		(2)		(3)		(4)		(5)		(6)		(7)		(8)	
-Foreign in a binational couple	020	★	0.21	★	0.20	★	0.20	★	0.20	★	0.20	★	0.18	★	0.18	★
-National in binational couple	0.06	★	0.06	★	0.06	★	0.06	+	0.05	★	0.04	+	−0.03		−0.02	
-Age			0.01	★	0.01	★	0.01	★	0.01	★	0.01	★	0.01		0.01	★
-Gender			0.03	+	0.03	+	0.03	+	0.02		0.03		0.03		0.03	
-Binational parents			−0.02		−0.02		−0.02		−0.02		−0.02		−0.02		−0.02	
-Average parental education			0.02	★	0.01	+	0.01	+	0.01	+	8.0E-03		8.0E-03		8.0E-.03	
-Number of countries visited before 17			5.0E-03		4.0E-03		5.0E-03	+	4.0E-03		4.0E-03		4.0E-03		3.0E-03	
-Education	0.02	★			0.02	★	0.02	★	0.02	★	0.01		0.01		0.01	
-Unemployed							−0.02		−0.02		−0.02		−0.02		−0.01	
-Housework							5.0E-03		2.0E-03		1.0E-03		−2.0E-03		2.0E.03	
-Student							−0.06		−0.06		−0.07		−0.07		−0.06	
-Other							−0.10	+	−0.11	+	−0.11	★	−0.12	★	−0.11	★
-High status occupation (managers, professionals, technical professions)							−0.04		−0.04		−0.05		−0.05		−0.05	
-Low status service occupations							−0.07	+	−0.07	+	−0.07	+	−0.07	+	−0.07	+
-Income (PPS)							0.00		−1.0E-03		−1.0E-03		−1.0E-03		−1.0E-03	

	1	2	3	4	5	6	7	8
-Number of languages known before meeting partner					0.03 ★	0.03 ★	0.03 ★	0.03 ★
-Duration of the relationship						-2.0E-03	-4.0E-03	-5.0E-03 ★
-Number of countries visited between 17 and living with partner								-1.0E-03
-Partner's education						0.01 +	0.01 +	0.01
-Number of countries visited since with partner								6.0E-03 ★
-Duration of the relationship★ Foreign in binational couple							2.0E-03	1.0E-03
-Duration of the relationship ★ National in binational couple							7.0E-03 +	6.0E-03
-Constant	-0.03	-0.41	-0.51 ★	-0.49 ★	-0.54 ★	-0.60 ★	-0.57 ★	-0.57 ★
R-square %	5.4	6.4	6.7	7.1	7.6	7.7	7.9	8.2
N					2115			

Controls for city of residence. +: Significant at 0.10 level, two-tailed; ★: Significant at 0.05 level, two-tailed.

164 Identities

Unlike Table 7.2, Table 7.4 shows that the number of countries visited since individuals began their relationship with their partner matters more than the number of countries visited in previous stages of the life cycle. The inclusion of this variable in the model cancels the positive effect of the duration of the relationship on the probability that nationals in binational couples choose Europe and the effect of the respondent partner's level of education (compare coefficients in columns 7 and 8). One possible interpretation for the findings above is that the duration of the relationship and the partner's level of education impact on people's choice by increasing opportunities to travel abroad, which in turn increases the salience of Europe as a category of identification.

Solidarity in binational and national couples

One can evaluate the depth of European identification, by examining how it translates at the practical level. In recent years, the literature on public opinion and European integration has turned its attention to the topic of European solidarity. This new focus of attention stemmed from the acrimonious debate that ensued from the debt crisis of 2010–2011 regarding whether the European Union, and very especially its richer member states, should help those states most deeply affected by the crisis.[5] Scholars have addressed three main questions: how prevalent is European solidarity? What is the scope of European solidarity? What are the determinants of European solidarity? On a practical level, horizontal fiscal solidarity and solidarity with countries overburdened by the refugee crisis has proven to be limited and conditional. Empirical studies, however, suggest that trans-European solidarity is highly prevalent and wide in scope (Díez Medrano et al., 2019; Gerhards et al., 2019). There may not be contradiction here. Gerhards and co-authors, for instance, also find that citizens still attach priority to the needs of co-nationals over those of other European nationals.

Binational couples provide a context where both partners get unique access to information about another country. No matter the selective and biased character of this information, it is reasonable to expect that national partners to such couples have more information on their European foreign partners' countries than do national partners to national couples. In general, one would also expect that, because their partner comes from elsewhere in Europe, national partners in binational couples would express greater solidarity to other European countries and people than do partners in national ones.

The *Eumarr* study measured solidarity through two items in the survey questionnaire. The wording of the items was as follows:

- The government in this country proposes a special contribution to assist another region in your country that has experienced a natural catastrophe. Please indicate how much of your yearly earnings you would be prepared to donate to help assist this region economically.

– The government in this country proposes a special contribution to assist another European country that has experienced a natural catastrophe. Please indicate how much of your yearly earnings you would be prepared to donate to help assist economically this country.

Respondents were asked to report their answer on a 10-point scale, where 1 means "None," and 10 means "A great deal." Needless to say, the first item has a completely different meaning for national and for foreign partners. For the latter, the national region is a foreign region as well. Although residence in the country may lead them to favor regions in the country of residence over other European countries, the fact that they are nationals from another European country may lead them to favor foreign European countries over regions in their country of residence other than the one in which they live.

Tables 7.5 and 7.6 show that the averages lie between 2 and 4, across different combinations of country, education, and type of married or cohabiting couple. This finding suggests that European identification, as measured in previous sections, is not particularly deep. It is more an expression of awareness than an expression of feelings of oneness with other Europeans. Except in Zurich, solidarity is generally higher among partners in binational couples than among partners in national ones. Also, solidarity is always higher among university educated respondents than among less educated ones. Then, a comparison between Tables 7.5 and 7.6 reveals that solidarity with the country of residence is higher than solidarity with another European country, although among highly educated foreign respondents the contrast is slightly less sharp. Finally, Table 7.6 shows that solidarity with another European country is slightly higher in the Spanish cities than in the other cities. In general, the contrasts across groups are not impressive.

TABLE 7.5 Average Levels of Solidarity with Country of Residence Region by Type of Couple, Education, and Country

		Spanish Cities	Belgian Cities	Dutch Cities	Swiss City
	National	3.58	2.60	2.62	4.01
		(120)	(30)	(29)	(200)
No university education	Binational	4.00	2.72	3.65	3.32
	(national partner)	(55)	(53)	(40)	(72)
	Binational	3.20	3.21	3.31	3.29
	(foreign partner)	(43)	(29)	(37)	(67)
	National	3.83	3.17	3.62	4.01
		(149)	(41)	(103)	(234)
University education	Binational	4.07	3.40	3.80	3.73
	(national partner)	(60)	(118)	(187)	(132)
	Binational	3.72	3.72	3.75	3.40
	(foreign partner)	(64)	(138)	(177)	(191)

( ) Number of respondents.

166 Identities

TABLE 7.6 Average Levels of Solidarity with European Region, by Type of Couple, Education, and Country

		Spanish Cities	Belgian Cities	Dutch Cities	Swiss City
	National	2.96	1.58	2.17	2.89
		(120)	(30)	(29)	(200)
No university education	Binational	3.62	2.13	3.10	2.46
	(national partner)	(55)	(53)	(40)	(72)
	Binational	2.91	2.72	2.84	2.63
	(foreign partner)	(43)	(29)	(37)	(67)
	National	3.46	2.50	2.96	3.03
		(149)	(41)	(103)	(234)
University education	Binational	3.51	2.91	3.32	2.89
	(national partner)	(60)	(118)	(187)	(132)
	Binational	3.30	3.25	3.25	3.16
	(foreign partner)	(64)	(138)	(177)	(191)

( ) Number of respondents.

Multiple regression analysis confirms the impression conveyed by the multivariate contingency tables. For our purposes, the most important finding is that being in a national or a binational couple is not associated with the degree of solidarity with other European countries (columns 5 and 6 in Table 7.7). Partners in binational couples express a stronger European identification than do partners in national ones, but this reflects greater situated awareness than genuine greater feeling of membership in a post-national community formed by all Europeans. Table 7.7 also shows that foreign partners express less solidarity with regions in the country of residence than do nationals, but this is to be expected (Columns 1 and 2). Another relevant finding is that theoretically relevant variables hardly contribute to the explanation of solidarity as measured in this survey, although the associations conform to expectations. Not shown here for space limitations is the observation that European solidarity is stronger among residents in the Spanish cities than among residents of the other cities, before and after the statistical models control for potentially confounding variables. This is consistent with the expectation that expressions of solidarity should be greater in countries that are more likely to need foreign assistance than in those that, because of their high level of development, do not need foreign assistance to cope with natural disaster (Díez Medrano et al., 2019). Spain being the poorest of the countries in the study, the finding that Madrid and Barcelona residents express more solidarity than do residents of other cities is consistent with the literature.

Table 7.7 also reveals that education correlates with the two solidarity items (columns 1 and 5) and more so with solidarity with other European countries. Then, both European identification and cosmopolitan identification as a citizen of the world are also associated with greater solidarity with other

TABLE 7.7 Association between being in a Binational Couple and Regional and European Solidarity, Controlling for City of Residence, and for Socio-demographic and Transnational Background and Experience Variables (OLS)

	Solidarity with Region in CoR (1)	Solidarity with Region in CoR (2)	Solidarity with Region in CoR (National) (3)	Solidarity with Region in CoR (Foreign) (4)	Solidarity with European Country (5)	Solidarity with European Country (6)	Solidarity with European Country (National) (7)	Solidarity with European Country (Foreign) (8)
-Foreign in a binational couple	−0.30 ★	−0.34 ★	·		0.08	−0.04		
-National in binational couple	−0.15	−0.22	−0.14		−0.03	−0.17	−0.16	
-Age		−0.01	−0.01	−0.01		0.01	0.03	−2.0E-03
-Gender		0.06	0.15	−0.15		0.14	0.16	0.10
-Binational parents		0.06	0.27	−0.33		−0.01	0.07	−0.17
-Average parental education		0.03	0.04	0.04		0.07 ★	0.09 ★	0.06
-Number of countries visited before 17		−4.0E-03	0.01	−0.03		7.0E-03	0.03	−0.02
-Education	0.10 ★	0.02	−0.05	0.18 +	0.16 ★	0.06	0.00	0.18 ★
-Unemployed		−0.04	−0.14	0.02		−0.30	−0.41	−0.15
-Housework		−0.01	−0.44	0.60		−0.03	−0.27	0.28
-Student		−0.26	−0.76	1.79		0.20	−0.18	2.03 +
-Other		−0.33	−0.53	0.11		−0.21	−0.20	0.27
-High status occupation (managers, professionals, technical professions)		−0.12	−0.20	0.06		−0.11	−0.19	−0.01

(Continued)

	Solidarity with Region in CoR	Solidarity with Region in CoR	Solidarity with Region in CoR (National)	Solidarity with Region in CoR (Foreign)	Solidarity with European Country	Solidarity with European Country	Solidarity with European Country (National)	Solidarity with European Country (Foreign)
	(1)	(2)	(3)	(4)	(5)	(6)	(7)	(8)
-Low status service occupations		0.02	−0.24	0.43		−0.06	−0.29	0.28
-Income (PPS)		5.0E-03 +	4.0E-03	6.0E-03		−2.0E-03	−4.0E-03	2.0E-03
-Number of languages known before meeting partner		−2.0E-03	−0.08	0.18 +		0.01	−0.01	0.11
-Duration of relationship		6.0E-03	−5.0E-03	0.04		−4.0E-03	−0.02	0.03
-Number of countries visited between 17 and living with partner		0.02 +	0.01	0.05 ★		7.0E-03	−0.01	0.04 ★
-Partner's education		0.01	0.05	−0.03		0.06	0.08 +	0.02
-Number of countries visited since with partner		0.01	0.03 +	−0.03		9.0E.03	0.02	−0.03
-European identification		0.02	0.00	0.06		0.06 ★	0.05 +	0.09 +
-Identification as citizen of the world		0.04 +	0.03	0.05		0.06 ★	0.05 ★	0.07 ★
-Agrees that non-European should adapt better		−0.12 ★	−0.20 ★	0.10		−0.26 ★	−0.36 ★	−0.03
-Constant	3.08 ★	3.21 ★	4.22 ★	−0.07	1.72 ★	1.06	1.45 +	−0.68
R-square %	1.2	2.6	3.7	8.5	2.4	6.9	8.6	8.7
N					1920			

Controls for city of residence. +: Significant at 0.10 level, two-tailed; ★: Significant at 0.05 level, two-tailed.

European countries (columns 6, 7, and 8), whether one analyzes national and foreign partners as part of the same statistical model (column 6), or separately. No study that I know of has established whether the relationship is causal or simply reflects that people have internalized a particular framing of what it means to be European. Since the wording of the item on solidarity with the region in the country of residence does not invoke Europe, however, the fact that the statistical coefficients obtained among foreign partners for the item on solidarity with the national region and solidarity with another European country are virtually identical (columns 4 and 8), whereas they differ significantly for national partners (columns 3 and 7), can be read as mild support for a causal interpretation.

One caveat with the *Eumarr* questionnaire is that it did not include items on people's left–right orientations, which as some publications show, is related to solidarity. To capture this effect, the statistical models include an item that measures attitudes to non-European immigrants instead. It is based on a four-point disagreement-agreement scale that measures answers to the following statement:

> *Non-Europeans* who live in [Country of Residence] should adapt their way of life more closely to the [National] way of life.

Arguably, and based on the literature on attitudes to migrants, the item should capture both tolerance of cultural diversity and left–right orientations (but only among national partners, since among foreign partners the fact that they themselves are migrants should take precedence over their left–right orientations when they answer the question). Columns 3, 4, 7, and 8 show that empirical associations are consistent with expectations. The association between the item and both national and European solidarity obtains only for nationals. This interaction also explains why the associations between education and solidarity disappear among national partners but remain strong among foreign partners after controlling for attitudes to the migrants' cultural assimilation.

Affective support for the European Union and binational and national couples

Since the early days of European integration, scholars have been interested in describing and explaining public opinion on European integration and the European Union. As European integration has gained in scope and depth, it has also become more politicized and controversial, which has in turn increased the relevance of this research (for a synthesis, see Hooghe and Marks, 2009). Over the years, researchers have proposed myriad explanations, some of them emphasizing the role of rational economic calculus, other emphasizing cognition and affect, some focused on the role of individual characteristics, others focused on the regional or national context. Economic interest, political views, and cues offered by political parties; interest in and information about European integration;

170 Identities

identification, both European and national; and trans-border activity are the individual variables that have received most attention in the literature.[6]

Intuitively, one would think that if partners in binational couples are more aware of their European identity than are partners in national couples, then they would also be more emotionally attached to the European Union. This expectation rests on evidence of a positive correlation between identification as European and support for European integration. Members of binational couples perhaps appreciate that the removal of legal requirements to work across the European Union country and the lifting of barriers for transnational movement is what made it possible for them to meet and stay together.

The expectation above is confirmed by the data for the seven cities in this study. When asked whether they would feel sorry, indifferent, or relieved if the European Union were to be dissolved, a vast majority of respondents say that they would feel sorry. Also, in all countries but the Netherlands, the percentage of those who say that they would feel sorry is greater among members of binational couples than among members of national ones (See Table 7.8)

The results above are replicated when one examines the relationship between type of couple and emotional attachment to the European Union, this time controlling for potentially confounding variables (see Table 7.9). The probability of saying that one would regret the dissolution of the European Union is a few percentage points higher among partners in binational couples than among partners in national ones (columns 1 to 7). Also, the log-odds of saying that one would regret the European dissolution instead of being relieved by it are greater for national partners in binational couples than for national partners in national ones (column 8). Although one can assume that awareness of being European and

TABLE 7.8 Respondents Who "Would be Very Sorry" if the European Union were to Dissolve, by Type of Couple, Education, and Country (%)

		Spanish Cities	*Belgian Cities*	*Dutch Cities*	*Swiss City*
	National	55	38	48	57
		(120)	(26)	(21)	(170)
No university education	Binational	67	68	57	55
	(national partner)	(54)	(50)	(37)	(62)
	Binational	58	82	64	58
	(foreign partner)	(45)	(33)	(50)	(72)
	National	73	79	88	79
		(123)	(47)	(96)	(228)
University education	Binational	83	90	88	85
	(national partner)	(59)	(116)	(193)	(123)
	Binational	84	89	88	88
	(foreign partner)	(68)	(158)	(195)	(199)

() Number of respondents.

TABLE 7.9 Association between being in a Binational Couple and Anticipation of Regret if the European Union were Dissolved, Controlling for City of Residence and for Socio-demographic and Transnational Background and Experience Variables (OLS)

	(1)	(2)	(3)	(4)	(5)	(6)	(7)	(8) Regret vs. Relief
-Foreign in a binational couple	0.07 ★	0.07 ★	0.07 ★	0.07 ★	0.07 ★	0.08 ★	0.08 ★	0.38
-National in binational couple	0.06 ★	0.05 ★	0.05 ★	0.04 +	0.04 +	0.05 ★	0.05 ★	0.52 ★
-Age		6.0E-03 ★	6.0E-03 ★	6.0E-03 ★	6.0E-03 ★	3.0E-03	2.0E-03	−8.0E-03
-Gender		−3.0E-03	9.0E-03	4.0E-03	7.0E-03	3.0E-03	4.0E-03	−0.06
-Binational parents		6.0E-03	3.0E-03	2.0E-03	−3.0E-03	−3.0E-03	−3.0E-03	−0.07
-Average parental education		0.01 ★	0.01 ★	0.01 ★	0.01 ★	0.01 +	0.01 +	0.18 ★
-Number of countries visited before 17		8.0E-03 ★	8.0E-03 ★	7.0E-03 ★	7.0E-03 ★	7.0E-03 +	5.0E-03 +	0.05
-Education	0.08 ★	0.07 ★	0.07 ★	0.06 ★	0.07 ★	0.06 ★	0.06 ★	0.37 ★
-Unemployed			0.07	0.07	0.08	0.09	0.08	−0.23
-Housework			−0.05	−0.05	−0.04	−0.05	−0.04	0.03
-Student			0.15 +	0.15 +	0.15 +	0.16 +	0.16 +	1.38
-Other			0.02	0.02	0.03	0.02	0.01	0.83
-High status occupation (managers, professionals, technical professions)			0.04	0.04	0.04	0.04	0.04	0.39

(Continued)

	(1)	(2)	(3)	(4)	(5)	(6)	(7)	(8) Regret vs. Relief
-Low status service occupations			−4.0E-03	−4.0E-03	−8.0E-03	−5.0E-03	−4.0E-03	−0.13
-Income (PPS)			0.00	0.00	0.00	0.00	0.00	−4.0E-03
-Works for multinational					0.04 +	0.04 +	0.04 +	0.61 ★
-Number of languages known before meeting partner				0.02 ★	0.02 ★	0.03 ★	0.02 ★	0.08
-Duration of the relationship						6.0E-03 ★	7.0E-03 ★	0.06 ★
-Partner's education						0.02 ★	0.02 ★	−0.02
-Number of countries visited between 17 and living with partner							5.0E-03 ★	0.01
-Constant	0.11 ★	−0.18 +	−0.18 +	−0.22 ★	−0.22 ★	−0.23 ★	−0.19 +	9.46 ★
R-square %	10.3	11.4	12.0	12.2	12.4	12.9	13.2	14.8
N					2030			

Note: Last model represents logit coefficients based on a multinomial logit model. R-square for that model is the Cox-Snell's Pseudo R-square.
Controls for city of residence. +: Significant at 0.10 level, two-tailed; ★: Significant at 0.05 level, two-tailed.

interest both play a role in the explanation of this contrast, neither the research design nor the information that the *Eumarr* survey collected allow to disentangle the two. I could show that if one controls for European identification, as some authors do when studying attitudes to the European Union, the contrast between national partners in binational couples and national partners in national couples becomes smaller and is no longer statistically significant, which would suggest that European identification is the main mechanism at play. But this analytical approach is questionable. The European Union is a much more salient object than is European identification. Attitudes to the European Union are as likely to influence European identification as is European identification to influence attitudes to the European Union. One should also be mindful that, for all we know from quantitative and qualitative studies, indicators of European identification measure awareness more than emotional attachment. Finally, the contrast between partners in binational couples and partners in national ones does not change at all when one controls for many potentially confounding variables that presumably capture both identification and interest. Therefore, one reasonable and conservative interpretation of the statistical findings is that partners in a binational couple simply develop a mix of awareness of and goodwill toward the European Union, based on the realization that were it not for the freedom of movement in the Schengen space, meeting and organizing their lives together would have been more complicated.

Whatever the meaning of the association between being in a binational couple and attitudes to the European Union, its magnitude pales by comparison with the one involving education. Just a two-unit difference in people's level of education translates into circa 12% points increase in the probability of saying that one would regret the dissolution of the European Union. Moreover, it is not only a person's education that is associated to attitudes to the European Union. The parents' and the partner's level of education also correlate with these attitudes and being a student is associated with a 15% points greater probability of saying that one would regret the dissolution of the European Union. We know very little about the mechanisms that mediate between education and attitudes to the European Union, one of the strongest and most robust associations in the literature. The statistical models in Table 7.9 suggest, however, that expected benefits from membership in the European Union, as some have highlighted in the past (Fligstein, 2008; Gabel, 1998), are not as relevant to the interpretation. This is because the education effect holds even after controlling for socio-economic indicators like employment status, occupational status, and income, and for indicators of transnational experiences and skills.

No other individual feature correlates as much with attitudes to the European Union as does a person's level of education. Nonetheless, smaller empirical associations obtain as well, of approximately the same order of magnitude as the association between being in a binational couple and attitudes to the European Union. For instance, the longer people have been together with their current partner, the more they say that they would regret the dissolution of the

174 Identities

European Union. This applies both to partners in binational couples and to partners in national ones. Also, people who work for a multinational are more likely to say that they would regret the dissolution of the European Union than do people who do not work for a multinational. Finally, the more languages people speak and the more they travelled in their childhood and youth, the more likely they are to say that they would regret the dissolution of the European Union (columns 4 to 7). I could show that the associations involving work for a multinational, languages, and travel actually disappear when one controls for European identification. I interpret this as meaning that greater awareness of the European Union, combined with appreciation of the opportunities it provides for travel and exchange across borders, underlies this, but a different research design and more information would be needed to substantiate the validity of this interpretation.

National identity in binational and national couples

While centered on European identification, this chapter examines related dimensions of a person's identity. One of these is identification with one's country of nationality. Transnational practices and experiences may not as much contribute to the development of supranational identifications as reduce the salience that national and sub-national identifications have for individuals (Díez Medrano, 2011; Favell, 2008). For instance, playing down national and sub-national identifications may be an adaptive reaction by partners in binational couples to defuse the conflict potential inherent to them.

The section on European identification has shown that when situated in places outside Europe, the odds that a European citizen will prime his or her European identification over his or her national or subnational identifications are greater if in a binational couple than if in a national one. We also know from the statistical analysis above that this follows in part from increased awareness of one's European identity. Does it also result from less intense feelings of national belonging? Empirical evidence suggests that it does not. Nationals in binational couples do not differ from nationals in national couples, and foreign nationals do not display a clear pattern (Table 7.10).

The statistical results in Table 7.11 confirm the lack of a de-nationalizing effect resulting from being in a binational couple. At the same time, they provide interesting information regarding the impact of socio-economic status and transnational background on national identification (Table 7.11). Regarding the de-nationalizing effect, multiple regression models show that, indeed, the national partners' national identification is indeed as strong in binational as in national couples. Foreign partners systematically identify less with their country of nationality. Close inspection of the data, however, shows that this has less to do with migration or with being in a binational couple than with the large presence of Germans in the sample of foreign respondents and their concentration in Zürich, where average national identification is higher than in

TABLE 7.10 Average Identification with Country of Nationality, by Type of Couple, Education, and Country

		Spanish Cities	Belgian Cities	Dutch Cities	Swiss City
	National	7.02	7.62	8.48	9.18
		(151)	(29)	(31)	(223)
No university education	Binationa	7.69	7.95	8.09	8.60
	(national partner)	(70)	(61)	(53)	(88)
	Binational	8.62	8.40	7.55	8.74
	(foreign partner)	(58)	(35)	(66)	(94)
	National	6.78	8.32	8.74	8.92
		(166)	(53)	(115)	(261)
University Education	Binational	6.84	8.03	8.36	8.80
	(national partner)	(74)	(128)	(221)	(140)
	Binational	8.43	7.56	7.14	6.94
	(foreign partner)	(76)	(149)	(223)	(219)

( ) Number of respondent.

the other cities. Germans are indeed known for their relatively weak national identity (e.g. the International Social Survey Programme: ISSP, 1995; ISSP, 2003; ISSP, 2013). When I re-estimated the models controlling for whether the respondent was German or not (models not displayed here), the resulting estimates showed that the average strength of national identification among German partners in binational couples is one point below the average for the rest of the national and foreign partners and that levels of national identification among foreign partners in binational couples no longer differed from those among national partners.

Although tangential to this study, other statistical results in Table 7.11 are also interesting for what they say about national identification. They show that while earnings are associated with a stronger national identification, high occupational status is associated with a weaker national identification (columns 4 to 7). Also, while being in a binational couple does not impact on people's national sentiment, other transnational experiences do. People who have parents with different nationalities, in particular, express weaker national sentiment than do those whose parents have the same nationality. The de-nationalizing aspect of growing up in a binational couple has been examined by Varro (1995). If confirmed in further quantitative studies, it suggests an interesting story about the long-term social impact of binational couples. The storyline would be that binational couples contribute to making the partners to these couples somewhat more conscious of their European identity. When they have children, however, these children do not as much internalize their parents' stronger European consciousness as develop a weaker national sentiment. The role of the social environment, which still very much primes national identifications over a European one and

TABLE 7.11 Association between being in a Binational Couple and Identification with Country of Nationality, Controlling for City of Residence and for Socio-demographic and Transnational Background and Experience Variables (OLS)

	(1)		(2)		(3)		(4)		(5)		(6)		(7)	
-Foreign in a binational couple	−0.38	★	−0.41	★	−0.41	★	−0.43	★	−0.43	★	−0.42	★	−0.46	★
-National in binational couple	0.07		0.10		0.10		0.09		0.10		0.13		0.10	
-Age			−0.05	★	−0.05	★	−0.05	★	−0.05	★	−0.05	★	−0.04	★
-Gender			0.07		0.07		0.078		0.10		0.09		0.11	
-Binational parents			−0.31	+	−0.32	+	−0.33	+	−0.32	+	−0.33	+	−0.33	+
-Average parental education			1.0E-03		0.01		0.02		0.02		0.03		0.04	
-Number of countries visited before 17			−0.02		−0.02		−0.02		−0.02		−0.02		−0.02	
-Education	−0.03				−0.04		−0.03		−0.02		0.02		0.02	
-Unemployed							0.32		0.33		0.31		0.31	
-Housework							−0.06		−0.05		−0.03		−7.0E-03	
-Student							−0.56		−0.56		−0.52		−0.51	
-Other							−0.38		−0.36		−0.32		−0.31	
-High status occupation (managers, professionals, technical professions)							−0.35	+	−0.34	+	−0.33	★	−0.32	+
-Low status service occupations							0.07		0.08		0.08		0.08	
-Income (PPS)							6.0E-03	★	6.0E-03	★	6.0E-03	★	6.0E-03	★
-Number of Languages known before meeting partner									−0.09		−0.08		−0.08	
-Duration of the relationship													−0.02	
-Number of countries visited between 17 and living with partner													−0.02	
-Partner's education											−0.09	★	−0.09	★
-Number of countries visited since with partner													0.02	
-Constant	6.99	★	8.60	★	8.88	★	8.70	★	8.84		9.12	★	8.94	★
R-square %	20.3		20.9		21.0		21.6		21.7		21.9		22.0	
N							2115							

Controls city of residence and for identification with city and identification with region. +: Significant at 0.10 level, two-tailed; ★: Significant at 0.05 level, two-tailed.

the superficial character of European identification, more awareness than emotion, probably contributes to the lack of transmission of the parents' more cosmopolitan identification to their children.

Foreign partners and identification with the country of residence

As discussed in the introduction to this chapter, the literature on migration and on inter-marriage has focused on the migrants' assimilation to the host culture and thus to the extent to which they adopt the host country's nationality. I have shown that in contemporary Europe, and in the context of the freedom of movement for Europeans, there are alternatives to acculturation. Foreigners can also develop a European identification, just like recent generations of Asian and Latin-American migrants in the United States have developed pan-ethnic ones (Espiritu, 1992; Mora, 2014). In this section, however, I focus on the adoption of the host country's national identification. It is conceivable that being married or cohabiting with a national of the country of residence would instill some degree of attachment to the partner's country of residence. On the other hand, the foreign partners' strong national identifications speak against the likelihood that this happens.

At the empirical level, the forces against national assimilation win-out. Foreign partners in binational couples display very weak identification with the country of residence (Table 7.12). They assimilate to the host culture in many ways, but they do not *acculturate* at the level of identity. Weak identification with the country of residence contrasts with strong European and national identifications (Tables 7.1 and 7.10, respectively). On a scale from 0 to 10, the average value lies between 2 and 3, depending on people's education and country of residence. Because of equal citizenship rights for all citizens of the European Union, wherever they live, European Union migrants very rarely naturalize in their country of residence (see Favell, 2008). It is thus unlikely that these results reflect a selection process, whereby those who identify most with the country of residence naturalize.

Table 7.12 shows that less educated foreign partners identify more with the country of residence than do more educated ones. Whereas one in four foreign respondents with less than university education rate their identification with the country of residence as seven or more, one in six foreign respondents with university education do.[7] In the in-depth interviews that I conducted in Spain, this contrast between less educated and more educated foreign respondents was well illustrated by the two Romanian female respondents whom I introduced in Chapter 2. The first one, it will be recalled, completed high school in Romania and started but did not complete a degree in management (Interview # 3). She had hardly ever travelled out of her own country and the reason why she eventually migrated to Madrid was to join her Romanian husband. To her disappointment, however, she discovered that her husband did not want to be with her.

178 Identities

TABLE 7.12 Average Levels of Identification with Country of Residence, by Type of Couple, Education, and Country

		Spanish Cities	Belgian Cities	Dutch Cities	Swiss City
	National	7.02	7.62	8.48	9.18
		(151)	(29)	(31)	(223)
No university education	Binational	7.69	7.95	8.09	8.60
	(national partner)	(70)	(61)	(53)	(88)
	Binational	5.36	3.62	3.93	2.92
	(foreign partner)	(53)	(34)	(64)	(87)
	National	6.78	8.32	8.74	8.92
		(166)	(53)	(115)	(261)
University education	Binational	6.84	8.03	8.36	8.80
	(national partner)	(73)	(128)	(221)	(140)
	Binational	2.63	2.85	2.47	2.69
	(foreign partner)	(72)	(142)	(219)	(214)

( ) Number of respondents.

They still had a daughter together, but, soon after her birth, they divorced. She now shares her life with a younger Spaniard in a very modest apartment. After a short stint of unemployment, she currently works endless hours in part-time jobs to make ends meet, while her partner combines studying with coaching a neighborhood football team. The very tight economic situation in which the partners live has not discouraged her, however, and she is now making plans to eventually buy a house. She is also fully integrated in Spanish society. Not only does she maintain ties to the Romanian community in Madrid, which helped her when she came in her quest to save her marriage, but also to many parents in her daughter's school. She likes the food, the lifestyle, and the variety and affordability of consumer goods, like shoes, more difficult to find in her native Romania. She is also fully familiar with Spanish popular culture, whether it is TV series or music, and expresses little awareness or interest in European or world culture. In the survey questionnaire that she filled-out online a couple of months before our meeting, she had rated her feeling of identification as Spaniard a 10, which she confirmed as we approached the end of the interview, when she spontaneously told me, "In Spain I feel at home; I feel more Spanish than Romanian, although I AM Romanian. I don't know why; I just feel fine here" (Interview # 3).

The second female Romanian whom I interviewed lives in the same Madrid suburb but in a more prosperous middle-class neighborhood (Interview # 8). Her background and resulting world outlook could not be farther removed from the previous respondent's. A scientist, in her mid-thirties, she grew up in Ceaucescu's Romania, with only little and, when so, supervised access to the outside world. The fall of Communism, however, coupled with her stellar academic credentials, opened the world for her. She left Romania and lived and worked in several

European countries before meeting her current Spanish husband while they were both in [Western European country]. In the course of time, they moved to Spain and "landed" in the Madrid suburb where they currently live. Although her husband is also a well-travelled scientist, when it came to settle, this place located five minutes away from his parents' home, and where he stayed until well into his thirties, was his favored choice.

For our respondent, this "pathological" attachment to family is one of the many things in Spanish society that she cannot stand. Talking about her efforts to retain some independence vis à vis her in-laws, she commented to me wryly: "I am probably the revolutionary virus that has come to disrupt the quiet and beautiful life of this Spanish family" (Interview # 8). Other sources of frustration for her in Spanish society are nepotism and pervasive lack of consideration for others (e.g. officials or academic personnel who never answer letters or emails). Not that she thinks that there are sharp contrasts with Romania. She is as critical of Romania as she is of Spain. The point is that her perspective is no longer that of a Romanian who has come to Spain, but rather, that of a cosmopolitan researcher who having broken free from the shackles that bound her to Romania finds herself in a country that she perceives to be as constraining and parochial or more as her native land. She is particularly afraid that her children will be trapped in Spanish culture. Low salaries and the huge debt acquired as they bought a home in the middle of Spain's real estate "bubble" mean that the family cannot afford taking their kids to a school they like; instead, they have had to compromise quality for price and take the children to a religious school. For an intellectual agnostic like her the school's emphasis on religious education is hard to bear: "they spend their time learning religion, chants, all sorts of prayers, in some ways they beat my mother-in-law in terms of devotion!" (Interview # 8). She is also afraid that the economic constraints that the family is currently experiencing will thwart their efforts to provide their children with travel experience:

> We are quite cosmopolitan compared with the average or to the place where we live. There are people who have certainly travelled farther than we have, but in this setting, and especially if I think about my husband's family, we are quite cosmopolitan; the world for us extends well beyond this town, where everybody proudly carries a pin that says 'I'm from X, and I've never moved from here, except for the month of August every summer, and when I move somewhere in August I ask that they prepare my favorite local dish the way they do in this restaurant in my hometown'. We are not into this: we do not belong to a religious brotherhood and things like that, we do not participate in processions around the city and all that. Ideally, we would like our children to be open to the world. Their father dreams of his son becoming an engineer in Germany and of her daughter studying art in Paris. And this gives him hope that this will allow us to travel again, since in the current context we cannot afford it. He hopes that this will provide him with an excuse to travel, in order to visit his children.

180 Identities

> The current situation is very constraining. You realize that you keep telling your children about cities that we will at some time visit, such as Paris, (even if this means the obligatory visit to Eurodisney), you tell them that Paris is a beautiful place to go for walks and so on, but the time to travel there never comes. We cannot travel abroad. We cannot afford it.
>
> *(Interview # 8)*

As one would infer from this excerpt, this respondent's feelings of identification with Spain where not strong and in fact, in her online questionnaire she had rated them as a 2.

Intuitively, it is not obvious that less educated foreign partners would display a greater predisposition to develop a strong identification with the country of residence. The illustration above, for instance, presents us with two Romanian women who are poles apart, the objective experience of the former objectively much worse than the latter's experience. Although a more international experience makes the Romanian scientist more likely to identify as European, the other Romanian's less cosmopolitan outlook should be as inimical to the development of a hyphenated Spanish-Romanian nationality as it is to European identification.

Previous chapters provide the key to the explanation of why less educated foreign partners identify more with the country of residence than do more educated ones. We saw that they are more integrated in a social support network that includes relatives, in-laws, and close friends, some from the country of origin, some from the country of residence, and that provides them with practical and emotional support when they need it. I suggested that their habitus, "virtue out of necessity" as Bourdieu would say, probably also predisposes them to seek close relatives and friends when needed. As the examples above illustrate, the highly educated Romanian respondent is not all too happy about depending from her in-laws. A large social support network provides less educated foreign partners like the first Romanian respondent above with the kind of emotional security that, according to Lawler underlies group identification (Lawler, 1992). Nothing captures this sense of security better than this respondent's reference to Spain as "my home."

Multiple regression analysis supports the argument outlined above and exemplified by the two Romanian respondents. Column 1 in Table 7.13 shows that less educated foreign partners identify more with the country of residence than do more educated ones. Then, Columns 4 to 6 reveal that the coefficient for the association between education and identification with the country of residence drops from -0.26 to -0.23 once one controls for whether foreign respondents have relatives in the country of residence (column 5) and then drops even more, to a non-statistically significant -0.16, once one controls for the foreign partners' report of the help they receive when addressing and solving everyday problems and tasks (column 6). Meanwhile, the statistical coefficient for the association between having relatives in the country of residence drops from 0.20

TABLE 7.13 Association between Socio-demographic, Temporal, Network, Well-Being, and Cultural Assimilation Variables and Identification with the Country of Residence (Foreign Partners) (OLS)

	(1)		(2)		(3)		(4)		(5)		(6)	
-Age	−0.02		−0.04		−0.04		−0.04		−0.03		−0.02	
-Gender (1=Female)	−0.24		−0.31		−0.34		−0.34		−0.29		−0.35	
-Education	−0.32	★	−0.25	★	−0.26	★	−0.26	★	−0.23	★	−0.16	
-Years in CoR			0.09	★	0.08	★	0.08	★	0.06	★	0.06	★
-Duration of relationship			−0.05	+	−0.05	+	−0.05	+	−0.04		−0.04	
-Uses local language with partner					0.55	+	0.49		0.53	+	0.56	+
-Unemployed							−0.12		0.23		0.18	
-Housework							−0.48		−0.52		−0.56	
-Student							−3.23	★	−3.22	★	−3.56	★
-Other							−0.45		−0.44		−0.75	
-High status occupation (managers, professionals, technical professions)							−0.67		−0.67		−0.78	+
-Low status service occupations							−0.63		−0.62		−0.73	
-Income (PPS)							−4.0E-03		−3.0E-03		−4.0E-03	
-Perceived social position							0.20	★	0.20	★	0.16	
-Has relatives in CoR									0.69	+	0.51	
- Number of countries visited since with partner									−0.02		−0.03	
-Perception of help available											0.49	★
-Satisfaction with relationship											0.31	★
-Constant	5.94	★	5.83	★	5.40	★	5.53	★	4.98	★	1.74	
R-square	5.2		8.9		9.5		11.4		11.9		16.1	
N							556					

Controls for city of residence. +: Significant at 0.10 level, two-tailed; ★: Significant at 0.05 level, two-tailed.

182 Identities

to a non-statistically significant value of 0.16 after one controls for the amount of help foreign partners receive in addressing and solving everyday problems and tasks (column 6).

As emphasized in the literature, the foreign partners' identification with the country of residence also depends on the length of residence. Like in many other social situations, time creates bonds among individuals and between individuals and the groups or locations in which they find themselves. Selection processes can bias an empirical assessment of this effect among migrants in general, because those who are unhappy can easily go back to their country of origin, but when the focus is on married or cohabiting foreign partners in binational couples this bias is somewhat attenuated, simply because it is more difficult for a foreign migrant to leave the country when he or she is married to a local. Table 7.13 shows indeed that the longer foreign partners in binational couples have lived in the country of residence, the more they identify with it, irrespective of how economically successful they have been, and independently of how socially integrated they are and of how happy they are in their relationship. On the other hand, the longer the duration of the marriage or cohabiting relationship, the less foreign partners identify with the country of residence, slowing down the acculturation process to a crawl.

The literature on the immigrants' economic, social, and cultural integration and assimilation has also emphasized the paramount role of knowing the local language. It improves the foreign workers' competitive position in the job market, it facilitates their developing friendships with the local population, and it decreases their perception of distance between their culture of origin and the host country's culture (Benet-Martínez and Haritatos, 2005; Chen et al., 2008; Haritatos and Benet-Martínez, 2002). I already showed in Chapter 4 that foreign respondents who speak the local language with their partners improve their chances of getting a job. The statistical results displayed in Table 7.13 provide evidence that speaking the local language also matters for social and cultural assimilation. Foreign respondents who speak the local language with their partners express greater identification with the country of residence than do those who do not (although the association is only significant at the 0.10 level; b = 0.55; column 5). Once one controls for people's socio-economic status (e.g. employment, occupational status, income, and perceived economic standing), however, the association becomes smaller and is no longer statistically significant. This is mainly because foreign partners who speak the local language report a better economic position than those who do not (see Chapter 4). One can speculate that speaking the local language creates a feeling of achievement among foreign partners that is then reflected in stronger identification with the host country. It is also relevant that when one introduces additional controls, as in columns 5 and 6, the association between the use of the local language and identification with the country of residence is again stronger and statistically significant. It is conceivable that this change in the association reflects that foreign partners who speak the local language perceive less cultural distance between their country of nationality and the country of residence and are treated as legitimate members of the community, which in turn leads them to identify with the country of residence.

Finally, the statistical analysis in Table 7.13 shows that the happier foreign partners are in the relationship the more they identify with the country of residence (column 6). Although this makes sense intuitively, for positive emotions tend to travel to objects other than those that originate them and because foreign partners may simply project their feelings toward their partner into their feelings toward their partner's country, the finding becomes more interesting when one connects it with the fact that how people evaluate their relationship does not bear on their European identification (not shown). It buttresses the contrast between the cognitive, non-emotional character of European identification and the emotional load associated to national identifications. Partners in binational couples do not identify as Europeans because they are happy or because they want to please their partners, or even because they transfer their love to their partner to Europe. They do so out of greater awareness, whereas those who identify with the country of residence, do so out of affect. The fact that the foreign partners' satisfaction with their relationship is associated only to identification with the country of residence is a sign of the non-emotional character of European identification.

Identification with the city of residence

The literature has debated on the role that residence plays in defining one's identity in an age of permanent mobility. Needless to say, this debate is based on confounding the spectacular increase in mobility, especially short-term, with absolute levels of mobility, especially long-term and long-distance. Theory and speculation surrounding the question of the continuing relevance of the local in the global age loses much of its persuasiveness once one takes into account that the stock of migrants still does not represent more than 3% of the world's population and that most mobility is very short-term and short-distance. Early analysts of the surge in mobility anticipated that the local would soon cease to be relevant to people's identities.[8] Critics since then have emphasized the continuing relevance of the local and of local identifications. Friedmann, for instance, argues that having strong local roots is what makes mobility conceivable for many (Friedmann, 2002). Andreotti et al. show that even highly transnational managers in cosmopolitan cities practice strategies of *partial exit*, retaining and nurturing strong bonds to their place of residence, which in most cases, is the same neighborhood where they grew up (Andreotti et al., 2015). Savage et al. go further than most critics and vindicate the centrality of place, at the same time as they decouple mobility from sense of belonging and from people's willingness to engage with others (Savage et al., 2005). In the global age, they claim, and empirically substantiate, a person's sense of belonging depends foremost on her or his ability to meaningfully integrate the place of residence into her or his

184 Identities

personal biography. Mobility into a particular neighborhood or city that one has purposely chosen can thus provide individuals with a greater sense of belonging than does being stuck in one's birth place because of lack of opportunity to move somewhere else.

The two extreme positions of the debate above translate into different expectations about how binational couples relate to their place of residence. Those who emphasize the role of geographic mobility in breaking the identity bonds that link individuals to their place of residence would probably anticipate that partners in binational couples identify little with their place of residence and that they do less so than do partners in national couples. This is because being part of a binational couple entails a greater degree of geographic mobility, as one pays frequent visits to relatives and friends living abroad. They would also anticipate that foreign partners in binational couples, because of living in a city different from the one they grew up and thus being more mobile in practice than is their national partner, identify less with their city of residence than do national partners in these couples. Those who emphasize the continuing relevance of place, on the other hand, would anticipate that binational couples identify strongly with their place of residence and make no predictions as to contrasts between binational and national couples.

Table 7.14 displays average levels of identification with the city of residence, across cities, levels of education, and type of couple. Contradicting the hypermobility thesis, it shows that all groups identify quite strongly with their city of residence, although slightly less than they do with their country of nationality and with Europe. Table 7.14 also shows that partners in binational couples generally identify less with the city of residence than do partners in national couples

TABLE 7.14 Average Levels of Identification with City of Residence, by Type of Couple, Education, and Country

		Spanish Cities	Belgian Cities	Dutch Cities	Swiss City
No university education	National	7.26	7.55	6.48	7.53
		(148)	(29)	(33)	(221)
	Binational (national partner)	6.78	7.33	7.13	6.24
		(68)	(58)	(52)	(88)
	Binational (foreign partner)	7.40	5.41	6.00	4.70
		(55)	(32)	(62)	(90)
University education	National	6.86	7.37	6.46	5.97
		(164)	(52)	(114)	(259)
	Binational (national partner)	5.50	6.62	6.24	5.14
		(72)	(127)	(221)	(139)
	Binational (foreign partner)	6.05	5.90	5.53	4.40
		(73)	(145)	(217)	(220)

( ) Number of respondents.

and that national partners in binational couples generally identify more with the city of residence than do foreign partners in these couples. While these contrasts agree with the hypermobility thesis, for binational couples and the foreign partners in these couples are more mobile than nationals in both national and binational couples, they are also consistent with other interpretations. Partners in binational couples, for instance, may be self-selected for personality characteristics like openness to the world, which makes them less likely to emotionally attach to their place of residence; also, foreign partners in these couples may identify less with the place of residence because of being geographically cut from their family of origin (Savage et al., 2005). In general, and above and beyond the contrasts just examined, relatively high levels of identification with the city among all groups of respondents are more consistent with the expectations of authors who emphasize the continuing significance of place than with those of hypermobility theorists.

Multiple regression analysis, as in Table 7.15, allows to examine the contrasts above in more detail, at the same time as it provides insights into the explanatory mechanisms at work. Again, the results are more consistent with arguments in favor of the continuing significance of place than with those formulated by hypermobility theorists. First of all, because binational couples identify less with the city of residence than do partners in national ones even after controlling for indicators of geographic mobility, such as travel propensities at different stages in the respondents' lives. The effects of the travel variables on identification with the city are actually contradictory. Whereas travel at a young age has positive effects on identification with the city, travel in adolescence and early adulthood has negative effects and travel after people started their relationship with their current partner has no effects. Then, although coefficients in columns 1 to 2 reveal that foreign partners in binational couples identify less with the city of residence than do national partners in these couples, as hypermobility theorists would predict, once I control for the presence of relatives in the country of residence, as in column 3, average levels of identification with the city of residence among nationals and foreigners in binational couples are the same. It is thus not mobility *per se* that would seem to lead foreign partners in binational couples to identify less with the city of residence than do the national partners, but the fact that many among them do not live close to their relatives.

Throughout the book, and this chapter is no exception, I have emphasized differences between less educated and highly educated partners in binational couples. These differences reappear in the analysis of identification with the city of residence. Less educated partners in both national and binational couples identify more with the city than do more educated ones. This contrast persists after I control for the presence of relatives in the country and, in a model not shown here, after I control for the amount of assistance that partners receive in solving everyday problems. I can only speculate that it reflects cognitive aspects related to education not captured by fluency in foreign languages.

186 Identities

TABLE 7.15 Association between being in a Binational Couple and Identification with City of Residence, controlling for Socio-demographic and Transnational Background and Experience Variables (OLS)

	(1)		(2)		(3)	
–Foreign in a binational couple	−1.49	★	−1.44	★	−0.90	★
–National in binational couple	−0.91	★	−0.86	★	−0.88	★
–Age			0.03	+	0.04	★
–Gender			−0.10		−0.08	
–Binational parents			0.18		0.16	
–Average parental education			0.05		0.05	
–Number of countries visited before 17			0.08	★	0.08	★
–Education	−0.23	★	−0.20	★	−0.18	★
–Unemployed			0.50		0.55	
–Housework			0.30		0.28	
–Student			−1.45	★	−1.48	★
–Other			0.11		0.14	
–High status occupation (managers, professionals, technical professions)			0.12		0.14	
–Low status service occupations			0.46		0.50	
–Income (PPS)			−1.0E-03		−1.0E-03	
–Number of languages known before meeting partner			0.01		−2.0E-03	
–Number of countries visited between 17 and living with partner			−0.04	★	−0.04	★
–Partner's education			−0.04		−0.03	
–Number of countries visited since with partner					−0.03	
–Has relatives in CoR					0.74	★
–Constant	8.14	★	6.62	★	5.70	★
R-square %	8.4		9.8		10.2	

Controls for city of residence. +: Significant at 0.10 level, two-tailed; ★: Significant at 0.05 level, two-tailed.

The pages above reveal that partners in binational couples display a greater awareness of being European and express more emotional attachment to the European Union than do partners in national couples. They also identify less with their city of residence. On the other hand, they are as strongly attached to their nationality as are partners in national couples and do not express a stronger sense of obligation to other Europeans. Greater awareness of being European and greater attachment to the European Union reflect in part greater openness to the world, acquired through one's family, early socialization experiences (including travel), education, and the learning of foreign languages. This greater openness to the world is what predisposed many among them to enter a binational couple in the first place and partly explains observed correlations between being in a binational couple and European identification, identification with the city of residence, and emotional attachment to the European Union. The analysis of European identification has shown, however, that being in a binational couple independently contributes to greater European awareness and weaker identification with the city of residence. The binational couples' embeddedness in transnational networks involving kin and friends propitiates the development of this cosmopolitan outlook. Additional findings concerning the transmission of European and national identifications between binational parents and their children suggest that the contribution of binational couples to the emergence of a cosmopolitan society is not a multiplicative process and runs parallel to denationalization. This is because while partners in binational couples tend to be more aware of their European identity than are partners in national couples, their offspring distinguish themselves not by their stronger European identification but, instead, by their weaker national identification.

The chapter has also illuminated the process of cultural assimilation among foreign partners in binational couples. It complements Chapter 3 above by further delineating two worlds of experience in binational couples, corresponding to the distinction between less educated and more educated binational couples. This distinction roughly overlaps with traditional and new forms of migration. Foreign partners in binational couples who fall into the traditional migration category are usually less educated, have family in the country, and are embedded in social networks where mutual assistance is quite pervasive. They therefore tend to identify more strongly with the city and the country of residence than do foreign partners in binational couples who fall into the new migration category. These new migrants, *Eurostars* as Favell called them, are more educated, do not have relatives in the country of residence and even though their social networks are as big as those of the other category of migrants, they are less likely to ask and receive practical assistance from these networks. Because of this lesser dependence on the wider community, partly willed, partly unwilled, they do not develop as strong an identification with the city and the country of residence as do foreign partners in the traditional migration category.

The analysis of different forms of identification, geographical, and geopolitical, as well as of horizontal solidarity between Europeans, illuminates both the transformative potential and the limits of binational marriage and cohabitation and of social transnationalism in general. Researchers have tended to place different nested geographical and geo-political identifications in a continuum from parochialism to cosmopolitanism. They have also treated support for European integration as one-dimensional, failing to differentiate between models or projects of integration (e.g. more or less political, more or less social, involving less of more transfers of sovereignty) (see Díez Medrano, 2003, 2009). This chapter's findings invite a sharper distinction between socio-geographical and political identifications. The analysis above has shown that binational couples differ from national couples in the degree to which they identify as European and with their city of residence. European identification, however, is shallow, it does not translate into strong solidarity with other Europeans. The analysis shows that

188 Identities

binational couples are also more likely to express emotional attachment to the European Union, a political project indeed, but this emotional attachment by no means implies a positioning in favor of a federal Europe. It may simply reveal positive feelings to an institutional framework that makes their lives easier. The most political of all the identifications discussed in the text is national identification and here being in a binational couple does not seem to make much of a difference. Binational marriage or cohabitation thus seems to have a greater impact on people's mental and spatial horizons than on their political ones. It is more socially than politically transforming, a finding that extends to other aspects of social transnationalism such as studying abroad, spending holidays abroad, or simply frequently travelling abroad, some of which have been examined in this chapter.

Notes

1 Inglehart (1970), Inglehart (1977). See also Belot (2010), Bergbauer (2018).
2 Fligstein (2008), Risse (2010), Calligaro (2013), Forêt (2008).
3 Qualitative work strongly suggests that this is also a plausible explanation for why people who know foreign languages or have travelled a lot around Europe or studied abroad under the Erasmus program identify as European more often than does the rest of the population. See Díez Medrano (2010).
4 The finding that the effect of duration of marriage is greater among national partners in binational couples suggests that the effect of being in a binational couple is independent of the length of residence abroad (about the latter, see Recchi, 2015).
5 Bauhr and Charron (2018), Daniele and Geys (2015), Kleider and Stoeckel (2018), Kuhn et al. (2017), Stoeckel and Kuhn (2018), Verhaegen (2018), Bechtel et al. (2014), Bechtel et al. (2017), Gerhards et al. (2019), Díez Medrano et al. (2019).
6 Milestones in this vast literature are: Hewstone (1986), Gabel (1998), Díez Medrano (2003), Hooghe and Marks (2004), Kuhn (2015).
7 Less educated foreign partners in the Spanish cities are the only ones who deviate from this pattern with an average of about 5. These are predominantly Romanian and Bulgarian citizens. Explaining this interesting anomaly, however, lies beyond the scope of this book because the sample of Romanian and Bulgarian respondents in the other cities is too small.
8 E.g. Urry (2000), Urry (2007), Soja (2000), Castles and Miller (2003).

References

Andreotti, Alberta, Patrick Le Galès, and Francisco Javier Moreno-Fuentes. 2015. *Globalized Minds, Roots in the City.* Oxford, UK: Wiley Blackwell.

Bauhr, Monika and Nicholas Charron. 2018. "Why Support International Redistribution? Corruption and Public Support for Aid in the Eurozone." *European Union Politics* 19(2): 233–254.

Bechtel, Michael, Jens Hainmueller, and Yotam Margalit. 2014. "Preferences for International Redistribution: The Divide over the Eurozone Bailout." *American Political Science Review* 28(4): 835–856.

Bechtel, Michael, Jens Hainmueller, and Yotam Margalit. 2017. "Policy Design and Domestic Support for International Bailouts." *European Journal of Political Research* 56(4): 864–886.

Belot, Céline. 2010. "Le tournant identitaire des études consacrées aux attitudes à l' égard de l' Europe. Génèse, apports, limites." *Politique Européenne* 30: 17–45.

Benet-Martínez, Verónica and Jana Haritatos. 2005. "Bicultural Identity Integration (BII): Components and Psychosocial Antecedents." *Journal of Personality* 73: 1015–1050.

Bergbauer, Stephanie. 2018. *Explaining European Identity Formation: Citizens' Attachment from Maastricht Treaty to Crisis*. Cham, Switzerland: Springer.

Bollen, Kenneth and Juan Díez Medrano. 1998. "Who are the Spaniards?" *Social Forces* 77(2): 587–621.

Calligaro, Oriane. 2013. *Negotiating Europe: EU Promotion of Europeanness since the 1950s*. New York: Palgrave MacMillan.

Castles, Steven and Mark Miller. 2003. *The Age of Migration*. New York: Guilford Press.

Chen, Sylvia, Verónica Benet-Martínez, and Robert Bond. 2008. "Bicultural Identity, Bilingualism, and Psychological Adjustment in Multicultural Societies: Immigration-based and Globalization-based Acculturation." *Journal of Personality* 76: 803–838.

Chen, Juan and David Takeuchi. 2011. "Intermarriage, Ethnic Identity, and Perceived Social Standing among Asian Women in the United States." *Journal of Marriage and the Family* 73(4): 876–888.

Citrin, Jack and John Sides. 2004. "Can Europe Exist without Europeans? Problems of Identity in a Multinational Community." *Advances in Political Psychology* 1: 41–70.

Daniele, Gianmarco and Benny Geys. 2015. "Public Support for European Fiscal Integration in Times of Crisis." *Journal of European Public Policy* 22(5): 650–670.

Díez Medrano, Juan. 2003. *Framing Europe*. Princeton, NJ: Princeton University Press.

Díez Medrano, Juan. 2009. "The Public Sphere and Europe's Political Identity." In Checkel, Jeffrey and Peter Katzenstein (eds.), *European Identity*. Cambridge, UK: Cambridge University Press, pp. 81–108.

Díez Medrano, Juan. 2010. "Unpacking European Identity." *Politique Européenne* 30: 45–66.

Díez Medrano, Juan. 2011. "The Present and Future of Social Classes." In Adrian Favell and Virginie Guiraudon (eds.), *Sociology of the European Union*. New York: Palgrave MacMillan, pp. 25–50.

Díez Medrano, Juan. 2018. "Multilingualism and European Identification." *Sociological Inquiry* 88(3): 410–434.

Díez Medrano, Juan, Irina Ciornei, and Fulya Apaydin. 2019. "Explaining Supranational Solidarity." In Ettore Recchi et al. (eds.), *Everyday Europe: Social Transnationalism in an Unsettled Continent*. Bristol, UK: Policy Press, pp. 137–171.

Dribe, Martin and Christer Lundh. 2008 "Intermarriage and Immigrant Integration in Sweden." *Acta Sociologica* 51(4): 329–354.

Espiritu, Yen. 1992. *Asian American Panethnicity: Bridging Institutions and Identities*. Philadelphia, PA: Temple University Press.

Etzioni, Amitai. 2013. "The EU: The Communitarian Deficit." *European Societies* 15(3): 312–330.

Favell, Adrian. 2008. *Eurostars and Eurocities*. Oxford, UK: Blackwell.

Fligstein, Neil. 2008. *Euro-clash*. Oxford, UK: Oxford University Press.

Forêt, François. 2008. *Légitimer l' Europe*. Paris: SciencesPo Les Presses.

Friedmann, Jonathan. 2002. "From Roots to Routes. Tropes for Trippers." *Anthropological Theory* 2(1): 21–36.

Gabel, Matthew. 1998. *Interests and Integration*. Ann Arbor: University of Michigan Press.

190 Identities

Gerhards, Jürgen, Holger Lengfeld, Zsófia Ignácz, Florian Kley, and Maximilian Priem. 2019. *How Strong is European Solidarity in Times of Crisis?* New York: Routledge.

Haritatos, Jana and Verónica Benet-Martínez. 2002. Bicultural Identities: The Interface of Cultural, Personality, and Socio-Cognitive Processes. *Journal of Research on Personality* 36: 598–606.

Hewstone, Miles. 1986. *Understanding Attitudes to the European Community*. Cambridge, UK: Cambridge University Press.

Hobsbawm, Eric. 1990. *Nations and Nationalism since 1780*. Cambridge, MA: Harvard University Press.

Hooghe, Liesbet and Gary Marks. 2004. "Does Identity or Economic Rationality drive Public Opinion on European Integration." *Political Science and Politics* 37(3): 415–420.

Hooghe, Liesbet and Gary Marks. 2009. "From Permissive Consensus to Constraining Dissensus." *British Journal of Political Science* 39(1): 1–23.

Inglehart, Ronald, 1970. "Cognitive Mobilization and European Identity." *Comparative Politics* 3(1): 45–70.

Inglehart, Ronald. 1977. *The Silent Revolution*. Princeton, NJ: Princeton University Press.

Inglehart, Ronald. 1977. "Long Term Trends in Mass Support for European Unification." *Government and Opposition* 12(2): 150–177.

Kleider, Hanna and Florian Stoeckel. 2018. "The Politics of International Redistribution. Explaining Public Support for Fiscal Transfers in the EU." *European Journal of Political Research* 89: 5.

Kuhn, Theresa. 2015. *Experiencing European Integration*. Oxford, UK: Oxford University Press.

Kuhn, Theresa, Hector Solaz, and Erika van Elsas. 2017. "Practicing What You Preach: How Cosmopolitanism Promotes Willingness to Redistribute across the European Union." *Journal of European Public Policy* 95(4): 1–20.

Mau, Steffen. 2010 [2007]. *Social Transnationalism*. New York: Routledge.

Mora, Cristina. 2014. *Making Hispanics*. Chicago, IL: University of Chicago Press.

Pötzschke, Steffen and Michael Braun. 2019. "Social Transnationalism and European Identification." In Ettore Recchi and co-authors (eds.), *Everyday Europe. Social Transnationalism in an Unsettled Continent*. Bristol, UK: Policy Press, pp. 115–137.

Recchi, Ettore. 2014. "Pathways to European Identity Formation: A Tale of Two Models." *Innovation: The European Journal of Social Science Research* 27(2): 119–133.

Risse, Thomas. 2010. *A Community of Europeans?* Ithaca, NY: Cornell University Press.

Rother, Nina and Tina Nebe. 2009. "More Mobility, More European? Free Movement and European Identity." In Adrian Favell and Ettore Recchi (eds.), *Pioneers of European Integration*. Northampton: Edward Elgar, pp. 120–156.

Savage, Mike, Gaynor Bagnall, and Brian Longurst. 2005. *Globalization and Belonging*. London, UK: Sage.

Smith, Anthony. 1992. "National Identity and the Idea of European Unity." *International Affairs* 68(1): 55–76.

Soja, Edward. 2000. *Postmetropolis*. Critical Studies of Cities and Regions. Oxford, UK: Blackwell.

Stoeckel, Florian and Theresa Kuhn. 2018. "Mobilizing Citizens for Costly Policies: The Conditional Effect of Party Cues on Support for International Bailouts in the European Union." *Journal of Common Market Studies* 56(2): 446–461.

Urry, John 2000. *Sociology Beyond Societies*. London, UK: Routledge.

Urry, John. 2007. *Mobilities*. Cambridge, UK: Polity Press.

Varro, Gabrielle (ed.). 1995. *Les couples mixtes et leurs enfants en France et en Allemagne*. Paris: Armand Collin.

Verhaegen, Soetkin, Marc Hooghe, and Cecil Meeusen. 2013. "Opportunities to Learn about Europe at School. A Comparative Analysis among European Adolescents in 21 European Member States." *Journal of Curriculum Studies* 45(6): 838–864.

Verhaegen, Soetkin. 2018. "What to Expect from European Identity? Explaining Support for Solidarity in Times of Crisis." *Comparative European Politics* 16(5): 871–904.

Waters, Mary and Tomás Jiménez. 2005. "Assessing Immigrant Assimilation: New Empirical and Theoretical Challenges." *Annual Review of Sociology* 31: 105–125.

Weber, Eugen. 1976. *Peasants into Frenchman*. Palo Alto, CA: Stanford University Press.

CONCLUSION

Binational couples embody and contribute to cosmopolitan society. In this book, I have focused on two dimensions of cosmopolitanism: (1) the ability to skillfully and confidently navigate foreign locations and cultures and (2) identification with geopolitical spaces beyond the national state. The decision to marry or cohabit with a foreign national is arguably the quintessential cosmopolitan act. Once together, partners in binational couples become part of international and transnational networks of friends and relatives. This places them in a privileged situation to learn about and become competent in navigating different countries and cultures. In the course of their relationship, they acquire transnational skills, a greater appreciation for things foreign, and, under the right circumstances, a cosmopolitan identification.

The chapters in this book also demonstrate that the nature and spatial distribution of the binational couples' international networks uniquely structure the partners' lives and world outlook: they structure the character of social interaction and communication and the amount and quality of assistance that they receive, they structure and constrain seasonal routines, and they structure the partners' interest in local and world events. I have shown, for instance, that the social life of foreign partners in binational couples is more centered around work acquaintances and provisional friends than is the social life of nationals in both national and binational couples. I have also shown that foreign partners in binational couples are less prone to receive assistance in order to tackle everyday problems than are national partners in both national and binational couples. Further, binational couples are distinct in how they organize their lives during the year. While national couples enjoy some freedom in planning their holidays, binational couples are generally constrained into spending at least part of their holidays together with the foreign partner's relatives and friends, especially when they have young children. Finally, *Europe in Love* reveals that although binational couples are as well integrated into local civil and political life as national couples are, they show greater interest in international politics.

The features above distinguish binational from national couples. The book has emphasized, however, that they are more prevalent among binational couples formed by highly educated partners than among those formed by less educated ones. This is mainly because whereas the relatives of foreign partners in less educated couples often live in the couple's country of residence, the relatives of foreign partners in more educated couples generally live abroad. More educated binational couples can also better afford to travel abroad to visit friends and relatives than do less educated ones.

The synthesis above thus shows that binational couples are not only cosmopolitan in their practices; they constitute a distinct social group segmented along educational/class lines. In order to further evaluate the binational couples' social distinctiveness, I have examined the extent to which partners in binational couples differ in socio-economic terms. My inquiry suggests that their objective social position is by and large similar to that of partners in national couples. Only foreign males from new European Union member states suffer some disadvantage in the labor market when compared with nationals. Paradoxically, however, statistical analysis has also revealed that less educated foreign partners in binational couples, who generally come from these new European Union member states, tend to situate themselves in a higher social position than do less educated partners in national couples. My interpretation of this interesting finding is that this is because less educated foreign partners from new European Union member states compare their current life conditions with those in their home countries. Further research is needed to confirm or contradict these findings and interpretation.

Because of sample size limitations and space constraints, I have left out topics that may be of interest to those interested in intermarriage. For instance, although gender is part of the analysis, I have only discussed statistical interactions between gender and type of couple that were significant and large. Bigger samples may help discover additional ones. The same qualification and disclaimer applies to my analysis of contrasts between foreign partners in binational couples with different nationality combinations. Indeed, this book is hopefully only the starting point for further research that will dig into these and other relevant issues, including the comparative analysis of Euro-couples with other binational couples.

From Europe to the world

What this book describes for Euro-couples can be extrapolated to binational couples worldwide. International mobility and communication have increased dramatically. These developments have undoubtedly contributed to a significant increase in binational marriage and cohabitation all over the world. It is unfortunate, however, that we lack accurate statistical information to adequately measure the exact magnitude and geographical distribution of this increase. Based

194 Conclusion

on mobility and migration flows, one can nonetheless surmise that this increase mainly involves Westerners from affluent countries who enter into marriage and cohabitation arrangements with both other Westerners and non-Westerners. Intense international migration within both Africa and Asia may have translated into a greater prevalence of binational couples in these regions too.

Because mobility and migration into Europe and mobility and migration into rich Anglo-Saxon countries usually spans longer distances (e.g. Asia-United States; United States-Europe; Latin America-Europe; Africa-Europe; South-America-United States) and requires circumventing countless formal and informal bureaucratic hurdles, the lives of the binational couples that result from this mobility and migration probably differs somewhat from those of Euro-couples. I would speculate, for instance, that they more often involve the less educated as well as foreign immigrants with blood relatives in the country of residence. Also, partly because of this and partly because of the aforementioned longer distances and greater bureaucratic hurdles, face-to-face contact with relatives and friends in the foreign partners' countries of origin is perhaps less frequent. It is certainly less onerous and complicated for a Spanish-Romanian couple to travel to Romania during the holidays and for Romanian relatives to travel to Spain, than it is for a Spanish-Argentinian couple to meet Argentinian relatives and friends. Argentinian relatives traveling to Spain to visit a daughter or son married or cohabiting with a Spaniard, for instance, have to pay comparatively expensive plane tickets and are required to bring enough cash with them to prove that they can support themselves while in Spain. If they intend to stay with their son or daughter instead of a hotel, they must also carry with them a letter written by the couple and sealed by the Spanish police that confirms that they will indeed stay at the couple's address. Such visits thus often require months of careful planning.

Variations of the scenario above probably characterize face-to-face transnational communication between foreign partners in binational couples and their relatives and friends in their countries of origin. Although less frequent face-to-face contact may be compensated through more frequent telephone or internet communication, the national partner in these couples may remain largely cut-off from transnational networks and thus relatively insulated from the transformative experiential and cultural impact that being in a binational couple potentially entails for both partners.

The book's findings thus call for systematic comparative research on binational couples in different world regions in order to more rigorously assess their role in the emergence of a cosmopolitan society. In the meantime, the book's focus on Europe helps dispel two myths in the literature: one, that cosmopolitans are only middle class; two, that only those habituated to traveling abroad as part of childhood socialization become cosmopolitan. *Europe in Love* shows that binational couples formed by partners with low levels of education also become cosmopolitan, whether one focuses on the national or the foreign partner in these couples. While the idea that the label "cosmopolitan" applies to *less educated foreign partners* may seem obvious to authors whose work has already claimed it for the thousands of poor migrants from less developed countries (e.g. Brown, 2017; Glick-Schiller and Irving, 2014), it is perhaps less obvious when applied to *less educated national partners in binational couples*. When mobility is cheap and easy, however, as in Europe, marrying or cohabiting with a foreign national can provide a previously uneducated and sedentary national with a unique point of entry to a transnational lifestyle that makes her or him more cosmopolitan than are less educated nationals who marry or cohabit with nationals.

One aspect that probably distinguishes Euro-couples from other binational couples around the world is the extent to which the partners involved develop cosmopolitan identifications. This is because of the entitativity and salience of Europe as a potential focal identification. In the absence of salient cosmopolitan identifications that encompass the particular combination of nationalities in a binational couple, partners in these couples are unlikely to develop one. Schroedter, Rössel, and Datler, for instance, have demonstrated that partners in binational couples formed by Swiss and non-Europeans do not differ from partners in Swiss-Swiss couples in the extent to which they see themselves as "citizens of the world" (Schroedter et al., 2015). It can of course be argued that not being able to put a label to a cosmopolitan identification does not mean that one lacks one. To the extent, however, that self-concepts are performative, that the ability to put a name to one's cosmopolitan identification makes a difference and strengthens this identification, one can reason that the entitativity and salience of European as an identification not only allows partners in Euro-couples to label an emergent cosmopolitan identification but also makes them more aware of it and leads them to act on it. The binational couples' greater emotional rapport to the European Union when compared with national couples (see Chapter 7) perhaps reflects this.

Binational couples and other cosmopolitan groups

With Steffen Mau, I posit that binational couples are core cells of an emerging cosmopolitan society. This, of course, does not imply that they alone contribute to this development. Globalization and the internet revolution, and the ensuing intensification of international exchanges, mobility, and communication, have led to the emergence of other potential carriers of a cosmopolitan transformation. Among them, the literature has identified highly educated individuals in general and, more specifically, highly skilled long-term migrants and professionals and entrepreneurs engaged in transnational transactions and interaction.[1] Their rich cultural resources and comfortable economic position, as well as their professional activity, motivate them, cognitively equip them, financially allow them, and often require them to travel abroad and meet people from other nationalities, so that they gradually become cosmopolitan. In the European context, this also instils in them greater awareness of being European. What probably distinguishes partners in binational couples from individuals in these other groups more than

196 Conclusion

anything, especially if highly educated, is the duration, continuity, intensity, and depth of contact with foreign populations and countries. I have shown, for instance, that being in a Euro-couple contributes more to the frequency of contact with friends abroad than does education (see Chapter 3, Table 3.18).

A cosmopolitan society without cosmopolitan political project

The literature on cosmopolitanism has often conflated discussion of the emergence of a cosmopolitan society with discussion of progress toward a cosmopolitan polity (e.g. Beck, 2006; Beck and Grande, 2004; Risse, 2010). It is generally assumed that the former will naturally lead to the latter, especially when social developments are coupled with a gradual emergence of cosmopolitan identifications. Assessing the validity of this assumption is particularly relevant in the context of the Europe Union. Over the years, both Eurocrats and sociologically minded scholars have placed their bets on the intensification of cross-national exchange, interaction, and communication, in the belief that they will produce the social preconditions for the emergence and consolidation of a legitimate European polity. Of course, they should have known better. Close reading of Karl Deutsch's *Nations and Social Communication*—a book to which many sociologists of European integration refer to nowadays—leads to much more modest expectations (Deutsch, 1953). In a rarely cited passage (p. 176), Deutsch argues that the main obstacle to the emergence of a European *people* (i.e. *demos*) is that any intensification of communication and exchange at the cross-European level is simultaneous to even greater intensification of communication and exchange at the national one. More concretely, messages emphasizing a common European identification are canceled and overpowered by even more frequent and intense messages emphasizing national belonging. *Europe in Love* confirms Deutsch's fears: partners in binational couples are social cosmopolitans; they even identify as Europeans and show great sympathy for the European Union, which they take for granted, but, like most Europeans, they do not imagine anything beyond a Europe of cooperating sovereign states.

The *Eumarr* data only hint at the continuing primacy of the national, even among social cosmopolitans. They show that people generally identify more as nationals than as Europeans and that while partners in binational couples identify more strongly as European than do partners in national couples, their average level of national identification does not differ from that of partners in national couples. De-nationalization thus does not happen in Euro-couples. Partners in these couples just become more aware of being European.

Unfortunately, data to further support the claim that social cosmopolitans are not necessarily political cosmopolitans are hard to find, mainly because the *Eurobarometer* study has systematically neglected directly asking respondents whether they support majority-decision making in the European Union. All we have is extremely rich information on the European Union citizens' support of cooperation in different policy areas. In the book *Framing Europe*, however, I used information from qualitative interviews with ordinary British, German, and Spanish citizens to demonstrate that even those who enthusiastically supported European integration and the European Union blinked and looked utterly perplexed when asked about their willingness to give up national veto power (see also Duchesne and Van Ingelgom, 2013). The truth is that most ordinary citizens do not even conceive of that possibility and were they told that a rising and very significant amount of national legislation simply implements European Union law and that much of the European Union legislation is adopted through qualified majority, they would be dismayed. This is because, as data from the *Eurobarometer* study show, about 90% of European Union citizens actually believe that the majority of the laws and policies that affect their lives originate in national, regional, or local government instances. That national politicians have managed for so long to fool their citizens into believing this is one of the saddest episodes in the history of European integration.

Despite the *Eurobarometer*'s shortcomings, it remains the best source of public opinion data on the European Union and one can find survey items that come close to adequately measuring both social cosmopolitanism and support for a European Union with supranational power. In the 87.3 study conducted in May 2017, for instance, respondents were asked whether they favor that more decisions be made at the European Union level. They were also presented with a list of integration measures and asked whether they favored or opposed them. The list included, among others, the following: (1) A common foreign policy, (2) A common defense policy, (3) A common migration policy, and (4) The free movement of citizens. It lies beyond the scope of this discussion to interpret the overall results. Suffice to say that when one considers the population of European Union citizens as a whole, clear majorities support giving more decision power to the European Union and the adoption of the policies above. Ambiguity about how the respondents interpret the questions demands that one does not come to hasty conclusions. What interests me is the extent to which social cosmopolitans distinguish themselves for being more favorable to this range of proposals than are other, more rooted, segments of the population. In recent years, *Eurobarometer* has regularly included an item in its survey questionnaire that asks respondents how often they have socialized with other Europeans in the past twelve months. This is the closest one can get to a valid and reliable measure of the extent to which people are part of trans-European social networks.

When one cross-tabulates answers to the socializing item with support to the different European integration proposals listed above, one discovers that the contrasts between those who have socialized with other Europeans and those who have not are always less than 12% points. The contrast is trivial on the issue of giving more decision power to the European Union (less than 3% points) and greatest for a common migration policy and the freedom of movement of people (between ten and 12% points).[2] While these findings are consistent with the argument that social cosmopolitanism and political cosmopolitanism go hand in hand, the contrasts are quite small.

198 Conclusion

Surveys other than the *Eurobarometer* series further question the assumption of a strong relationship between social and political cosmopolitanism. The ISSP 2003 and 2013 studies, for instance, asked respondents about their feelings of attachment to their country and to Europe, as well as about the electoral preferences. If social cosmopolitans (i.e. those who interact frequently with other Europeans and also identify as Europeans), are simultaneously political cosmopolitans, one would assume that they also shy away from populist far-right parties. This is because while generally endorsing European integration and the European Union, these political parties advocate an inter-governmental approach based on cooperation and firmly oppose significant transfers of sovereignty. The ISSP surveys, however, reveal trivial correlations, most of them below 5%, between how close people feel to Europe and vote for the far right (i.e. Austria, 2003, Poland, 2003, the Netherlands, 2003, Germany, 2003, and Denmark, 2013). Stronger correlations, around 14%, obtain for France and Germany in the 2013 surveys, but they are still quite small. This means that many social cosmopolitans are willing to support the populist right, the implication being that while they support European cooperation, they are reluctant to give up national sovereignty.

In all, triangulation of information originating in different surveys invites the conclusion that the emergence of a cosmopolitan society does not imply a simultaneous increase in the demand for supranational forms of governance. This conclusion is all the more justified when one takes into account that the cosmopolitan vision that the European Union represents is an exception and that in most parts of the world, large numbers of people are becoming cosmopolitan without contemplating for one moment the creation of a supranational polity.

I began *Europe in Love* with a reference to *Les Deux Anglaises et le Continent*. It is thus fitting that I conclude the book by going back to Roché's 1956 novel, which Truffaut faithfully translated into film. This is because we encounter structural features in Roché's story that speak to the sociological themes discussed in this book: in 1899, Anne, an aspiring young sculptor (not English as the title says, but actually Welsh!) crosses the English Channel to practice her French and simultaneously immerse herself in Paris's *fin de siècle* thriving artistic atmosphere. Her mother, a middle-class widow who lives with her two daughters in a rural Welsh parish, has arranged that she introduce herself to an old friend of hers, Mme. Roc, also a widow. Mme. Roc, in turn, acquaints Anne to her son Claude, a young art student. Claude and Anne soon become good friends and Anne invites Claude to visit Wales and meet her sister Muriel, whom, she thinks, he will like. Claude visits Wales and a complex and tortured love triangle develops. Some critics have compared this love triangle to the one portrayed in *Jules et Jim*, another of Roché's novels and also filmed by Truffaut. Initially committed to Muriel, Claude will propose her in marriage and will even contemplate finding work and settling in Wales. The marriage will never take place, however. A forced one-year separation orchestrated by both mothers, "skeptical of international marriage," and, later on, deep emotional confusion resulting from a brief but inconsequential love affair between Claude and Anne during this interlude will tear them apart.

Like in Roché's and Truffaut's story, contemporary binational relationships between Europeans generally involve educated members of the middle class. Also, just like in Roché's and Truffaut's story, partners in these relationships often come from well-traveled families that have invested in providing their children with transnational cultural capital, in the form of experience abroad and fluency in foreign languages. Major transformations have taken place since nineteen hundred, however. In particular, the European Union was created and, with it, heightened opportunity to visit, study, live, and work in other European countries. Because of this, the number of Euro-couples keeps increasing and includes both highly educated members of the middle class and less educated members of the lower classes. Binational couples between Europeans are now a normal feature in cities across Europe, a reflection of greater mobility, an expression of cultural similarity across Europe, and the source of multiple international ties between Europeans. The latter is especially relevant in light of Europe's current retrenchment into nationalist politics and helps relativize the social implications of Brexit. *Les Deux Anglaises et le Continent* can be viewed as a metaphor of the very tortured relationship between the United Kingdom and Europe, of the marriage that did not work, even though, in contrast with Roché's story, it came to be. Paradoxically, however, the United Kingdom is probably one of the countries in Europe that hosts more Euro-couples, just as thousands of Britons have married or cohabit with Europeans abroad. The British–European ties forged by these couples will not become undone with Brexit and may even contribute to a future re-integration of the United Kingdom in the European Union. In Europe, and especially in the rest of the world, movement toward a cosmopolitan society, as carried forward by binational couples and other social groups, does not necessarily proceed in step with movement toward a cosmopolitan polity. Cosmopolitan society lays the ground for a cosmopolitan polity, however, and, makes it difficult to unravel once some of its architecture has been put in place. Or, at least, this is what this author hopes.

Notes

1 Andreotti et al. (2015), Favell and Recchi (2009), Fligstein (2008), Mau (2010).
2 All contrasts are greater than those obtained for the comparison between the attitudes of respondents with university education and respondents without university education, before and after controlling for country of residence.

References

Andreotti, Alberta, Patrick Le Galès, and Francisco Javier Moreno-Fuentes. 2015. *Globalized Minds, Roots in the City*. Oxford, UK: Wiley Blackwell.
Beck, Ulrich. 2006. *Cosmopolitan Vision*. Cambridge, UK: Polity Press.
Beck, Ulrich, and Edgar Grande. 2004. *Cosmopolitan Europe*. Cambridge, UK: Polity Press.
Brown, Bernardo. 2017. "Unlikely Cosmopolitans: An Ethnographic Reflection on Migration and Belonging in Sri Lanka." *Anthropological Quarterly* 91(1): 209–236.

200 Conclusion

Deutsch, Karl. 1953. *Nationalism and Social Communication*. Cambridge, MA: MIT Press.

Duchesne, Sophie, and Virginie Van Ingelgom (eds.). 2013. *Citizens Reactions to European Integration Compared: Overlooking Europe*. London, UK: Palgrave-MacMillan.

Favell, Adrian, and Ettore Recchi (eds.). 2009. *Pioneers of European Integration*. Northampton: Edward Elgar.

Fligstein, Neil. 2008. *Euro-Clash*. Oxford, UK: Oxford University Press.

Glick-Schiller, Nina, and Andrew Irving (eds.). 2014. *Whose Cosmopolitanism?: Critical Perspectives, Relationalities, and Discontents*. New York: Berghahn Books.

Mau, Steffen. 2010 [2007]. *Social Transnationalism*. New York: Routledge.

Risse, Thomas. 2010. *A Community of Europeans?* Ithaca, NY: Cornell University Press.

Schroedter, Julia, Tom De Winter, and Suzana Koelet. 2015. "Beyond l'Auberge Espagnole: The Effect of Individual Mobility on the Formation of Intra-European Couples." *European Journal of Population* 31(2): 181–206.

APPENDIX 1

SURVEY METHODOLOGY

The *Eumarr* project was sponsored by the European Social Science Foundation and funded by the national research agencies of Belgium, the Netherlands, Spain, and Switzerland.[1] The survey part of the project was conducted in seven large and cosmopolitan cities: Brussels, Antwerp, Amsterdam, The Hague, Barcelona, Madrid, and Zurich.

The questionnaire

The *Eumarr* survey was designed to be implemented as a web-survey. Respondents were able to read and fill-out the survey in any of the country or regional official languages, or in English. At a later stage, and in order to increase the participation rate, respondents were also offered the possibility of filling-out a paper version of the questionnaire, also in different languages. There were only minor formatting differences between the web and paper versions of the questionnaire.

The questionnaire was addressed to only one respondent per household. When required, this respondent was responsible for providing information on the partner. The questionnaire content and structure were virtually identical across countries, although national teams were given freedom to adapt some questions to the local context or add new ones. The book's analysis is based on common content in all surveys only.

The questionnaire structure was as follows:

1. Information on the respondent's birthdate, birthplace, and nationality/ies
2. Information on the respondent's parents' birthplace and nationality/ies
3. Information on the respondent's partner's birthdate, birthplace, and nationality/ies

202 Survey methodology

4. Information on the history of the relationship between the two partners (e.g. when and where it started, circumstances in which the two met, when did the couple began to live together).
5. Information about the perceived quality of the relationship
6. General information about the number of children from this and previous relationships
7. Stays abroad
   a   Residence
   b   Short trips
8. Fluency in different languages and use in different contexts (including information on the parents' knowledge of foreign languages)
9. Transnational networks and social capital
10. Consumer taste and practices
11. Identification
12. Political participation, social engagement, and attitudes to migrants
13. Socio-demographic information

A preliminary version of the questionnaire was written in English and then translated into the different languages in which it was provided to the respondents, depending on the country: Spanish and Catalan in Spain; French and Flemish in Belgium; Dutch in the Netherlands; and German in Switzerland. Then, pretests in the different language versions were conducted in all participating countries. Based on the results of the pretests, the English version was modified accordingly and translated into the different versions made available to the respondents.

Samples

All city samples followed strictly random procedures and used population registers as their sampling frame. Also, all city samples included a control group, formed by partners in cohabiting or married national couples, and an experimental one, formed by partners in cohabiting or married couples where one of the partners is national and the other partner is a national of another European Union country. Finally, the comparative study did not target binational couples in which none of the partners is a national of the country of residence, for they represent an insignificant segment of the population of binational couples. A letter of invitation that was sent to all individuals included in the city samples stated that the survey was part of a larger European project on the lifestyles, attitudes, and experiences of couples in Europe. In order to encourage participation in the study, the letter informed addressees about the possibility of winning an iPad in a lottery that would take place at the end of the fieldwork phase.

Beyond these similarities, the city samples differed by country, because of differences in the information conveyed by the population registers, because of differences in the criteria used by each national team concerning the desired size of the control and experimental groups, and because of different criteria concerning the inclusion of same-sex couples. For instance, whereas the Spanish survey aimed at similar group sizes for the experimental and control groups and for the representation of binational couples where the foreign partner came from old European Union member states and binational couples where the foreign partner came from new European Union member states, the other surveys did not. Also, whereas the Swiss study targeted all binational couples in the city of Zurich and a slightly broader age cohort, the others only targeted binational couples in which one of the partners was a national of the country of residence and the other partner was a national of another European Union member state. The book, however, only focuses on national couples and on binational couples formed by a national and a foreign European Union citizen, and only on respondents in the 30 to 46 age bracket. Since only Belgium included same-sex couples in the study, and since they only represent 6% of the cases in the Belgian working sample, no distinction in the analysis was made between these same-sex couples and the heterosexual couples.

Spain

The official data source for the sampling was Spain's Population Register (with two different dates of reference: January 1st and December 31st 2012) and, more specifically, population register data for the provinces of Spain's two biggest provinces, Madrid and Barcelona. The provinces of Madrid and Barcelona are mainly urban. The provinces' populations are concentrated around and economically integrated with the cities that give them their name and largely coincide with the cities' metropolitan areas.

Spain's Population Register does not report the family connections between the members of the household and thus does not allow for a direct selection of couples. Therefore, the sampling procedure consisted of two stages:

- In the first stage, households where two adults (30–46) of opposite sex reside were randomly selected. This was done both for households formed by nationals and for households where at least one eligible person was Spanish and at least one eligible was a national from any of the European Union countries with which Spaniards married most often in the 2005–2009 period: British, French, German, Italian, Portuguese, Romanian, and Bulgarian.

The Spanish team's goal was to secure a target final sample size of about 600 respondents, equally split between Madrid and Barcelona. Also, to maximize the possibility of comparisons while controlling for a sufficiently large number of variables, the team aimed toward achieving three approximately equally large groups in both Madrid and Barcelona: national couples, binational couples formed with foreign partners from old European Union member states, and binational couples formed with foreign partners from new European Union member states. It was assumed, however, that the average level of education

204 Survey methodology

of partners in binational couples where the foreign partner comes from a new European Union member state would be lower than that of binational couples where the foreign partner comes from old European Union member states. Since web-surveys overrepresent more educated segments of the population, there was a risk that the control group formed by national couples would display a higher average level of education than would the experimental group. Therefore, and in order to preclude this problem, the Spanish research team decided that the control group would consist in equal size samples of individuals with less than university education and individuals with university education.

The objectives above guided the sampling of households in this first stage. In addition to this, consideration was given to the prospect that only a very small percentage of those being selected as part of the sample would actually reside at the address listed in the Population Register, would be eligible to participate, and would then agree to participate in the survey. This concern led to drawing a sample of households that was about ten times bigger than the target sample (N = 6504).

- In the second stage, one adult was randomly chosen in each of the selected households, making sure that the resulting sample equally represented men and women.

The fieldwork phase of the survey started on May 16th, 2012, and ended on June 23rd, 2012.

Belgium

In Belgium, the study was restricted to the metropolitan areas of Brussels and Antwerp, including all 19 municipalities of the Brussels-Capital Region and all 9 districts of the city of Antwerp.

The Brussels sample was drawn from the National Population Register and the Antwerp sample from the Municipal Population Register, both containing information on current nationality. The sampling procedure was designed in three steps:

- In the first step, all individuals were selected who were 30- to 46-year old and reported either the Belgian nationality or any of the six most frequent European Union nationalities in binational couples formed in Belgium in the 2005–2009 period: French, Dutch, Italian, German, Polish, and Spanish. These selected individuals were subsequently grouped by household. The Belgian survey focused on both heterosexual and homosexual couples, unlike the remainong ones, which focused on heterosexual couples only.
- In the second step, only households with two potential partners among the remaining household members were kept in the household file. Potential partners were (1) a reference person and a person identified as married to the

reference person, (2) a reference person and a non-related person, (3) a son/daughter and a son-/daughter-in-law, or (4) a son/daughter and a non-related person. Households with more than two potential partners among the remaining household members were not selected to avoid errors in pairing up potential partners and their nationalities.

- In the third step, one partner per household was randomly selected.

The initial sample drew 2,000 addresses, based on a predicted response rate of 25% (1.600 binational couples and 400 uninational couples). Antwerp's "Dienst Stadsobservatie" and the National Brussels Register each drew 1,000 addresses for Antwerp and Brussels, respectively. In the process of data cleaning, however, the Belgian team noticed that a misunderstanding had led the National Register to draw two-person households only, instead of households with only two potential partners. The Brussels sample thus did not include households with children. To correct this mistake, an additional sample of 1,000 addresses was drawn for Brussels, using the right selection algorithm. Only those among the selected households in which there were children were kept (to match the original sample of respondents without children) and, from these, one adult was chosen randomly. This supplementary exercise added 750 more individuals to the sample.

The original fieldwork started on April 26th, 2012, and finished on June 15th, 2012, whereas fieldwork for the additional sample took place between January 9th, 2013, and February 26th, 2013.

Netherlands

In the Netherlands, the survey was conducted in The Hague and Amsterdam. The Hague's and Amsterdam's municipal population registers GBA (gemeentelijke basisadministratie) were the official source for the sampling of national and binational couples. The register includes information on people's birth date, country of birth, nationality, and marital status. Hence, identification and selection of couples with the right characteristics was done directly.

In The Hague, the sample included 350 national and 1109 binational couples. One person from each couple was then randomly selected. The initial plan was that the sample of binational couples only include the four most frequent European Union nationalities in these couples during the 2005–2009 period, British, German, Dutch, and Polish. Low numbers, however, eventually recommended that all European Union nationalities be included.

In Amsterdam, the sample included 256 national and 836 binational couples. For similar reasons as in The Hague, all European Union nationalities were considered when creating the sample of binational couples.

The target sample size was 2551 individuals. Fieldwork started on May 26th, 2012, and ended on July 6th, 2012. Nine-hundred and forty-six individuals agreed to participate in the survey.

206 Survey methodology

Switzerland

The Swiss survey was conducted in Zurich. The sample was drawn by using Zurich's Population Register. Sampling proceeded in four stages.

-   In the first stage, all 30- to 45-year-old men and 18- to 57-year-old women, with Swiss, European, Algerian, Brazilian, Dominican, Lebanese, Moroccan, Peruvian, Philippine, Thai, Tunisian, or United States citizenship, were included in the sample.
-   In the second stage, information on people's addresses was used to match individuals at the household level. Only households including at least two adults of opposite sex were kept in the sample. In households where more than two individuals met the criteria above, priority was given to married partners. In those cases where there was no indication as to whether those living in the household were part of a couple, two individuals of opposite sex were chosen at random.
-   In the third stage, the couples left in the pool were classified into five groups.
    1   Couples in which both partners have a Swiss citizenship.
    2   Couples in which one partner is Swiss and the other has European Union citizenship.
    3   Couples in which one partner is Swiss and the other is a citizen of a European country that is not part of the European Union.
    4   Couples in which one partner is Swiss and the other has a citizenship of one of the following non-European countries: Algeria, Brazil, Dominican Republic, Lebanon, Morocco, Peru, Philippines, Thailand, Tunisia, and United States of America.
    5   Couples in which both partners have a citizenship of one of the EU27 countries.
-   In the fourth and last stage, up to a maximum of 2,500 couples in each group were randomly selected and one individual within each of these couples was also drawn randomly.

The resulting sample included 2500 individuals for group 1, 2500 individuals for group 2, 928 for group 3, 680 for group 4, and 833 for group 5. Only those in groups 1 and 2, and only respondents whose age lies within the *Eumarr* research design range (30–46) were retained for the comparative analysis in this book.

The fieldwork period lasted from June 6th, 2012, to October 31st, 2012.

Response rates

Response rates for the survey were low, as expected in mail surveys in general and in web-surveys in particular (see table below). The *Eumarr* survey combined features of both. While it approached potential participants by mail, it required the completion of a web-survey. The low response rates in the Spanish survey stands out from the rest. The reasons for this are unclear, although the two best candidate explanations are that (1) whereas other countries automatically update information on address changes, in Spain, it is left to individuals to update this information, and they often do not do it, and (2) in 2012, internet access was less prevalent in Spain than it was in the other countries in the study.

Response Rates over the Target Samples

	Sample Size	Response Rate %
Antwerp	380	38.0
Brussels	496	28.3
Amsterdam	454	42.9
The Hague	492	34.0
Barcelona	318	15.5
Madrid	417	9.4
Zurich	1925	38.5

Although it is unlikely that those who participated in the survey are a random representative sample of the target samples, there are no obvious reasons why low response rates should bias the findings, once one controls for relevant socio-demographic characteristics like education, as I do in the book. Assertions regarding the entire population have only been made occasionally, when the results for less educated and more educated segments of the population agree.

Obtained and working samples

It must be noted, as I do in Chapter 2, that the working sample used in the book differs in one important aspect from the achieved samples above. The goal of the book is to systematically compare partners in national couples with partners in binational couples. Yet, as mentioned in Chapter 2, many participants in the survey had more than one nationality. After much thought, I decided that instead of conducting the analysis by distinguishing more than two groups, through taking into account whether individuals had one or more nationality, and on the nationality combinations themselves, or instead of arbitrarily taking the first nationality as the relevant one, I would only retain partners in "pure" national and binational couples. Individuals in "pure" national couples are those who hold the country of residence's nationality only and whose partner holds the country of residence's nationality only. Individuals in "pure" binational couples are those in couples where one of the partners holds the country of residence's nationality only and where the other partner holds one or more nationalities from other European countries only.

Obtained and Working Samples

	Obtained Sample	Working Sample in Europe in Love
Belgium	876	530
Netherlands	946	744
Spain	735	628
Switzerland	1925	1100

Note

1 Project entitled "Toward a European Society: Single Market, Binational Marriages, and Social Group Formation in Europe (Eumarr)" (EUI2010-04221). The Spanish part of the project was funded by the Spanish Ministry of Economy and Competitivity, former Ministry of Science and Innovation (09-ECRP-044); The Belgian part of the project was funded by the Fonds voor Wetenschappelijk onderzoek Vlaanderen (09-ECRP-044, FWO finance number G.0994.10N); the Dutch part of the project was funded by the Netherlands Organization for Scientific Research (NWO); finally, the Swiss part of the project was funded by the Swiss National Science Foundation (FNS-SNF) (No. of the Project: 105515_127818).

APPENDIX 2

IN-DEPTH INTERVIEWS

The Spanish *Eumarr* team supplemented the web-survey with in-depth interviews to a group of volunteers among the participants. At the end of the web-survey, respondents were asked whether they would be interested in participating in a more qualitative interview. Then, once the fieldwork process was over, the team proceeded to contact some among the volunteers, with the aim of interviewing equal numbers of highly educated and less educated respondents. In the end, I interviewed fifteen people, of which seven of them had less than university education and eight had more than university education. Also, ten were women and five were men. Finally, twelve among them were foreign nationals whereas three were nationals (see table below).

The purpose of the in-depth interviews was to provide information that would illuminate the quantitative findings and enrich the analysis. In retrospect, the interviews would have been richer had they been conducted at the end of the quantitative analysis than just after the fieldwork was completed. It is unlikely, however, that one would have been able to locate many of them and obtain their cooperation.

The in-depth interviews lasted between one and one and a half hours. They were digitally recorded and transcribed in their entirety.[1] They covered many of the topics in the main survey questionnaire. The main sections were as follows:

- Synopsis of the couple's history together
- Daily and yearly routines
- Expectations for children (for those with children)
- Transnational experiences and social networks
- World and national outlook (including impressions about the European Union)
- Hobbies and consumer practices
- Lasting memories concerning recent history

210 In-depth Interviews

In general, respondents were quite involved when discussing the couple's history together, daily and yearly routines, expectations for children, and transnational experiences and social networks. They were much less comfortable and eloquent when discussing world and national issues or lasting memories concerning recent history. Finally, they generally had relatively little to say when discussing hobbies and consumer practices, whether music, sports, or film.

Interview Number	Respondent's Nationality	Gender	Education	Partner's Nationality
1	Spanish	Woman	University	German
2	French	Woman	Less than university	Spanish
3	Romanian	Woman	Less than university	Spanish
4	Italian	Man	University	Spanish
5	British	Woman	University	Spanish
6	Portuguese	Woman	University	Spanish
7	British	Woman	Less than university	Spanish
8	Romanian	Woman	University	Spanish
9	Spanish	Man	Less than university	Italian
10	British	Man	University	Spanish
11	Italian	Woman	University	Spanish
12	French	Woman	Less than university	Spanish
13	Spanish	Woman	Less than university	German
14	German	Man	University	Spanish
15	Italian	Man	Less than university	Spanish

Note

1 I would like to thank Dr. Irina Ciornei for her assistance in locating the respondents and in transcribing the interviews.

APPENDIX 3

VARIABLES USED IN THE STATISTICAL ANALYSIS

	Minimum Value	Maximum Value	Mean or Proportion	Median	Standard Deviation
Socio-Demographic and Psychological Variables					
Barcelona	0	1	0.1	0.0	0.3
Madrid	0	1	0.1	0.0	0.3
Brussels	0	1	0.1	0.0	0.3
Antwerp	0	1	0.1	0.0	0.3
Amsterdam	0	1	0.1	0.0	0.3
The Hague	0	1	0.1	0.0	0.3
Zurich	0	1	0.4	0.0	0.5
Binational parents	0	1	0.1	0.0	0.3
Foreign in binational couple (1=Yes)	0	1	0.3	0.0	0.5
National in binational couple (1=Yes)	0	1	0.3	0.0	0.5
Poor country (Yes=1)	0	1	0.1	0.0	0.3
Not poor country (Yes=1)	0	1	0.2	0.0	0.4
Duration of relationship	0	29	10.7	10.0	5.6
Satisfaction with relationship	0	10	8.9	9.0	1.4
Gender (1=Woman)	0	1	0.5	1	0.5
Age	30	46	38.0	38.0	4.2
Has child (1=Yes)	0	1	0.6	1.0	4.8
Number of children with current partner	0	8	1.1	1.0	1.1
Education (9=Doctoral)	1	9	7.0	7.5	1.5
Partner's education	1	9	6.9	7.0	1.6
Parents' education (9=Doctoral)	1	9	5.3	5.5	2.0

(*Continued*)

212 Variables Used in the Statistical Analysis

	Minimum Value	Maximum Value	Mean or Proportion	Median	Standard Deviation
Currently employed (1=Yes)	0	1	0.8	1.0	0.4
Partner employed (1=Yes)	0	1	0.8	1.0	0.4
High status (managerial, professional, technical) occupation (1=Yes)	0	1	0.6	1.0	0.5
Low service occupations (1=Yes)	0	1	0.1	0.0	0.3
Works for multinational (1=Yes)	0	1	0.2	0.0	0.4
Income (PPS) (Yearly-€ 1000s)	4.0	123.8	36.2	29.9	24.0
Ln(Income) (PPS) (Yearly € 1000s)	1.4	4.8	3.4	3.4	0.7
Individual contribution to household income	0	100	53.5	50.0	25.2
Unemployed (1=Yes)	0	1	0.0	0.0	0.2
Student (1=Yes)	0	1	0.0	0.0	0.1
Housework (1=Yes)	0	1	0.1	0.0	0.3
Other occupational status (1=Yes)	0	1	0.0	0.0	0.2
Social position	0	10	5.9	6.0	1.6
Household size	2	13	3.2	3.0	1.1
Homeowner (1=Yes)	0	1	0.5	1.0	0.5
Psychological well-being (10=Worst)	0	10	2.3	2.4	1.9
Best Friends' Origin					
Children's school (1=Yes)	0	1	0.3	0.0	0.4
Work (1=Yes)	0	1	0.6	1.0	0.5
Partner's work colleagues (1=Yes)	0	1	0.2	0.0	0.4
Neighborhood (1=Yes)	0	1	0.3	0.0	0.5
School/University (1=Yes)	0	1	0.6	1.0	0.5
Partner's friends/acquaintances (1=Yes)	0	1	0.5	0.0	0.5
Clubs and associations (1=Yes)	0	1	0.3	0.0	0.4
Relatives and Friends					
Has relatives (in CoR) (1=Yes)	0	1	0.7	1.0	0.5
Has in-laws (in CoR) (1=Yes)	0	1	0.6	1.0	0.5
Has friends (in CoR) (1=Yes)	0	1	0.9	1.0	0.3
Has friends in another EU country (1=Yes)	0	1	0.7	1.0	0.5
Has friends in a non-EU country (1=Yes)	0	1	0.4	0.0	0.5
Has relatives in another EU country	0	1	0.5	0.0	0.5
Has in-laws in another EU country	0	1	0.4	0.0	0.5
Number of native friends (out of five best) (foreign partners)	0	5	2.2	2.0	1.7

Variables Used in the Statistical Analysis 213

	Minimum Value	Maximum Value	Mean or Proportion	Median	Standard Deviation
Number of relatives and in-laws (6=11 or more)	0	6	4.4	6.0	2.4
Number of close friends (6=11 or more)	0	6	4.0	4.0	2.0
Meet (relatives/in-laws) (0=does not have; 8=daily)	0	8	4.2	4.5	2.1
Meet (friends) 0=does not have; 8=daily)	0	8	4.4	5.0	2.2
Telephone (0=does not have; relatives/in-laws)	0	8	4.6	5.0	2.4
Telephone (friends)	0	8	4.4	5.0	2.3
Internet (0=does not have; relatives/in-laws)	0	8	4.0	4.0	2.4
Internet (friends) 0=does not have; 8=daily)	0	8	4.7	5.0	2.4
Visit (relatives/in-laws) (EU) ★ (7=daily)	0	7	1.7	2.0	1.4
Visit (friends) (EU) ★(7=daily)	0	7	1.3	1.0	1.2
Get visited (relatives/in-laws) (EU) (7=daily)	0	7	1.6	2.0	1.3
Get visited (friends (EU) (7=daily)	0	7	1.2	1.0	1.1
Telephone (relatives/in-laws) (EU) (7=daily)	0	7	3.0	3.0	2.6
Telephone (friends) (EU) (7=daily)	0	7	2.0	2.0	1.9
Internet (relatives/in-laws) (EU) (7=daily)	0	7	2.8	3.0	2.5
Internet (friends) (EU) (7=daily)	0	7	2.5	3.0	2.2
Amount of Assistance Received					
Perception of help available (10=all needed)	0	10	6.6	6.7	2.1
Health (7=all information and assistance)	1	7	5.7	6.0	1.6
School help (7=all information and assistance)	1	7	4.9	4.0	1.6
Jobs (7=all information and assistance)	1	7	4.9	5.0	1.7
Rent/buy house(7=all information and assistance)	1	7	4.9	5.0	1.7
Small repairs(7=all information and assistance)	1	7	5.1	5.0	1.7
Child care (7=all information and assistance)	1	7	4.9	4.0	1.6
Taxes (7=all information and assistance)	1	7	4.5	4.0	1.9

(Continued)

214 Variables Used in the Statistical Analysis

	Minimum Value	Maximum Value	Mean or Proportion	Median	Standard Deviation
Languages Known					
Speaks English (1=yes)	0	1	0.9	1.0	0.3
Number of languages known before meeting partner (4=4 or more)	1	4	2.8	3.0	1.0
Languages known (4=4 or more)	1	4	3.0	3.0	0.9
Uses local language with partner (1=Yes)	0	1	0.8	1.0	0.4
Residence Abroad and Travel					
Years of residence in CoR (Foreign partners)	0	44	11.5	10	7.9
Countries visited before age 17	0	22	4.3	4.0	3.6
Countries visited between 17 and meeting partner	0	28	8.2	8.0	5.5
Number of states visited since with partner	0	30	7.8	7.0	5.0
Number of trips to neighboring EU countries in last 12 months	−4	102	3.4	2.0	6.4
Number of trips to other EU countries in last 12 months	−4	60	1.9	1.0	3.9
Interest in Politics					
Interest in politics (100=maximum)	0	100	53.7	51.0	21.3
Interest in city politics (4=very and Extremely Interested)	1	4	2.9	3.0	0.9
Interest in national politics (4=very and Extremely Interested)	1	4	3.2	3.0	0.8
Interest in European politics (4=very and extremely interested)	1	4	3.0	3.0	0.9
Interest in world politics (4=very and extremely interested)	1	4	3.0	3.0	0.9
Interest in local politics (8=very Strong)	0	8	4.4	4.0	1.9
Interest in supranational politics (8=very Strong)	0	8	4.1	4.0	1.9
Relative interest in home and residence politics (foreign partner) (−4=great interest in national; minimum interest in CoR)	−4	+4	1.7	0.0	1.0

Variables Used in the Statistical Analysis **215**

	Minimum Value	Maximum Value	Mean or Proportion	Median	Standard Deviation
Membership in Organizations and Associations					
Participation in civil activities and associations (number of activities/associations)	0	9	1.7	1.0	1.6
Sports club–outdoors organization (1=yes)	0	1	0.4	0.0	0.5
Organization for cultural or hobby activities (1=yes)	0	1	0.2	0.0	0.4
Religious organization (1=yes)	0	1	0.1	0.0	0.4
Organizations for peace, humanitarian aid, human rights, minorities, immigrants (1=yes)	0	1	0.2	0.0	0.4
Parents' organization in school (1=yes)	0	1	0.3	0.0	0.4
Organizations for environmental protection (1=yes)	0	1	0.2	0.0	0.4
Organization for animal rights (1=yes)	0	1	0.2	0.0	0.4
Club: social, for the young, for the elderly, women, a friendly society (1=yes)	0	1	0.1	0.0	0.3
Other organizations (1=yes)	0	1	0.1	0.0	0.3
Political Mobilization					
Political participation (7=maximum)	0	7	1.1	1.0	1.4
Contact a politician, government or local government official (1=yes)	0	1	0.1	0.0	0.3
Worked in a political party or action group (1=yes)	0	1	0.0	0.0	0.2
Worked in another organization or association (1=yes)	0	1	0.0	0.0	0.2
Worn or displayed a campaign badge/sticker (1=yes)	0	1	0.1	0.0	0.3
Signed a petition (1=yes)	0	1	0.4	0.0	0.5
Took part in a public demonstration (1=yes)	0	1	0.1	0.0	0.3
Boycotted certain products (1=yes)	0	1	0.2	0.0	0.4
Identifications, Europe, and Immigration					
Identification with city	0	10	6.2	7.0	3.5
Identification with nation	0	10	8.0	9.0	2.7

(*Continued*)

216 Variables Used in the Statistical Analysis

	Minimum Value	Maximum Value	Mean or Proportion	Median	Standard Deviation
Identification with country of residence (foreign partners) (10=highest)	0	10	2.3	2.0	3.2
Identification with Europe	0	10	7.6	8.0	2.8
Choice of European identification (1=yes)	0	1	0.2	0.0	0.4
"Would be Very Sorry" if the European Union dissolved (1=yes)	0	1	0.8	1.0	0.4
Non-Europeans should adapt better (4=completely agree)	1	4	2.9	3.0	0.8
Solidarity with region in CoR (10=would donate a large sum)	0	10	3.6	3.0	2.4
Solidarity with European country (10=would donate a large sum)	0	10	3.0	2.0	2.2
Taste in Music					
Jazz (1=yes)	0	1	0.4	0.0	0.5
Folk (1=yes)	0	1	0.3	0.0	0.5
Contemp. classic (1=yes)	0	1	0.3	0.0	0.4
Classic (1=yes)	0	1	0.5	1.0	0.5
Pop (1=yes)	0	1	0.6	1.0	0.5
Rock (1=yes)	0	1	0.5	1.0	0.5
Singer-songwriters (1=yes)	0	1	0.4	0.0	0.5
Likes pop from country of residence (foreign partners) (1=yes)	0	1	0.6	1.0	0.5
Likes rock from country of residence (foreign partners) (1=yes)	0	1	0.6	1.0	0.5
Likes folk from country of residence (foreign partners) (1=yes)	0	1	0.3	0.0	0.5
Likes singer/songwriters from country of residence (foreign partners) (1=yes)	0	1	0.5	0.0	0.5
Taste in Film					
American (1=yes)	0	1	0.8	1.0	0.4
Country of residence (1=yes)	0	1	0.6	1.0	0.5
Non-National, Non-Anglo, European (1=yes)	0	1	0.6	1.0	0.5
Non-National, Non-Anglo, Non-European (1=yes)	0	1	0.5	0.0	0.5
Original version (1=yes)	0	1	0.7	1.0	0.4

Variables Used in the Statistical Analysis **217**

	Minimum Value	Maximum Value	Mean or Proportion	Median	Standard Deviation
Likes film country of residence (foreign partners) (1=yes)	0	1	0.5	1.0	0.5
Likes film in original version (Spanish cities and Zurich) (foreign partner) (1=yes)	0	1	0.6	1.0	0.5
Likes film in original version (Belgian and Dutch cities) (foreign partners) (1=yes)	0	1	0.9	1.0	0.3
Cuisines Liked					
Number of national cuisines liked	0	24	9.5	9.0	5.3
Likes Asian food	0	10	4.6	4.2	3.1
Likes French (1=yes)	0	1	0.6	1.0	0.8
Likes German (1=yes)	0	1	0.3	0.0	0.8
Likes Greek (1=yes)	0	1	0.5	1.0	0.8
Likes Italian (1=yes)	0	1	0.8	1.0	0.8
Likes Polish (1=yes)	0	1	0.1	0.0	0.3
Likes Scandinavian (1=0)	0	1	0.4	0.0	0.7
Likes Hungarian (1=0)	0	1	0.3	0.0	0.7
Likes CoR food (1=0)	0	1	0.6	1.0	0.5
Likes CoR food (foreign partners) (1=0)	0	1	0.5	1.0	0.5
Other Consumer Practices					
Book in foreign language (1=Yes)	0	1	0.6	1.0	0.5

INDEX

acculturation 11, 153–4, 177, 182
actor-network theory 127
age at start of life together 34–5
age gap between partners 34–6
Amsterdam 13, 29, 31, 201, 205
analytical methodology 32
Andreotti, Alberta 8, 17–18, 49, 51, 67, 183
Antwerp 13, 29, 31, 201, 204–5, 207, 211
Argentinian 30, 194
assimilation 4, 177, 187; and knowledge of
  the local language 182; and migration 28,
  47, 80, 117, 142, 146, 169, 177, 182; and
  taste 142, 146–8
assistance received with everyday tasks 16,
  51–4, 64–7, 75
associations 7, 105–6, 108–13, 122
attachment to place 8, 18, 49, 119, 183–5

Barcelona xvii, 13, 29, 31, 39, 60, 67–9, 74,
  159, 166, 201, 203
Belgium xvii, 4, 12–13, 14, 32, 36–7, 40,
  43, 62, 69, 114, 132, 134, 136, 140, 147,
  201–4, 208
bi-ethnic marriage see intermarriage
binational couples i, xvi, 1–2; and book's
  analytical strategy 29; and book's focus
  10, 27; and class or education iii, 4,
  15–16, 28–9; and core cells of European
  society iii, 9; and cosmopolitanism 2, 3,
  9, 10–11, 13, 15; and country of origin;
  and de-nationalization project iii, 9;
  and Favell 9; and freedom of movement
  12–13, 17; and globalization 10; the

literature and 9–11, 13–15; and Mau 9;
  prevalence of 28; and research design
  29, 30; and social transformation 3; and
  working sample 31; working definition
  of Euro-couple 30–1
binational friendship 7, 12, 28, 56, 62
bi-national identity 8
binational marriage see binational couples;
  and acculturation 11, 153–4, 177, 182
binational parents 41–2; and identification
  175–77, 187
blood relatives and friends in country of
  residence iii, 4, 15–16, 19, 48–9, 51–4,
  57; and assistance received with everyday
  tasks 47, 51–4, 64–7
Botev, Nikolai 6
Bourdieu, Pierre 20, 127, 130, 148, 180
Bowling Alone 106
Braudel, Fernand 28
Brexit 199
British 1, 21, 33, 61–2, 69, 73, 156, 159, 197
Britons 21, 199
Brussels 13, 29, 31, 62, 152, 201, 204, 205

Castro-Martín, Teresa xvi, 3, 12
Chicago School 28
childcare 17, 48, 53, 97, 113
children: binational couples 9, 14–15, 17,
  19, 44, 48, 65, 94, 98, 108, 110, 112–13,
  140, 153, 175, 177, 187, 192, 199; contact
  with family and friends 14, 49–50, 68,
  93; residence close to family 67; class 127
citizen of the world 166

220 Index

citizenship 11, 45, 152, 153, 177, 206, 208
civil engagement 3, 109, 110–13
class: lower- iii, 1, 2, 15–17, 44, 64, 67, 74, 199; middle- i, iii, 1, 2, 13, 15–16, 44, 69, 73, 178, 194, 198–9; segment 1–6, 8, 11, 17–18, 35, 44, 100, 122, 193
Classic assimilation theory 80
coinciding social and cultural cleavages 3, 11, 15
communication with friends and relatives 51–4, 56, 63–4, 68–75, 192, 194; in general 5, 7, 10, 106–7, 122, 159, 193, 195–6; theory 6, 160, 196
Communist 33, 52
consumer taste 3, 20, 79, 100, 145–6, 148, 202
consumption 15–16, 20, 126–7, 130, 145, 148
contact with family and friends *see* communication with friends and relatives
context for establishing friendships 49–51, 57–63
Cortina, Clara xvii, 21
cosmopolitan: society i, 4–5, 7–10, 12, 16, 20, 187, 192, 194–6; individuals iii, 1, 2, 6, 8–11, 13, 15, 17, 20, 144, 151–2, 156, 166, 177, 187, 192, 195
cosmopolitanism i, 5, 9, 15; and class iii, 1, 2, 4, 13, 51, 56, 122, 194; definition of 2, 14, 192; social and political 2, 3, 20, 196–8
cosmopolitics 127
Cotts-Watkins Susan 6
countries visited 2, 41, 88, 160, 164
country of origin: and employment 80, 88; and integration 19, 29; life in 98; opportunities in 81; relatives and friends from 15–16, 107, 180; and selection of immigrants 81; subjective comparisons with 4, 19, 22, 94, 99, 100; ties to 47, 97
criteria for city selection 29
cross-national mobility: and civil and political engagement 105, 122; and class 8, 48, 74; and cosmopolitanism 7–8, 9, 17; and de-nationalization 9; and education 8, 48; and European policy 2, 27, 34; and the formation of states and polities 7; and friendship ties 56, 107; and globalization 5, 8, 16, 122, 140; and identification 7, 17, 152; and intermarriage 9–10, 12, 16; and sense of belonging 8, 18–19, 47, 183–6; and

solidarity 9; types of 7, 8, 12, 47, 107; *see also* international mobility
currency 7, 152

Datler, Georg 15, 195
Delhey, Jan 9
democracy 105–6
democratic deficit 105
de-nationalization thesis 17, 19–20, 187, 196
de-nationalized project 9, 11, 17–18, 48
De-regulation 28
Deutsch, Karl 6, 160, 196
Díez Medrano Juan i, 3, 12, 20–1, 28, 41, 45, 82, 85, 138, 152, 154–5, 159, 164, 166, 174, 187–8
discrimination 19, 80, 81, 91, 99, 101, 108
disposition 11, 48, 74, 127, 130, 140, 180
Duby, Georges 28
duration of relationship: and civil and political engagement 112, 121; and identification 1–2, 20, 156, 159, 161, 164, 182, 188, 196; and language transmission 4; in sample 31, 34; and support for European integration 173
Durkheim, Emile 2, 105
Dutch 14–15, 32–3, 45, 132, 134, 142, 152, 154–5, 202, 204–5, 208

earnings 15, 19, 68, 88–93, 109
economic returns 8, 19, 85
education: and attachment to the European Union 173; and binational marriage or cohabitation 41, 82; and civil and political Engagement 109; and contrasts between binational couples 15, 28–9, 48, 57, 63, 65, 83, 95, 97, 98, 100, 108, 122, 193; and cultural consumption 126, 130, 134, 136, 148; and European solidarity 166, 169; and family formation 21, 32; and identification 159–61, 177, 180, 185–6; and geographical mobility 52, 111; and sample distribution 30, 32, 34, 203–4; and socio-economic achievement 19, 80–3, 98, 100, 108
elective belonging 18
employment status 19, 79, 80–3
English language 7, 86, 88, 138
Ethnic: bias 45; bi-ethnic 14, 45; music 128–9, 132; pan-ethnic 8, 10, 11, 177; political salience of ethnic cleavages 2; tolerance 2, 127
Eumarr project xvi–xvii, 3–4, 12–13, 29–32; 201–2

Euro-couple *see* binational couples
Euro-marriage 23; and cosmopolitan
 identifications; incidence of 28; and
 transnational networks 13; trends
 in 12–13
European couples *see* binational couples
European identification 15, 17, 20–1,
 151–66, 173–4, 177, 180, 183, 186–7, 196
European solidarity 9, 20, 128, 151–2
 164–9
European Union xvi, 2, 4, 9, 11–13, 16–17,
 20–1, 27–8, 30, 32–3, 37, 41, 44, 45, 47,
 56, 75, 91, 105–6, 114, 140, 151–2, 154,
 164, 169, 170, 172–4, 177, 186–8, 193,
 195–9, 202–6, 209
Eurostars and Eurocities 19, 59, 75, 94, 100,

family and friends abroad 16 54–7, 62,
 68–74, 107, 112, 160, 184, 193, 196
Favell, Adrian xvi, 4, 8–9, 17 19, 21, 29, 40,
 47–8, 57, 59, 64–5, 74–5, 81, 93–4, 97,
 100, 187
film categories in survey 132
film taste 132–38
Fligstein, Neil xvi, 9, 17
foreign friends 60, 63
foreign partners: countries of origin 32–4;
 and cultural taste 130, 134, 142–8; and
 employment status 83–5; and experience
 of discrimination 19, 99, 101, 108;
 and identification 17–18, 20, 37, 113,
 154 156, 174–5 177–83, 185, 187; and
 interest in politics 114; and native friends
 59–62; and occupational status 83–5;
 and personal income 16 88–93 95 100;
 and relatives in country of residence 4,
 14–15, 16, 19, 48, 57, 59–64, 67, 74, 97,
 180, 185, 187, 193–4; and self-reported
 social position 4, 16, 19, 79, 93–9; and
 work for multinationals 85–8; and years
 of residence in country 15, 36–7
Framing Europe iii, xvi, 197
free movement 11, 197
free trade 7
freedom of movement iii, 2, 12, 16, 19, 28,
 36, 173, 177, 197
Friedmann, Jonathan 183
friends abroad 17, 55–6, 68–9, 72–3, 94,
 107, 112, 196
friends introduced by partner 59, 63, 74
*From Provinces into Nations: Demographic
 Behavior in Western Europe, 1870–1960* 6
Fukuyama, Francis 105

gastronomic taste 20, 128, 140–5, 147–8
gender 14, 32, 40–1, 44, 45, 50–1, 75, 80,
 83, 88, 92–3, 100–101, 108–9, 128,
 130, 193
geographers 8
Gerhards, Jürgen xvii, 2, 164
Germans 21, 33, 174–5
Germany 12, 38, 61, 69, 72, 179, 198
globalization 2–3, 6–10, 16–18, 27, 85,
 106–7, 122, 127, 140, 144, 148, 195
Granovetter, Mark 54
group cohesion 11, 105
group identification 10, 180

Hague the 13, 29, 31, 201, 205
happiness in relationship 14, 113, 183
holidays 28, 37, 40, 44, 72–3, 75, 81, 112,
 188, 192, 194
homeownership and civil and political
 engagement 139
hybrid identity 8, 10–11
hypermobile world 8, 184–5
hyphenated identity 8, 10–11, 153, 180

identification: and awareness 128, 153–6,
 159–61, 165–6, 170, 173–4, 177, 183,
 186–7, 195; with city of residence 16, 18,
 20, 113, 119, 183–7; communication and
 5–7, 160, 196; and cosmopolitanism 187,
 192, 196–8; with country of nationality
 4, 17, 20, 113, 120, 151, 174, 184; with
 country of residence 2, 16–17, 177–83;
 European 15, 17, 20–1, 151–6, 159,
 160–1, 164–6, 173, 177, 180, 183, 186–7,
 196; and European Union xvi, 2, 9, 11,
 17, 151–2; and geographic mobility 5,
 8, 184; and globalization 6–7, 16–17,
 195; and intermarriage 6, 9, 153–54;
 measurement 154; perceived cultural
 distance and 10, 182; situated character
 of 174; and state legitimacy 151–2, 196
imagined communities 5–7
immigrants: and identification with country
 of residence 2, 16–17, 177–83; and social
 capital 48, 81–2, 94, 98, 106–7
immigration policy 7
importance of music in people's lives
 129–30
income *see* earnings
industrial revolution 5
Inglehart, Ron 9, 11, 159, 188
integration: European i, iii, xvi, 1, 105,
 144–5, 151–2, 169, 196–7; frames about

Index

Europe 154; the immigrants' 4, 38, 47, 60, 62, 82, 107–9, 118, 122, 182; support of European 152, 164, 169–70, 187, 197–8
interest in politics 16, 109, 114, 118–19
inter-group marriage *see* intermarriage
intermarriage 6, 9, 16, 21, 27, 99, 193
inter-marriage *see* intermarriage
internal market xvi, 5, 7
international mobility 9, 16, 48, 140, 193
international regulatory agencies 7
internet 35–6, 51, 56, 68, 75, 194–5
interview # 1 40, 132, 153
interview # 3 26, 177, 178
interview # 4 68, 73
interview # 5 39, 61, 68, 73, 156, 159
interview # 6 59, 62, 74
interview # 8 27, 99, 178–80
interview # 9 40, 59, 63
interview # 10 40, 69
interview # 11 40, 67
interview # 12 72
interview # 13 39, 72
interview # 14 60
interview # 15 69
Italian 33, 140, 144, 203–4
Italy 12, 40, 134

Jules et Jim 198

Kaelble, Hartmut 20
knows local language 59, 86, 91, 182
Kocka, Jürgen 3
Koelet, Suzana 14, 21, 48, 69
Kriesi, Hans-Peter 3, 9
Kuhn, Theresa 9, 17

labor market segmentation 81
language spoken at home 86–7
languages known 41, 43, 51, 72, 138–9, 159–60
Latour, Bruno 127
Le Galès, Patrick 8, 18
leisure 11, 15
length of residence 91–3, 118, 182, 188
Les Deux Anglaises et le Continent 1, 198–9
liberalization 7, 13, 28
lifestyle 1, 3, 15, 18, 28, 30–1, 41, 126, 178, 195, 202
Lizardo, Omar 126–7, 130
longue durée 4
love i, 10, 12, 28, 30, 40, 57, 83, 183
Lyon 18, 51, 67

Madrid xvii, 13, 18, 29, 31, 51, 67, 69, 72, 140, 166, 177, 178, 179, 201, 203
Making Democracy Work 105
Maloutas, Thomas 51
Manchester 18
Mann, Michael 3
marriage dissolution 28, 31, 45
Mau, Steffen xvi, 9, 11, 16
meeting context 35–6
migration: and assimilation 4, 28, 146; and binational marriage and cohabitation 12, 193–4; causes of 12, 33; and civil and political engagement 19, 106, 122; and cross-national ties 107, 114; and diversity 51, 107; gender 83; and globalization 8; group formation and 6, 47; and identification 47, 174, 177, 187; and industrialization 6; origins and destination of 37; policy 7, 36, 81, 197; selection 82; and socio-economic status 79–93; taste and consumption 140; trends 12, 49, 80; types and logics 12, 16, 48, 57, 74, 81, 187
Milan 18, 51, 67
mixed marriage, *see* intermarriage
Mobile Europe 3, 4, 106
moral economy 16, 82
Moreno, Javier 8, 18
motivation 2, 8, 12, 80, 83, 91, 93, 111, 140, 144
multilateral governance 7
multiple nationalities 30
musical taste 20, 128–32, 134, 144–7, 210

national and international solidarity 9, 20, 128, 151–2, 164–9
Nations and Social Communication 196
native friends 60–1
Netherlands the xvii, 4, 12–14, 31–2, 37, 45, 69, 114, 132, 134, 136, 138, 142, 147, 170, 198, 201–2, 205, 208
Norris, Pippa 9

occupational status 79, 82–5
open-mindedness 1

Paris 18, 51, 67, 179
Peasants into Frenchmen 5
place of first meeting 35–6
Poland 12
political engagement 3, 11, 15–16, 79, 105–10, 113–22
Population, Space, and Place 12, 28, 33
Portes, Alejandro 21, 80, 117

preference for film in the original language 132, 134, 136, 138, 146–8
Prieur, Annick 130
psychological 10, 13–14, 109–10, 118, 121–2
Putnam, Robert 105–6, 110

reads books in foreign languages 128, 138–9, 145
Recchi, Ettore xvi, 3, 4, 9, 106–7, 113
Roché, Henri-Pierre 1, 198–9
Romania 12, 45
Romanian 33, 91, 97, 99, 188
Rössel, Jörg xvii, 3, 15, 195

Saito, Hiro 127–8
sample iii, 18, 29–34, 38, 41, 43, 45, 82, 91, 114, 144, 174, 188, 193, 202–7
Savage, Mike 8, 18, 129, 130, 183
Schengen 7, 11, 13, 16, 21, 27, 31, 36, 45, 154, 173
school 48–9, 50–1, 57, 59, 62, 65, 94, 108, 110, 112
Schroedter, Julia 14–15, 21, 195
Segmented assimilation theory 80
self-reported social position 16, 19, 79, 83, 93–100, 193
Simmel, Georg 28
Skiles, Sara 127, 130
social mobility 3–4, 47
socio-demographic 19, 109, 114, 129–30, 140, 147, 202, 207
socio-economic 3–4, 16, 29, 57, 79, 81, 109, 122, 156, 173–4, 182, 193
Spain xvi–xvii, 3, 5, 12–13, 28–9, 32–3, 37, 45, 114, 119, 132, 134, 136, 138, 140, 142, 147, 152, 154, 166, 177, 201–3, 206–7
state formation 3, 6
stratification iii, 32, 79–80, 82, 93, 95, 99–100

support for European Union 152, 169–74, 197
Sweden 12, 45
Switzerland xvii, 4, 12–13, 21, 30–2, 36–7, 45, 201–2, 206

Tocqueville, Alexis 93, 105
transnational ties 54–6, 68–74, 106–7
travel: binational couples and 15, 69, 72, 85, 199; and civil engagement 113; and class and education 13, 42, 56, 68, 97, 193–5; and familiarity with other cultures 85; and foreign friends 51, 72, 74; globalization and 28, 62, 107, 140; and identification 160–1, 164, 185–6, 188; and omnivorous taste 140, 142; and political mobilization 121; and Schengen, 194; and support for European integration 174, 177, 186; and work for multinationals 88
Truffaut, François 1, 198–9

unemployment: 80, 88, 109–10 178
United Kingdom 12, 21, 45, 199

Valk de, Helga xvii, 3, 14–15, 28, 45
Van Mol, Christof 14–15
Van Wissen, Leo xvii, 3, 15

Weber, Eugen 5, 21
Weber, Max 148
West European Politics in the Age of Globalization 3
Winter de, Tom 14
work for multinationals 85–8, 91–3, 174
World Values Study 11

Zürich 13, 15, 21, 29, 31, 45, 51, 132, 134, 136, 138, 148, 154–5, 165, 174, 201, 203, 206